MY PRETTY BABY

PRAISE FOR *MY PRETTY BABY*

"Correa is an engaging wordsmith and fills her stories with detailed descriptions . . ."

—*Kirkus Reviews*

". . . *My Pretty Baby* offers a journey not just through one woman's choices, but the music, mindfulness, and meanings that result in a better, more peaceful life. . . ."

—*Midwest Book Review*

"A beautifully brave coming-of-age story that follows a young girl from 'being' to 'becoming' and how she uses her brokenness as a superpower to break inherited and hurtful cycles, *My Pretty Baby* mixes memories of music, motherhood, and meditation as Wendy Correa composes the notes for the song of her new life—one that silences the cacophony of generational trauma."

—Bridey Thelen-Heidel, author of *Bright Eyes*

"Born into a chaotic family, full of painful, confusing experiences and few guides to give her clarity, Wendy never gives up her quest for safety and purpose. Finally, she finds her own winding path to teachers, spiritual practices, love and healing."

—Priscilla Warner, *New York Times* best-selling author of *Learning to Breathe*

"*My Pretty Baby* is an enjoyable, captivating roller coaster ride through family dysfunction, alcoholism, spiritual seeking, and iconic cultural moments in music history."

—Leslie Johansen Nack, author of *Nineteen*

"Wendy's journey to heal the tender roots of childhood trauma and family scars leads to a transformation of inherited pain into a beautifully told story of self-discovery."

—Kathleen Rose Morgan, author of *The Seller of Secrets*

MY PRETTY BABY

Seeking Truth and Finding Healing

A Memoir

Wendy B. Correa

SHE WRITES PRESS

Published in 2025 by
She Writes Press, an imprint of The Stable Book Group

32 Court Street, Suite 2109
Brooklyn, NY 11201
https://shewritespress.com
Library of Congress Control Number: 2025911603
Print ISBN: 979-8-89636-004-9
E-ISBN: 979-8-89636-005-6

Interior Design by Tabitha Lahr

Printed in the United States of America

Names and identifying characteristics have been changed to protect the privacy of certain individuals.

For Nacho and Mateo

One day you will tell your story of how
you overcame what you went through, and
it will be someone else's survival guide.

—BRENÉ BROWN

Your job as a writer is to love and to mourn, to tell the unbearable story so that others might feel less alone in theirs.

—STEVE ALMOND

CONTENTS

PART III BELONGING

AUTHOR'S NOTE

The late author, Dorothy Allison famously said, "If you're going to make someone out to be an asshole in your memoir, you damn well better make yourself an asshole too." While I agree with the sentiment, my hope is not to portray assholes, but to reveal imperfect, wounded humans—each yearning to be loved, understood, and accepted. These are people who struggled, often failing, to express those needs.

This is a work of nonfiction, though certain names and identifying details have been altered for privacy. Dialogue has been reconstructed to the best of my memory. This story is mine—shaped by artifacts like photographs, journals, emails, and letters as well as by lived experience, perception, emotional truth, and memory etched deeply into the recesses of my mind.

Part I
BEING

CAMELOT

Blaring lights suddenly flashed on in the gymnasium, and the movie reel we were watching from our seats on the wooden floor abruptly halted as we looked around at each other and blinked our eyes against the intrusive disruption.

"Attention students and teachers, please listen carefully," the principal announced over the loudspeaker. "President Kennedy has been shot."

I burst into tears.

Three years earlier, I'd stood next to my mother in a black-cloth-shrouded box, only slightly big enough for her and me to fit in. I'd inhaled her Estee Lauder Youth Dew perfume—delicious-smelling, with scents of vanilla, rose, and patchouli. At four years old, I'd had a perfect view of her nylon-stockinged legs and black high heels, and I'd reached out and touched her smooth calf.

Knowing that other people were also in secret little boxes near us, I'd whispered my question: "What are we doing here?"

My mother had responded giddily, "We are electing John Fitzgerald Kennedy to be president!"

Even at that young age, I'd understood that this was an important and momentous day and that my mother was proud to be contributing her part. She loved the romantic *Camelot* story of JFK and Jackie.

But now—three years later, on Friday, November 22, 1963—their fairy-tale story seemed to be ending.

I numbly and quietly shuffled back to my second-grade classroom. Seated, we prayed out loud and cried. I laid my head on my desk, unable to stay upright.

After a short while, the intercom in my classroom crackled to life.

The principal cleared his throat and then, after a long pause, announced, "Teachers and students, I am sorry to report to you that in fact President Kennedy has died." His voice faltered, choking on the words. "This is a very sad day in our country, in America."

I walked home alone in a daze. I knew that my mother was at work but that my father, who'd recently had another heart attack, would be resting in bed when I arrived.

As I walked along, I pulled my wool coat closer. The crisp November air suddenly turned bitter, and a chill ran up my spine as I thought about what it meant to be dead. Suddenly, I remembered standing barefoot in the freezing cold snow, staring at the spinning red light on the ambulance as I watched the paramedics slide my daddy, who was lying on a stretcher with an oxygen mask on his face, into the ambulance. I nervously wondered if he would be all right.

That awful night had taken place three Christmases ago, not long after JFK's election. When my father came home from the hospital after Christmas, he'd stayed in bed to recuperate, covered by starchy white sheets, and worked on a paint-by-number kit—black, white, and brown-spotted paint horses grazing in a field of colorful wildflowers. I'd inhaled the paint fumes as I stood in the doorway and waited for him to look up at me and invite me to sit on the bed and watch him dab the colors on the canvas.

When my dad was feeling well, I loved to follow him around the yard while he tended to his garden and the fledgling mini-orchard of peach and pear trees that he and my mom had planted the same summer they built the house. I watched him dig holes and plant weeping willow saplings, soaking the ground to give them a good drink of water. Sometimes, though, I wished I hadn't followed him outside.

Once, I heard him angrily mutter, "Damn gophers," right before he put the running hose in one mound hole and then stood several feet away at the other end of the tunnel mound, feet spread wide, rifle aimed at the hole. When the gopher poked its head out of the hole, the rifle blasted, startling me to the brink of tears.

And now, only three years after my mom and I had voted for JFK, my dad had suffered yet another heart attack. Would he die like JFK had? I always thought that he was mean to the gophers, but I didn't want my daddy to die.

I arrived home and went quickly to my father, lying in bed. With tears in his eyes, he patted the spot next to him. I climbed up and watched with him, on the black-and-white television, as CBS news anchor Walter Cronkite choked back tears and gave the sketchy details of the assassination.

"This is so sad, Daddy," I said, tears welling up in my already swollen eyes.

"Yes, this is very sad," he replied with the same look in his brown eyes that I had seen when I had found his book of horrific images from WWII—a look that said, *I am so sorry that my sweet little girl has to see this.*

Looking at my father's gray skin and drawn eyes, I also sensed a deeply personal sadness within him. I didn't know the details of what he had seen as an army private during WWII except for the images I'd seen in that book, but in this moment, I saw sorrow in his expression. Did he fear, as I did, that he might be on the brink of death himself?

Monday, November 25, 1963, was declared a National Day of Mourning. Watching the televised funeral procession along with the rest of America, I felt connected to JFK's children, Caroline and John-John, by my sense of foreshadowed loss.

What would it be like to lose my father? I wondered.

A couple of weeks later, my father was admitted into the hospital again. He was still there on Christmas morning when I opened a Barbie dollhouse present. Though I didn't like or own a Barbie, I did have a Tammy doll and a Ken doll, and the house was perfect for them.

My mom didn't even try to pretend that Santa had brought the gift, nor did she mince her words. "Your father put that house together for you before he went into the hospital, so you should take care of it," she told me. "It might be the last gift you ever get from him."

Her words ran cold up my spine, and I knew them to be true.

We went to the hospital to see my father the next day. The nurses had removed the oxygen tent, and he was sitting up in bed. As usual, he patted the bed and asked me to climb up next to him.

Everyone was smiling, but I worried as I listened to his labored, rattling breathing and watched beads of sweat gather on his brow. I reached out to touch his hand, but it felt cold and waxy.

Earlier that week, Donna, my next-door-neighbor playmate, had said something to me that ended with "when your father comes home from the hospital."

"I don't think my father *is* coming home," I'd replied—and was just as startled to hear those words come out of my mouth as Donna was.

Now, remembering what I'd said, I felt guilty.

"He was in good spirits, and his color was good," my mom exclaimed on the way home. "Plus, he didn't need the oxygen tent!"

But I couldn't share in her enthusiasm; all I felt was troubled.

I was so busy working on my letter shapes in class that I barely noticed when my teacher, Mrs. Burton, was called to the principal's office our first Monday back at school after the Christmas break.

Five minutes later, she returned to the classroom with the school secretary.

"Wendy, your mom is here to pick you up. Please come to your cubby to get your coat and your things." Mrs. Burton's voice was soft and reassuring. She helped me put my coat on.

"Should I take my lunch box too?" I wondered how much of the school day I might miss, and I thought about that leftover Twinkie I hadn't finished at lunch time.

"Yes, honey, take all your things with you," she answered.

Honey? I thought. That was weird. She'd never called me that before.

Speechless and worried, I was escorted to the main office with Mrs. Burton and the secretary, who rested her hand on my shoulder as we walked. The air was thick with unsaid words.

Inside the office, my mom stood with the principal facing me, and by their faces I knew something was wrong.

Without hesitation my mom blurted out, "Wendy, your father died."

It was so abrupt. The words felt like a cold slap across my face.

Unable to process the thought, I lashed back, "No, Mom, that's not true. You're lying!" As much as I'd feared my father's death with incessant uneasy thoughts, I couldn't believe that he had really died.

Clearly irritated, my mom snapped, "Wendy, I would not lie about something like that."

Unable to comprehend what was happening, unable to grasp the significance of the moment, unable to even know how to begin to think about what was happening, I went numb. I haltingly followed my mom to the car, where my nineteen-year-old sister, Sharon, was waiting behind the wheel. I climbed into the back seat with my fourteen-year-old brother, Mark, whose eyes were focused on his hands, folded in his lap.

No one spoke to me. I didn't know where to look. Finally, my gaze landed on the only comfortable and distracting place I could find: the back of my sister's head. Her auburn hair was ratted and piled high into the current beehive style. I had watched her meticulously apply her makeup and style her hair many times, noting her pride in perfection. Aqua Net hairspray held every loose hair in place. (I knew the tool she used to lift the pile higher was called a "rattail" comb, and the name, combined with the idea of "ratting" hair, made me unsure I wanted to do that when I got older.) So that she wouldn't mess up her hair after styling it, she'd taped a note on her vanity table reminding herself, *Put on sweater first, then hair*.

My daydream was interrupted by matter-of-fact voices as Sharon and Mom discussed plans for a viewing in Riverside and a funeral in St. Louis, six hours away.

"We need to make a list of everyone to call," Mom said. "Call your grandmother first, of course. And then your dad's brother. Then call my sisters and brothers. Then we can call the funeral parlor in Riverside to arrange a viewing and the funeral parlor in St. Louis to plan the funeral."

The talking and planning seemed endless and made me sleepy. I felt relieved that the details of death were all up to the adults and not for me to figure out.

At home, Sharon and Mom began making the necessary phone calls, and Mark went out into the snow-covered backyard to throw a football straight up into the air. I watched him throw the ball up and catch it repeatedly. Looking out the window at him, I felt an ache all over my body. Something frightening rushed through me. I feared I might burst, that I couldn't contain all my feelings.

It was the first time I'd felt separate from others in this way—alone in my thoughts, alone in my body. I inhaled and exhaled deeply to shake it off.

I wanted to be physically close to my mom, to climb up into her lap so she could scratch my back and comfort me, but she was impatient with me.

"Not now, Wendy," she said. "Go play at Donna's house."

Donna's mother greeted me at the door, then rejoined her husband on the couch to continue watching the CBS Evening News. As I turned toward Donna's bedroom, her father casually asked, "Wendy, how is your dad?"

I didn't know how to respond. A tangled mess of emotions welled up inside me, clogging in my throat and knotting in my stomach. I was afraid and sad and numb. But I didn't want to appear to be rude to my elders by not answering.

Unable to breathe and choking back tears, I hesitatingly stuttered out, "H-he died." The words tasted like rusted metal in my mouth.

Both adults jumped up—eyes wide, foreheads crinkled, faces contorted in shock. Their mouths twisted open, but they were speechless.

Their frozen looks frightened me so much that I ran to Donna's room.

There, in the safety of my friend's room, I relaxed a little. But we weren't playing for very long before Donna's mom came to the door and gently said, "Wendy, honey, I think it would be better if you went home to your family."

I thought that I would rather stay at my friend's house playing with dolls than go home to a house heavy with gloom. But I didn't know how to articulate that, so I just nodded silently and shuffled back to my house.

As soon as I got home, I walked into my parents' bedroom and began to look through my father's drawers. Since I could no longer touch and smell him, I at least wanted to touch and smell his things.

On the bureau, I laid out his shaving strap, straight razor, shaving cream cup, cuff links, high school ring, handkerchiefs, underwear, T-shirts, and bottle of Old Spice aftershave.

I felt a profound urge to gather his belongings and display them.

I went to find my mom.

She was sitting at the dining room table, staring into space, her hands wrapped around a steaming cup of black coffee.

"Maybe we should gather Daddy's things," I said tentatively.

She just laughed.

Hurt by her reaction, I clamped my mouth shut and turned away.

It wasn't until a few days later, at the viewing, when I would realize why she laughed.

"Wendy thought we were supposed to bury his things with him," she said to my Aunt Hazel, and once again laughed.

That wasn't what I had meant at all.

My father's funeral was held three hundred miles south, in St. Louis, Missouri—the city where my mother and father had met and where my father's mother and brother and other family members still lived.

My mother was one of ten siblings, all with large families of their own, so the funeral parlor was packed with people from babies to the elderly. Of all the cousins, my two-year-old twin girl cousins and I, at age seven, were the youngest. The twins were adorable: blonde-ringlet-haired, blue-eyed little girls in matching yellow dresses lined with white crinoline to fill out the skirts. Outside the room where my father lay in his casket, we played on a giant powder-blue ottoman, all three of us in white socks trimmed in lace and shiny black patent leather shoes.

People were milling about and chatting as if they were at a cocktail party. I caught my mom's beautiful, toothy smile and sideways glance toward me as she spoke with a relative. I thought my mom was so pretty with her ash-blonde hair and beautiful green eyes. She always took pride in dressing stylishly and wore sweet-smelling Youth Dew perfume. As she talked, I saw her hand—the one our family called her "little hand"—twitch.

Mom had been born with a rare congenital condition in which all her fingers and thumb on her right hand were underdeveloped, a fact that had garnered her the nickname "Stub" from one of her beloved big brothers (only he could call her that). But it never occurred to me that her birth defect detracted in any way from her beauty.

Watching my family, I wondered if other families laughed at funerals. Weren't we supposed to be sad? My father was dead, and they were all laughing and having a good time.

Eventually, we all filed into the large room where my father lay in his casket. Once everyone sat down, the funeral began.

I barely heard what the minister said because my focus was on my dead father lying in his casket, his face waxy and unreal, his stiff body dressed in his favorite suit and cushioned by soft white satin. There was a wall of shelves behind his casket, filled with what seemed like hundreds of vases bursting with carnations. Pink carnations. White carnations. Red carnations. The stench was disgusting and overwhelming. The room reeked of carnations and death. I could hardly breathe.

Finally, the service concluded. People began to stand up and file out. I popped up out of my seat eagerly; I couldn't wait to get out of that nauseating room and into the fresh air.

And then, right in front of me, someone closed the satin-lined lid of the casket on my father's face.

I inhaled my breath sharply and trembled. Although I understood that my father was dead, the idea of him being trapped in a casket and buried in the ground made me panic. Scared and shaky, my breath caught in my throat, I looked at my mom, brother, and sister, but their expressionless faces seemed dead too.

Feeling as if somehow *I* was in that casket, unable to breathe, I gulped in deep, desperate breaths—only to once again draw in the stench of those carnations.

I wanted to run away, so I left my body and pretended I could fly to the ceiling.

At the frozen January gravesite, we sat on hard metal chairs. As I struggled to keep my cold legs covered with my short black wool coat, I thought about my father—enclosed in a casket, being lowered into the ground, covered with dirt, and buried forever.

Suddenly, the loud explosion of the three army honor guardsman blasting their rifles into the air startled me out of my frightening reverie. Unaware that they used blank cartridges, I worried about the birds they must have killed and scanned the trees for falling dead bird bodies and was relieved there were none. A white-gloved and gold-buttoned soldier reverentially and ceremoniously folded the American flag into a triangle as the bugle played the wailing sound of "Taps" and then presented it to my mom like it was a prize.

No one explained anything to me. No one said it was very sad that my dad had died but he was very sick, and his body was too worn out to heal. No one said that we would miss him very much and we would always remember him. No one said he loved me very much and was very sorry he would not get to see me grow up. No one said we could see him in the moon and the stars, and that I could always talk to him. No one said that he would want me to be happy even though he was dead. No one said that I needn't worry—that even though my father had died, my mother was healthy and young and would not die. No one said that everything was going to be okay. That we would grieve properly, and missing him would hurt, but we would all be okay.

I wondered why God would take my father away from me. I needed him more than God did, didn't I? I was mad at God. He'd taken Caroline's daddy, and now he'd taken mine. I worried that I might be doomed for life for being mad at God.

But even scarier than that was this thought: *Will my mom die too?*

I felt so alone—unsteady on my own two legs, overwhelmed by the weight of the world. I knew that JFK had been only forty-six when he died. My father had been only forty-five.

What if I die when I'm forty-five?

I did my second-grade arithmetic. *Forty-five minus seven. Five minus seven, then borrow a one from the four and carry it over to make it fifteen. Fifteen minus seven*—I counted on my fingers—*equals eight, carry the three down. Thirty-eight.*

Thirty-eight! What if I only had thirty-eight years left to live? What should I do with those years? Life was short. Maybe even shorter than I knew.

Although no one spoke to me about my grief, about my fears and my feelings, I felt less alone when I thought of JFK's daughter. I thought that the two of us belonged to a special club of little girls who had lost a father.

For many years, I thought that Caroline and I were the only members of that club.

ACCIDENTAL BAPTIST

On Sunday, February 9, 1964, Mom turned on the TV to watch *The Ed Sullivan Show*. The screaming was so loud we could barely hear the music that the glowing smiling mop-topped young men on the screen were playing. The Beatles, they were called, according to Ed.

Transfixed, I moved right up to the TV. Tired by the past month of dog paddling and floating in a sea of sorrow, I suddenly felt like a life buoy had been thrown to me by those boys on the stage and the screaming girls in the audience. I sensed I had something to look forward to, something to be hopeful for.

My nineteen-year-old sister sat on her upholstered chair, legs tightly crossed, smoothing her beehive hairdo. With disdain, she blew smoke from her Salem cigarette and scoffed. "Oh, that is just ridiculous."

I took a moment to register my sister's attitude toward the band and fans on our TV, but once I did, I realized right there and then how different we were. Ever since my father had died, everything in my world had been frozen and morose. But now, feeling this new music in my body, my heart lightened and brightened.

If only I could be standing in that crowd, I thought, wide-eyed with awe.

In April, three months after my daddy died, the frozen ground began to give way to melting snow and mud. The irises and daffodils poked their fledgling buds into the world, announcing spring. Resurrection. New life.

Mom and I made pastel-colored, vinegar-dipped, hard-boiled eggs the night before Easter Sunday, and I woke up to find that the Easter Bunny had delivered chocolate eggs, hollow chocolate bunnies, and multicolored jellybeans nestled in a bright green, grass-filled basket covered in cellophane and wrapped with a pink satin bow.

Later that morning, my mother, brother, sister, and I went back to the church we'd attended when my father was alive: the First Church of the Nazarene, an evangelical Baptist church. Sitting in the wooden pew, I imagined one of the men in the choir as my father. If I squinted my eyes just so, he looked like him, and I could almost convince myself that my daddy was still alive.

After the sermon we sang another song, and then it became quiet. The preacher began to admonish the congregation for being "sinners that needed to be saved." He implored people to come up to the pulpit and accept Jesus Christ as their Savior.

"If you ask for forgiveness," he boomed loudly, "Jesus will forgive you of your sins and will save you from going to hell when you die."

Scary. My stomach churned with tightness and butterflies, and I found it hard to breathe—the same feeling I'd had at my daddy's funeral. I wanted out of there. I looked to the ceiling and wondered, *Did my daddy go to heaven or hell?*

Now near tears, the preacher continued to beg people to save themselves.

Then everyone started to sing:

> *"Just as I am, and waiting not,*
> *To rid my soul of one dark blot,*
> *To Thee whose blood can cleanse each spot,*
> *O Lamb of God, I come, I come!"*

People walked up to the pulpit, and the preacher put his hand on their heads and exclaimed, "Thank you, Jesus! Praise the Lord!"

I felt sick to my stomach and tight in my chest. I looked over at my mom.

Stoic and tight-lipped, she offered no comfort.

Left to my own devices, I started to analyze the situation.

I am a good girl. I do what my mom says. I brush my teeth and go to bed when she says. I don't talk back. I clean up my messes. How have I sinned? I don't believe this man. Who is this man? He doesn't even know me. How does he know I am a sinner? Jesus knows I am not a sinner. Jesus wouldn't make me go to hell. If the only way to go to heaven is through Jesus, Jesus would tell me. Why do I have to talk to God through Jesus anyway? I talk to God all the time. Is that a sin? I ask him questions like: How can you let a bad man take Caroline and John John's daddy from them? How can you take my daddy away from me? How can you let bad people kill those four Black girls while they were at church? But then I also beg him, because the idea petrifies me. *Please don't let my mommy die too!*

"Mommy," I whispered, tugging on her sleeve. "I'll wait for you outside."

She looked at me quizzically but nodded.

I slipped from the pew and practically sprinted to the wooden door.

The next Sunday when mom wanted to go to church, I felt sick and vomited up my oatmeal, and we stayed home. After that we didn't go back to the First Church of the Nazarene or any other church. It seemed we had reached a silent understanding that we didn't need that sort of thing in our lives.

Sitting in the back of our car, my winter-white legs sticking conspicuously out of my JCPenney flowered cotton shorts and matching top, I stared out the window as my sister drove us down bucolic country roads past row upon row of burgeoning cornfields, white farmhouses trimmed in green with red barns nearby, and horses and cows grazing in the pastures with their new babies. It was finally summer break, a beautiful, sunny day in June, and we were on our way to an open house Mom had read about in the paper and wanted to go to.

When we arrived, I got out of the car and noticed a robin's-egg-blue sky filled with whimsical, cotton ball clouds. All around us were maple and oak trees bursting with full canopies, and the smell of fresh-cut grass filled the air.

I thought we were at a beautiful place until Mom explained that we were about to tour Dixon State Mental Hospital.

I didn't know what that was, but I didn't like the sound of it.

Along with a handful of other people, we gathered around the tour guide outside the entrance of a large building.

"Built in the cottage-style architecture of 1918 with one large main building that included the hospital ward and surrounded by numerous smaller cottages," the tour guide explained, "patients are housed according to their social and mental abilities."

Social and mental abilities? I looked around the group and noticed there weren't any other children present.

"Originally built as the Illinois State Colony for Epileptics," she continued, "the facility has evolved to include the care of the 'feebleminded,' and a new school was built for the learning disabled."

Feebleminded? What is that? I wondered. Feeling nervous and scared, I reached out to hold my mom's hand.

The buildings were perched on top of a hill with a rolling green lawn filled with oak and sycamore trees and surrounded by flower beds that teemed with fragrant roses. The big white brick building with white columns loomed larger than life. It looked to me like the White House, which made me think of President Kennedy and Caroline and my dead father.

As we moved into the main building, I realized there was nothing *normal* about this tour. Several people were lined up along the halls in wheelchairs, while still others were tethered to their metal chairs with sheets as if they were on display. Many of the patients were making frightening sounds—wailing, crying, whimpering. One man's head rolled around while he made guttural sounds, and I noticed that cloudy cataracts covered the pupils of his wide-open eyes.

I clung to my mom's side, wishing that I was small enough for her to carry. I didn't understand what I was seeing, I didn't understand why we were there, and I felt sorry for those people who were being gawked at.

We reached a gymnasium, and a crowd of people gathered around the open glass front door. I couldn't see, so I wiggled my way between adult legs toward the front of the crowd.

The stench of feces and urine hit my face before I could see anything. But when I could see, I couldn't believe my eyes. Teenage boys were running around the gymnasium freely, wildly, screaming and laughing maniacally. Some of the boys were completely naked. One boy appeared to have been scratched by himself or others; the skin on his arms and legs was red and raw.

I didn't want to see what I was seeing, but I couldn't look away, either.

Finally, Mark grabbed me by the shoulder and pulled me away from the door. He seemed angry, but not at me.

I walked back to the car in a daze. *Why are these children in this place?*

The sun was now low in the sky and my flesh was covered with goose bumps. I was shivering from my fear of this place and felt a gripping sensation in my chest. I'd just seen so many things I didn't understand.

Arriving at the car, I was relieved to jump into the sun-baked back seat—the smell of the warmed leather upholstery so comforting.

In the front seat, my mom and sister chatted away as if there was nothing unusual about what we'd just witnessed, and we slowly drove down the winding, tree-lined driveway. Reminiscent of the day my father died, my somber fourteen-year-old brother sat looking at his folded hands. No one spoke to me. I didn't know what anyone was thinking. I didn't know how to even form the words for the questions in my own mind.

The summer breeze blew the faintest scent of those sweet roses through my open window, and I turned to look out the rear window. As Dixon State Mental Hospital began to fade into the distance, I inhaled deeply and thought I could taste the roses.

That, I decided, was what freedom must taste like.

Thinking of my father in his casket and the suffocating feeling I had experienced as I watched the lid being closed on his face, I shivered again and began to take deep breaths, reminding myself that I could breathe. But I would never be able to erase the memory of my dead father's waxy face and hands and that horrible, carnation stench-filled funeral parlor from my mind.

God, are you listening? What happened to these people? Why do bad things happen to good people? Why do some people die so young? What can I do? When I'm big, I want to help people. God, I think you are listening. I feel you in my heart, but I don't know about religion or church. Why don't you just tell us which is the right religion? Will I ever know the answers?

Maybe there weren't any answers. Even if there weren't, though, I decided I must make the most of my life. I would live for those kids, stuck in that wretched place, and for all the people who didn't get to live anymore, like my daddy.

In July, just after I turned eight, my mom sent me and Mark to St. Louis to spend a few weeks with our paternal grandmother—Clara, our German grandma—while she sold our house and moved us to an apartment. I liked our house. I liked my school. I liked my friend Donna. Having to say goodbye felt like something that would never end.

Grandma Clara was a soft, round seamstress with short, curly, steel-gray hair and round, gold-rimmed glasses. She loved to go to her Baptist church for the ice cream socials and potluck gatherings, and to dress up in her Sunday best.

That first Sunday morning with Grandma Clara, I sat in the pew next to her, squirming to keep my dress under my thighs so they didn't stick to the wooden pew. As I studied the netting and pearls on her pastel purple pillbox hat—perfectly matched to her pastel purple dress with pearl buttons—the refrains of a familiar song startled me to attention:

"Oh, Lamb of God, I come, I come!"

But what surprised me even more was watching Mark step out of a pew and walk up the aisle to the minister at the podium.

Afraid to be separated from my brother, I jumped up and ran to the podium next to him.

He gave me a scowling look that said, *You little brat. Why did you follow me?*

"Do you accept Jesus Christ as your Savior?" the minister asked us.

My heart was beating so hard it made my body shake, and so loudly that I couldn't hear anything else, but I must have responded yes, because the next thing I knew they were leading us to another room. A man was filling the rectangular baptismal tub in the middle of the room with water. A woman gave me a thin cotton dress. "Go into the bathroom and put this on," she instructed me.

When I emerged, the minister was fully clothed but barefoot, standing in the tub. "Cross your arms over your chest," he instructed.

I did as I was told and descended the few steps into the freezing water. As soon as I got waist-deep, my dress began floating to the surface. Embarrassed and struggling to keep my dress down, I forgot about crossing my arms over my chest.

The minister put one hand behind my head and pinched my nose closed with the other, then dunked me backward into the water. "In obedience to our Lord and Savior Jesus Christ," he intoned, "and upon your profession of faith, I baptize you, my sister, in the name of the Father, Son, and Holy Spirit. Amen."

I felt the fresh, cold water on my goose-bump-covered skin and heard his words, but I didn't really understand what any of it meant.

I shivered and shook as I stepped out of the tub and, dripping wet, walked back to the bathroom. I struggled to change into my dry clothes because no one had given me a towel to dry my dripping hair and my wet underpants.

When I finally finished changing, I stood on the concrete steps in front of the large wooden doors of the church in a daze, unsure of what to do. All I wanted was to go back to Grandma's apartment to change my wet clothes and eat some of her delicious crispy fried chicken and creamy mashed potatoes with white gravy and green beans that she'd cook in our breakfast bacon lard.

As I stood there, old and young congregants smiled at me and shook my hand and congratulated me. "Don't you feel wonderful?" they asked me. "Don't you feel clean?"

Yes, yes, I did. But as Grandma, Mark, and I got into the taxi to go to Grandma's house, I wasn't sure if it was because I really felt that way or because they were telling me I *should* feel clean.

Or was it just the cold bath I'd been given?

The following week, back home in our new two-bedroom apartment in Forestville, a suburb north of Riverside, my friend Cheryl called to ask if I would like to go with her and her family to Pearl Lake to go swimming.

I'd learned at the St. Louis church that Baptists believed exposing your body in a swimsuit and swimming and dancing were sins. But it was a hot, clothes-stick-to-your-body muggy July day, and the idea of swimming in a cool lake sounded heavenly. Plus, I loved swimming—and dancing too.

I considered my options for a moment, then decided I was an accidental Baptist anyway.

"Yes!" I told Cheryl eagerly. "I'll be right there."

TRIPLE A

Mom was a buxom, long-legged, blonde, and youthful forty-seven-year-young beauty, and Paul was a handsome, raven-haired, thirty-four-year-old Marlon Brando type—a tough-guy character with dark brown eyes behind metal-rimmed glasses that crinkled into small slits when he laughed.

My mom seemed happy with Paul. She laughed and giggled more and sang along with her favorite songs on the radio. But I was confused as to how I should feel.

He wasn't my dad. My dad was dead—and it hadn't been so long since he died, just a year and a half. Were we supposed to just forget him?

It didn't seem to matter much what I thought or felt, though. I met Paul for the first time in the spring, and by the end of summer he was living with us. Before long, my sister moved out, my brother was relegated to the couch, and my mom and Paul took over my brother's bedroom.

"Goddammit, here they are," my sister spat, her angry presence startling me as she joined me on the balcony.

I'd just run to the balcony after hearing my mom's laughter in the parking lot below our apartment, ecstatic that my mom was home—but now my sister was shouting curses at her and Paul and tossing Paul's clothes over the second-floor balcony railing.

My mom and Paul stopped laughing and stooped to pick the clothes up. When they rose and looked up at Sharon again, their faces turned somber.

During their twenty-three years of marriage, my mom and dad had never traveled beyond Missouri and Illinois, so when Paul asked my mom to go to Mexico, she'd jumped around gleefully like a little kid. Then she'd called June—an old neighbor back in Collinsville, a day's drive away—to see if my brother and I could stay with her.

June had agreed. But after a week or so, Mom and Paul still weren't back—and when June asked us when they would be picking us up, of course neither of us had any idea. So, June had called Sharon, who'd told June to put us on a bus back to Riverside.

"I can't believe she would do this," she'd fumed when she picked us up from the bus station. I couldn't understand what she was so mad about.

My siblings and I met Mom and Paul on the landing as they walked toward the apartment. Mom was tanned, beaming, and looked refreshed with a big, ridiculous Mexican sombrero on her head. I ran to hug her, but my sister got to her first—and the sombrero went flying.

Sharon had just *slapped* our mom. I couldn't believe it.

"How dare you abandon your children!" she screamed, her voice shrill. "You should be ashamed of yourself!"

"I didn't abandon my children. They were safe with June." My mom spoke softly and calmly but she looked stunned, and she seemed to choke on the words.

"I almost called the police!" Sharon snapped.

"Sharon, what are you talking about? You knew where we were, and you knew the kids were safe." Mom's beautiful face looked pained and sad.

Paul and Mark stood sheepishly to the side, looking just as helpless as I felt. I ran to Paul's side, and he put his hand on my shoulder. I looked at his face to clue me in on what to do. His concerned gaze was fixed on my mom, and his jaw muscles twitched.

I had never seen my family in this kind of emotional tangle. Shaking, I started to cry. I was afraid that my sister had hurt my mom. I only wanted her to be happy, and if she wanted and needed Paul in her life to be happy, then I did too.

My sister angrily stomped away, still shouting at my mom that she was a terrible mother and had neglected her children.

What did this all mean? Why couldn't Sharon just be happy for Mom?

In that instant, I decided I would *never* fight with my mom. I was so afraid she would die like my dad. I only wanted to take care of her and make her happy.

In October we moved from the apartment into a new rental house, and I started the fourth grade in a new school. The semester passed by in the blink of an eye; before I knew it, it was Christmas.

On Christmas Eve, we visited my mom and Paul's friends and their kids.

The trendy drink of choice that year was a nasty-smelling Swedish concoction called glögg. Served hot in mugs, it was supposed to be a remedy for taking off the cold winter chill, and the adults all happily accepted numerous refills that night.

It was the host family's custom to allow their children to open their presents on Christmas Eve. I watched these children squeal with delight with each present they ripped open as I awkwardly smiled. Naturally, there was nothing there for me or my brother. I tried to be happy for them and not act like a brat. I knew that my presents were already under the tree at home.

Later, after we arrived at home, Mom turned on the magical Christmas tree lights so we could gaze at them for a few minutes before bedtime. I got into my pajamas and sat on the hardwood floor, picking up the presents labeled with my name, shaking and squeezing them to try to guess the contents. Having anxiously watched those kids open all their presents, I was exploding with excitement about Santa coming, although that myth had already been debunked.

"Oh, Mom, could Mark and I open just *one* present?" I pleaded.

"I guess it wouldn't hurt to open one," Mom said, and she handed me a hastily wrapped soft package.

But as I opened it, Paul blurted out, "No, goddammit, it's not Christmas yet!"

"Oh, what's the big deal?" Mom said. "It's just a pair of socks."

"I told you *no*, goddammit, and I meant *no*."

He lunged for the heavily decorated Christmas tree and threw the whole thing—icicles, delicate bulbs, and all—to the floor.

Hot piercing fear exploded in my gut and my heart. I tried to breathe as I watched the brightly colored ornaments crash into glass splinters, but the air felt like sharp ice. The broken glass pieces mixed with the shimmering icicles as they slid across the wooden floor.

I lifted out of my body; the seconds went by in slow motion. The lights continued to blink as if nothing had happened. *What is wrong with Paul?* The air was infused with the glögg he had drunk, and he suddenly was a different person. *How could he do that to our tree?*

Paul wheeled around, his bloodshot wide eyes bulging with rage. He was a solid, muscular man. I'd learned that he had a brown belt in karate, which meant he was strong, and his arms and hands were hardened from years of working in manual labor and factories.

My frightened mother mewed, "Now, Paul, look what you've done. I know you didn't mean to do that."

"The hell I didn't! I'll kill everybody!" he roared, his face as red as a forest fire. He wrung his hands as if he was looking for something else to throw.

I froze at the threat of death. It tasted bitter in my mouth. Images of my dead father in his casket rushed into my mind. The next image was of my nine-year-old body in a child-size casket.

Paul pushed my mom into the tiny bathroom, using his whole body like a bulldozer, and forced her to step into the open bathtub.

I followed along, crying and pleading for him to stop, terrified he would hurt my mom. "Please, Paul, stop! I'm so sorry I asked to open a present. It's all my fault. Don't hurt my mom! It's *my* fault." I begged and shook and cried. I had to save my mom.

"Leave our mom alone!" Mark cried, running into the bathroom.

It took only one swoop of Paul's muscular arm to pin my thin, lanky brother to the wall.

"Stop it, Paul, stop it now," Mom pleaded. "You don't know what you're doing. You're drunk. I know you don't mean this. Come on, Paul, let the kids go. I'll call Sharon to come get them."

Mom kept talking, and finally Paul released Mark and walked out of the bathroom. We watched, eyes wide, as he went upstairs to the bedroom and Mom went to the kitchen to call Sharon.

I raced after Mom and clung to her as she picked up the phone, and I saw red and purple marks emerging on her arms. My heart pounded, but at least Paul was no longer next to us. Still, what would happen when we were gone? Would things get worse or better? I wanted to stay and protect my mom. But what could I do?

Mark and I sat in a daze on the couch, slack like airless balloons. Our coats covered our pajamas, and we tried not to look at each other while we waited for our twenty-one-year-old sister to come pick us up.

Sharon pulled into the driveway, and Mom rushed us out to the car and told Sharon to take us to our aunt and uncle's house, where we would spend the night. Sharon cursed and muttered the whole way there about Paul being crazy and how she did not approve of Mom being with him. When we arrived at my aunt and uncle's house, they clicked their tongues and said as much too as they led me and Mark into my older cousin's childhood bedroom, empty now that he had moved out on his own.

I fell asleep tired, confused, and hoped and prayed that Santa Claus would fix everything.

On Christmas day, our aunt and uncle tried to be cheerful, but their lips were pursed, and a heaviness filled the house.

"I'm sorry we don't have presents for you kids. I mean, of course we didn't expect you to be here Christmas morning." My Aunt Hazel stated all this matter-of-factly, but her voice was edged with judgment and sarcasm, and she was scowling. "I just don't know what your mom is doing with him. She's better than him—isn't she, Willie?"

My uncle just grunted in response.

"He's just a no-good troublemaker is what he is," she finally declared.

All the angry sniping about my mom made my stomach hurt even though I loved the hot chocolate my aunt had served me. *Maybe I don't deserve any presents from Santa for being such a brat and asking to open a present before Christmas and making Paul go crazy.*

Christmas afternoon, Sharon finally brought Mom to pick us up. I ran to the door to give her a big hug and breathed in her scent, relieved to see that she seemed to be all right.

"Well, it's good to see that you are okay. Are those bruises on your arm? What in the world, Elda?!" my aunt exclaimed.

My sister shook her head grimly and glanced up at my aunt and uncle, lips squeezed together.

"Everything is okay," Mom said calmly. "Paul just had a bit too much to drink. He's sorry. Thank you for letting the kids come here last night. Let's go, kids."

She ushered us out to the car. As we drove home, she said, "Mark and Wendy, you must know that Paul doesn't even remember what he did. He was drunk, and he didn't mean to do that. He is sorry for what he did."

If that's what glögg does to a person, then maybe you shouldn't drink it, I thought. But my mom was okay, and that was all that mattered.

When we got home, there was no apology from Paul. Everyone just went on about their business.

Some inner voice told me that none of this was my fault, even though I'd asked to open a present. Deep down, I sensed that Paul's behavior was unacceptable, that there must be something wrong with him.

"Remember his good side too," Mom said. "He is a good person even though he drinks."

I wasn't sure I agreed with her, but I just wanted my mother's love. To make sure she wouldn't leave me, I'd do anything she said.

It was May, a few months before I turned ten years old, and a cool, wet April had nurtured the vegetation back to life in Forestville. The lilacs were in full bloom in every yard I passed as I walked to school. I skipped down the road, and the intoxicating aroma followed me from bush to bush. I ran up to each lilac bush and buried my nose in the fresh purple flowers. I broke off a sprig of lilacs and shoved it into my pocket. With each inhalation of those lilacs, I felt that I was waking up to life all around me.

Today, though, I was viewing our neighborhood's lilac-filled streets through our car window; it was Saturday morning, and my mom and Paul were driving me somewhere.

"Where are we going, Mommy?" I asked.

"Triple A," she nonchalantly answered.

My heart raced, and I felt relief. Mom and I had taken a taxi to one Al-Anon meeting a few months before. I'd learned at that meeting that drinking alcohol could be dangerous and harmful, both to the person drinking and to those around them. I thought Triple A meant AA, and we were going to get some help for Paul.

"You mean . . . we're going to Alcoholics Anonymous?" I asked hesitatingly.

"No!" Mom replied, and angrily snapped her head around to face me in the back seat.

Oh. Too late, I realized that my mom had not told Paul that she and I had gone to that Al-Anon meeting.

"Where in the world did you get that idea?" she said quickly. "Triple A, not AA. We're going to get some maps at Triple A."

"Oh." So we weren't going to get help from those nice, concerned people. My shoulders sank, and I hung my head.

Paul looked at my mom, and she looked back. I tensed. Would Paul explode?

But no, he looked away—he was letting it go. My body relaxed.

I looked out the window. After what I'd witnessed on Christmas Eve a few months earlier, and Paul's bad mood every holiday and weekend that he drank, I thought we *should* be going back to Al-Anon or AA. But I knew better than to say that.

As we drove along, I thought of the previous week when Mom and I were home alone and I'd had the courage to ask her, "Mom, why is Paul so angry? What is wrong with him?"

"Wendy," she began haltingly, "he's only starting to tell me things. His father used to beat him and his mother. He has a younger sister, Shirley, and a younger brother, Ernie, and he had an older sister, Betty, who died of encephalitis, a brain disease, when she was young. Paul had to leave the house when he was twelve and go to live on a neighboring farm. He lived in the barn and worked for the farmer. I think his father is already dead, though."

That was a lot to learn about Paul's life, but I wanted to know more. "Where is his mom and brother and sister?" I asked. "Why doesn't he see them?"

"I don't know yet, Wendy, but there is something else I do know."

I held my breath as I waited for the rest of the sentence.

"Paul was married before, and he has five kids."

The concerned look on her face and her mysterious tone worried me. "What?" I whispered. "He has children that he doesn't see anymore?" I asked, horrified. "Do you know where they live? How old are they? What are their names? Why don't we see them?"

It was all so confusing to me. How could such a sad story be true?

"Whenever he tried to see his kids, his ex-wife would call the cops and have him thrown in jail." My mom shrugged. "I made him go to the courthouse and pay up all the child support he owed and set up monthly payments. The kids live in Wisconsin and are all much older than you. The youngest was just a baby when he left."

"Can we meet them?"

Mom said she didn't have any more answers yet.

From the backseat of the car, I gazed out the window at the blur of purple lilac bushes rushing by, and I thought about Paul's five kids who he never saw. I wondered who this man was that lived with us. Would I always have to be afraid when he drank? Evidently, I was the only one in the car who knew that instead of going to Triple A for maps, we should be headed to AA for a road map back to sanity. I never wanted to be afraid like I had been at Christmas ever again, and I never wanted to see my mom in danger or have another holiday ruined.

Sighing, I pulled yesterday's crumpled lilac cluster from my pocket; buried my nose in the soft, purple flowers; and inhaled deeply.

ROCKY MOUNTAIN HIGH

"Happy birthday, Wendy! Pack your bags! We're going out west to Colorado!" Mom brushed the hair from my eyes, kissed my cheek, and smiled broadly, flashing those beautiful white teeth. "Why don't you invite your friend Cheryl to come along?"

Open-mouthed with delighted surprise, I picked up the phone to call Cheryl. Her parents immediately approved when I asked if she could join us.

Mom and Paul had been poring over the glossy brochures they'd picked up at Triple A that day in May for over a month now, and they were ready for an adventure. And they were going to take me—and a friend too! Mom was the best mom. And maybe Paul was cool too. This was going to be amazing, our very first ever family vacation.

Well, "family" vacation. It wouldn't include Sharon, who was already living on her own, or Mark, who had become very dedicated to his Baptist church recently. But I didn't dwell on that fact for very long. I was too excited for the trip.

"You want to go for a hike with me, Wendy Beth?" Paul asked.

"Sure!" I said, jumping up from my seat.

I didn't really know what a hike entailed, but I was flattered to be invited. So while Mom and Cheryl stayed back at the cabin to rest, I eagerly joined Paul for a hike around Lake Granby.

We'd driven the green Rambler—full of blankets and pillows, AAA books and maps, and a cooler filled with sandwich makings, potato chips, soda pop, and beer—all the way to Granby, Colorado, where we were staying at a dude ranch. For the last few days, we'd ridden horses on breakfast trail rides and, in the evening, joined campfire sing-alongs under black skies laden with bright falling stars and an array of constellations the likes of which I had never seen before. Cheryl and I were two Midwest, flatland, corn-fed kids in awe of this land of mountain peaks, roaring mountain rivers, and real cowboys and cowgirls. It was like living inside an episode of the TV show *The Wild Wild West*, which I loved watching back home.

Lake Granby was a sparkling turquoise lake surrounded by stately mountains rising tall into the vast, azure sky. Paul and I made our way around it without saying much, quiet in our own thoughts.

Walking along behind Paul, I noticed he was drinking a beer, and my heart sank a little. Knots had formed in my stomach over the months since Christmas. I constantly worried about him drinking now, even though Mom always said to focus on his good side, and I felt guilty worrying in this moment, since he'd brought me to breathtaking Colorado.

Anyway, since no one talked to me about my feelings, I sometimes wasn't sure if I even had a right to feel them.

Still, I was wary of Paul, and I watched him when he drank, wondering how many it would take before his mood changed from happy-go-lucky to angry and violent. Even when he wasn't drinking, he often seemed upset and used curse words I had only heard from the bad boys at school, like *goddammit* and *fuck*.

All this worried me so much that I'd started having severe stomachaches. The pain had become so bad, in fact, that mom had taken me to the doctor a couple of months back. He'd diagnosed my condition as a "spastic colon" and prescribed medicine for me to take called Librium. But after she watched me go through a full week of severe grogginess, to the point that I was unable to get out of my bed, my mom flushed the pills down the toilet and said enough of that.

So far on this trip, though, Paul seemed okay, and when he stopped to sit on a large boulder, I sat next to him.

The sun reflected off the emerald-green lake and created rainbows of light. Paul looked so peaceful sitting there, taking in the beautiful sight. I gazed at the deep shadows on the distant, ponderosa pine-covered mountain slope as if I was gazing into a crystal ball. I looked into the future and imagined a peaceful life filled with awe and lightness and a contented happiness that I had never known. I inhaled the thin Colorado mountain air and peered at the clearest, deepest blue sky I'd ever seen. I didn't really understand what I felt except that I felt more at home there than I did in my actual home back in Illinois. I felt somehow lightened and free.

I decided right then and there that when I grew up, I would live in Colorado.

Paul didn't say anything, but I could tell the landscape before us calmed him too.

After a few minutes of absorbing the view, he stood and dusted off his pants. "We should get back."

I nodded and followed his lead.

From Granby to Glenwood Hot Springs to Yellowstone National Park, our trip was just as amazing as I'd hoped it would be. I really took to traveling; I felt carefree and content as I experienced the vast world outside of Forestville, Illinois.

Perhaps the best part of all, though, was that Paul didn't drink much on our trip. He seemed easygoing and relaxed, and I felt calmer around him.

I wished we could just stay on the open road forever, where Mom and Paul and I were happy and lighthearted and at peace.

The fall after that summer trip, I entered the fifth grade.

I wasn't typically allowed to do anything that cost money. There were no after-school programs or summer camps. I didn't have piano or violin lessons, or dance, or gymnastics, or any sports or art classes. I wanted to, but I didn't dare ask for any of it. If it wasn't offered for free at school, I didn't get it.

Thankfully, listening to the radio and watching TV were free, and *American Bandstand* and *Soul Train* and Motown were the bright lights in my life. I listened to the Chicago AM radio station WLS, which famously introduced new music and recording artists and played the Top 40, Top 10 R&B hits, and the greatest oldies in those days (in February of 1963, WLS was the first US radio station to play the Beatles' record "Please, Please Me"). When I turned on the radio in the living room and sang along to Four Tops, the Beatles, Herman's Hermits, the Mamas & the Papas, the Supremes, the Box Tops, and the Jackson 5 and danced the way I had seen the girls on TV dance, I felt hope and happiness, and my fear of Paul and his moods disappeared from my mind.

From time to time, Paul also surprised me with an occasional unexpected kindness.

One day he came home and handed me an LP. I laughed at the cover, which had the Mamas & the Papas lying in an empty bathtub, and I rushed to put it on the stereo turntable. It was the group's first album, and I especially loved the song "California Dreamin'," which I'd heard many times on the radio.

"Thank you, thank you!" I jumped up and down with excitement. How had he known I would love it so much?

He grinned. "You're welcome. I thought you might like to have your very first LP. Keep singing along. You're a good singer, like your mom."

In that moment, it was easy to focus on his good side.

It was Saturday night, and my mom and Paul were gone for the evening. I invited Dorothy, Sheila, Rhonda, and Gina—four new friends since the beginning of fifth grade—over for a sleepover.

It turned out that these girls were a bit rough for being only ten years old. They talked about sex and giggled about boys, and they previously taught me how to smoke in Sheila's bedroom.

I had tried smoking once before, when I was eight; and as a latchkey kid, I was home alone and lit up a Salem cigarette butt with the marks of my sister's red lipstick on the filter. I'd done it because my sister made it look so grown up to smoke and because I was a little afraid and sad being home alone. So now, when Dorothy handed me a Winston cigarette, I felt smug and grown up; I thought I knew what to do.

I put the cigarette in my mouth, struck the match, and put the flame to the cigarette—but forgot to puff on the cigarette. My friends fell into a heap of laughter on the bed. I started to choke and cough, and tears spilled down my cheeks.

Before long, though, I would be an expert smoker, French inhaling and blowing smoke rings.

That night at our sleepover, we practiced singing the Box Tops' big hit "The Letter" and performed the accompanying dance we'd made up for the school talent show. We wore our matching flowered, sleeveless shift dresses that we'd purchased from Riverside Dry Goods, the department store where the wealthy kids shopped (a rare occasion for the five of us).

After we finished practicing, we piled blankets and pillows on the living room floor to make a pallet to sleep on.

"Wendy, have you ever snuck into your parents' booze?" Rhonda asked, flashing her bright blue eyes and deep dimples.

"Nooo, of course not," I stated vehemently. But looking around at the other girls' faces, I realized that all the rest of them *had* done it. "What? You all *have*?" I exclaimed, suddenly nervous.

"It's easy," Dorothy said. "We just add water back into the bottle, so they don't notice any missing."

I had always wondered why Paul drank—what it did for him. Now seemed like the time to find out. "Okay," I conceded. "Let's do it!"

We jumped up, squealing with excitement about doing something bad and dangerous. We gathered up Paul's numerous bottles of vodka, gin, whiskey, and tequila; piled them on our blanket pallet; and took a few swigs off each bottle, carefully noting how full each bottle was and adding water back in as we moved from bottle to bottle.

"My whole body feels warm," I slurred, laughing after numerous gulps.

We giggled and laughed as we heard each other speak with funny, garbled voices, and we swayed and fell on the pallet and talked about how numb our faces felt until we all passed out.

It was the first time in a long time that I didn't feel fear rumbling in my stomach.

So that's what Paul feels when he drinks, I thought.

I exhaled. It felt good to be drunk and numb.

SUMMER OF LOVE

The summer of 1967 was called the Summer of Love. Jimi Hendrix burned his guitar, Janis Joplin belted and boozed, Jim Morrison wanted to "light my fire," and the Grateful Dead and Jefferson Airplane played free concerts in Golden Gate Park. It was the be-ins, sit-ins, love-ins; psychedelic, velvet, black light, glow-in-the dark posters; and "bell-bottomed Elvis married beehive-haired Priscilla" kind of summer.

For me, however—an eleven-year-old kid from Forestville, Illinois—the Summer of Love was another summer out exploring the country with my mom and Paul.

Paul sold the Rambler and bought a VW van. He built out the back of the van to fit a double mattress bed where he and my mom would sleep. Then he built a low rectangular box with compartments for dishes, pots, pans, and camping equipment, covered on the top with a soft foam cushion for sitting and, for me, sleeping on at night.

I was already learning at this tender age that human beings are complicated, unpredictable creatures with good and bad traits. I was beginning to understand that good people do bad things and bad people do good things. Paul's scary dark side showed up to mar his good side more often than I liked—but during our vacation to Colorado the previous summer, his good side had won out the whole time. So, I was excited to be embarking on our second cross-country vacation together. This time, just the three of us.

I loved lying on the mattress in the back of the van, listening to the radio piped in through box speakers that Paul rigged and gazing out the window at the clouds as we rolled west down the wide-open highway. For hours at a time, I also sat on a makeshift stool close to Mom and Paul's front bucket seats and asked them to tell me stories.

"Mom," I prompted one day, "tell me about your family history. Who are our ancestors?"

"Well, you know we are a large, loving Missouri family with ten kids, except my little sister Helen died when she was young of pneumonia," she told me. "I think we have French, English, Scottish, and a little bit of Illinois Kaskaskia Native American roots."

"Really?" My eyes widened. "How do you know that? And who was the first person to come to America?"

"Oh, I think on my mom's side there were two French explorers who came to North America in the 1600s and eventually built and lived at Fort de Chartres in southern Illinois, where they lived with the Native people, then the family eventually crossed the Mississippi into French territory when the British took over. Your cousin George has researched the family tree. We'll get a copy from him."

Her details were sketchy, but even so, I was enthralled by these stories of my adventurous and tough ancestors. I often dreamed about being an early explorer myself.

"What were songs you liked to sing as a kid?" I asked next. I plied her with questions as if I had never met her before.

"Oh, I loved this one," she said and then launched into the funniest song I had ever heard called "Mairzy Doats".

She taught me the lyrics and then we sang them as fast and garbled as we could until we broke down in hysterical laughter.

"Here's another one you should know, Wendy," she said. "I learned this one from our Black granny midwife who delivered all of us kids at home."

"Little mouse in yonder's well,
Lingo little makimbo
If he ain't got out he's in there still,
Lingo little makimbo
Kid a makay dose a malary kid a ma, kid a ma kimbo
Jump straw diddle and a baldy no,
Lingo little makimbo!"

Mom's deep, resonant voice rang out as she sang.

Barbed wire fences enclosed open ranges as far as the eye could see on both sides of the highway, filled with grazing cattle and rolling hills sparsely dotted with trees. Mom taught me all four verses of "Lingo Little Makimbo" until I could sing it with her, starting slowly and speeding up faster and faster through the verses.

Suddenly Paul said, "I've got a story for you, Wendy Beth."

He began telling me a story about his ex-wife and first-born child, Betty, who was named for his sister who had died. He'd never told me about any of them before—he'd never even mentioned his ex-wife or kids—but I knew some of the story through what Mom had already told me, including the fact that his sister had died young of an inflammation of the brain called encephalitis.

Mom looked out the window as Paul spoke, and I stayed quiet, pretending that I didn't already know any of what he was recounting; I wanted him to tell me more.

"Well," Paul continued, "it was a beautiful and snowy but bitter-cold Illinois winter day. Man, it was so cold you couldn't hardly even go outside, and if you did, your lungs and nose hairs immediately froze and you got icicles on your eyebrows. All we had to keep warm was a woodburning stove. I had already chopped a cord of wood for the winter and had a few days' supply stacked up in the cabin. I had to keep the fire going all night long for warmth, and that was no easy task if the wood was wet. We didn't have a crib for the baby, so I made her a bed from a dresser drawer and filled it with soft blankets and kept her close to the fire to make sure she was warm."

I could imagine yellow and red flickering flames licking the air from the cast iron stove, the snow drifts piled up to the windowsill, glistening crystal icicles hanging from the roof like stalactites. I could smell the earthy burning wood. I could hear the logs crackling and feel the warmth emanating from the fire on my face. It was such a simple story, but I loved it. I felt closer to Paul having learned how he cared for his infant daughter. It gave me a glimpse into his good side, the good side Mom always reminded me of. The story revealed that he felt tender and nurturing toward his baby girl, and I could sense a sadness within him just as I had sensed the sadness of my daddy before he died.

I wanted to ask, to plead, why he didn't see her, why we didn't know her, but I knew that was a taboo topic so instead I just said, "I love that story. Will you please tell me again?"

I sat back and stared out at the horizon, past the vast, open prairie, and wondered, *What kind of life do his five kids have? Do they also have a stepfather?* It seemed so odd to me that Paul now referred to me as his daughter when he introduced me to a stranger. He wasn't even married to my mom. How could he call me his daughter when he didn't see his other kids? *Should I call him "Dad"?*

Thinking about doing that felt like a betrayal of my real father. It was all too much for me to think about, and to feel the sadness in his story and my own.

I moved to the mattress at the back of the van, pulled a warm quilt over me, and was lulled to sleep by the gentle humming of the van's wheels turning, lightly hypnotized by streaks of brilliant baby blue and pink hues as the sun set across the vast Nebraska-prairie sky.

During this Summer of Love, we finally made our way to San Francisco and to the corner of Haight-Ashbury. The fog had burned off to reveal a crystal clear, sunny, and unusually warm San Francisco day. The streets were packed with people milling about, some carrying large banners that shouted MAKE LOVE, NOT WAR. A tangled nest of hippie kids marched by, led by a barefoot hippie with ratty long hair in an army jacket emblazoned with colorful peace signs. Like the Pied Piper, he led them to yell out the letters F-U-C-K as they belted out a protest song by Country Joe and the Fish. The stragglers flashed the peace sign and handed out wilting daises to the bystanders as they sauntered down the sidewalk. They seemed so innocent and friendly, and I looked at Mom and Paul to see their reaction. They just laughed and were amused. Mom even began to flash the peace sign back at the hippies and giggle.

We wandered in and out of shops heavy with an earthy, smoky scent that I learned was called incense. The shops sold T-shirts, flowy and flowered long skirts, jewelry, strange newspapers with naked people on the front, and large black light posters. Mom bought me a hippie love bead necklace that was out of place with my JCPenney matching short set, but I loved it and thought wearing it made me look so *groovy*—a word I'd recently learned and liked saying.

Overwhelmed with the sights, I wanted to stop and stare and take it all in.

"Can I stay out here and wait?" I asked as we walked toward the next shop.

She hesitated.

"I'll stand right here, and I won't go anywhere," I promised.

She nodded. "Okay. We'll be out in a few minutes. Don't move."

Young men and women walked by with their ragged bell-bottom blue jeans dragging around their bare feet, their long hair either braided or streaming down their shoulders, their faces painted with flowers and hearts. Some tossed flower petals into the wind, and I detected the smell of incense and what I would later learn was marijuana intermingling in the air.

I was so overwhelmed by the sights and smells I had to prop myself against a street sign for balance.

A young hippie walked up the sidewalk toward me. He must have been about sixteen, the same age as David Cassidy of *The Partridge Family* and the other dreamy boys in the teen magazines. His wide smile and sparkling dark brown eyes caught my attention, and once they did, I couldn't take my eyes off him. His sleeveless, fringed leather vest just slightly covered his bare chest, which was adorned with layers of necklaces made from pukka shells and silver and turquoise beads. His long, curly brown hair hung over his shoulders and down his back. I focused on his long, toned, tanned arms and the sprinkle of freckles across his nose.

He swaggered up to me, stroking a scruffy beard. His disheveled appearance belied the sweetness of the glimmer in his eyes and the mischievous, slightly upward turn of his lips. I'd never seen anything like this hippie boy back home, and his aura made me catch my breath.

He stopped in front of me, looked me up and down, and gestured to my hippie necklace. "So, are you a hippie or a yippie?" he said, his eyes twinkling.

Shocked that he was speaking to me, I struggled to find words. "I . . . I . . . I . . . I don't know what I am!" I finally managed to sputter, my face feeling hot and flushed.

"Oh, that's okay, kid!" he said cheerfully. "Most people don't know who or what they really are, but I have a feeling you'll find out, you'll find out. You have a good life now, okay?"

And just like that he disappeared into the meandering crowd, taking with him my breath and my heart, and leaving me wondering if what he'd said was true. Would I really find out who I was one day?

Sometimes I wasn't so sure.

Mom, Paul, and I climbed into the van to make our way to Chinatown. I noticed that Paul had purchased one of those newspapers with the naked people on it and put it under his seat, which made me feel squeamish.

I was still in a daze thinking about that hippie boy when my attention turned to the dragons, fish, and big lions adorning the ornate, pagoda-topped Dragon Gate at the entrance of Chinatown.

I was immediately overwhelmed by the sights, and again, I wanted to stop to take it all in, but Mom and Paul kept walking. I felt like I had been transported to a foreign country; I tried to make sense of the Chinese-style architectural facades, pagoda-topped buildings, gilded storefronts, and narrow, bustling streets and sidewalks. Even the lampposts were brightly painted and topped with intricate Chinese lanterns.

From a plaque on a wall, I learned that red, which symbolized good fortune and happiness, and yellow, which generated something called "yin and yang" or the center of everything, were the dominant colors in Chinese culture. Hundreds of red and yellow banners flapped in the wind amongst a sea of signs, their yellow Chinese characters popping out against red backgrounds. Gazing toward the sky, my sight was filled with red round Chinese lanterns that were strung across the street in rows as far as I could see. From the balconies and windows on the buildings, underwear and other laundry was hung out to dry.

Hundreds of small, family-owned shops and restaurants packed the streets. Shops with names like Peking Bazaar were filled floor to ceiling with souvenirs: intricately embroidered Chinese silk clothing, beaded slippers, plastic costume jewelry, Chinese porcelain tea sets, chopsticks, smiling golden Buddhas, and various trinkets made from jade and ivory in glass cases. With no room to spare, the entire ceiling was covered with Chinese lanterns in various sizes and colors.

Freshly slaughtered chickens and ducks hung by their intact claws, and piles of fish, eyes bulging, stared at me from their ice beds in the butcher shops we passed. The mix of the smell of fresh blood and raw fish made me gag.

All the shops were filled with vendors and buyers haggling in Chinese for the best bargain.

Struggling to take in all the sights and keep up with my mom and Paul as we darted through the sea of people meandering on the crowded sidewalk, my brain was also processing the sounds—multiple layers of voices, clanging metal, honking car horns, and music. The expressive, lively tone of Mandarin was foreign to me, but quite pleasing. Traditional Chinese folk music, with the twangy, playful sounds of the zither layered with the lilting melodies of the harp and lute, emanated from every shop we passed.

Inhaling deeply to keep my short legs moving, I was assaulted by car fumes mixed with the stench of bags of garbage piled on the sidewalk and spilling into the street as well as the more pleasant aromas of garlic and ginger emanating from all the restaurants—all that wafted in the breeze to my confused nose. I wondered how a place could be filled with such wonderful smells and awful smells at the same time. I also wondered how the people who lived there could live with the stench and the constant roar of sound and clanging.

I was grateful when we turned onto a quiet side street and found the herb shop that Paul had been looking for.

Inside the apothecary, we turned toward the long, well-worn wooden counter. Behind the counter, the wall was covered with hundreds of small wooden drawers with brass pulls and, above them, shelves full of gallon-size glass jars that rose nearly to the ceiling.

Paul handed the Chinese man behind the counter the recipe for "Chinese medicine," written in Chinese, that one of his sensei in Chicago had given him a while back. Supposedly, it was an ancient recipe used by martial artists. If we had a cut, bruise, sprain, hangnail, or any ache or pain in our house, Paul would say, "Put Chinese medicine on it."

The Chinese man nodded seriously, pulled a length of brown butcher paper from a large roll on a metal rod that was bolted onto the counter, ripped the paper from the roll, and laid it on the counter with a flourish. Then he began to pull open numerous wooden drawers from the wall and placed handfuls of what appeared to be bark, twigs, leaves, dried grasses, sliced roots, ferns, pods, seeds, and some orange furry thing that looked like dried flower petals on the paper. One handful of bark had a beautiful concentric, mandala-like pattern, and another sliced root had a strong medicinal smell. Out of the final drawer came black chunks of—what? Was that dung?

For his final act, the Chinese herbalist slid the wooden ladder over to reach one of the gallon jars near the ceiling, then placed on top of the pile a handful of the exoskeletons of cicadas. I was too fascinated to be grossed out by the bugs and dung.

He wrapped the whole thing up in the butcher paper and taped it closed.

The bitter, pungent smell of Paul's herbs filled the van all the way to Disneyland and back to Illinois. When we got home, he placed the contents of the package into a large gallon jar filled with alcohol, where it simmered and stewed for a few months until our next batch of "Chinese medicine" was fully brewed. It would last us for many sore, achy muscles, cuts, and bruises as well as treatments of my mom's arthritic hands in the coming years.

I had experienced so many magical and wonderful people and places on the trip. The whole thing had felt like going to Disneyland.

Despite its lovely name, Forestville looked more like Dullsville in comparison.

The previous year, Paul had decided to get a German shepherd puppy. A thoroughbred police dog, his full registered name was Sheba's Prince Tawny, but we called him Tawny.

I loved Tawny when he was a cute, soft puppy, but I became more and more afraid of him as he grew bigger and more aggressive.

Diagnosed with hip dysplasia, poor Tawny limped and was in obvious pain. Paul had no patience with him, and with no desire to spend money on learning how to train a dog, he beat him with a rolled-up newspaper whenever he misbehaved. My stomach knotted up and tears burst from my eyes every time this happened; when Tawny yelped and slunk into the corner with his tail between his legs, I felt his pain.

One evening shortly after we returned from our vacation, Paul spontaneously began a game of tag with me. I never had liked this game, even with other kids, but went along because Paul was acting like a friendly kid wanting to play—a rare occurrence. Although I knew to be careful around him, especially whenever he was drinking or just moody, I joined in on the game and let down my guard.

Tawny, excited by our running around the backyard, jumped straight up into the air, barking, straining at his chain.

Wanting the game to be over but also thinking I was being clever, I ran toward the house, slipped through the back door, and locked the screen. Before I had a chance to realize that was not a good idea, Paul pulled on the screen door so hard that he nearly pulled it off its hinges.

Entering the kitchen, eyes fierce and glaring, jaw and fists clenched, Paul stomped up to me and hissed, "Don't you ever lock me out of my own goddamn house ever again!"

I stood there shaking, my heart pounding with fear, wondering if he would kill me. Feeling like Tawny, I put my tail between my legs and ran to my room—to my Mickey Dolenz of the Monkees posters, to the Motown music on the radio, to my fantasy of fleeing from home.

During the day, while Mom and Paul worked and Mark and I were at school, Tawny was chained up outside next to his doghouse. One night when we went to feed him his evening meal, we noticed that his dog food bowl was out of his reach—strange, since we had left his breakfast for him in the morning, and we knew we'd put the bowl close to him. How had it gotten so far away?

When we put the full bowl next to him, he wolfed the food down hurriedly, as if he was starving, and acted nervous, like he thought his food would be taken away.

The same thing happened for many nights, until one night, while we were eating dinner, Tawny started barking. I looked out the back door—and there was a huge pig, pushing Tawny's bowl just out of his reach and eating his food.

Paul ran out the door and chased the pig away, but the pig kept coming back. Day after day, we came home to find the bowl just out of Tawny's reach, and Tawny starving.

Our rental house sat at the edge of a farmer's cornfield; I assumed the pig must belong to him. "Shouldn't we call the farmer and tell him his pig keeps getting out of its pen?" I asked.

Instead, Paul decided Tawny should have his revenge on the pig. The next time the pig showed up, he let Tawny off his chain.

I felt so scared for the pig. "Run, pig, run!" I cried.

And it did—but Tawny tore off after it. I could hear the pig squealing and the cornstalks breaking and crunching as it ran for its life through the cornfield.

A few hours later, Tawny came back home, and Paul tied him up to his doghouse.

I didn't sleep well that night, the sound of the terrified pig squealing played over and over in my head.

The next morning, we could not believe our eyes when we came outside: the mauled, bleeding, and half-dead pig, his neck and backside so chewed up it looked like raw, bloody hamburger, was lying on the ground next to the food bowl, just inches out of Tawny's reach.

Mom and Mark just shook their heads and grabbed me by the shoulder to go into the house. Paul told Mark to go get his gun and he'd "put the pig out of its misery."

He told us he buried him in the cornfield.

I tried listening to Motown on WLS when I went to bed at the end of that day, but that night and for many nights thereafter, I could still hear the terrified, squealing pig running though the cornfield.

Try as I might, I could not figure Paul out. I wanted to understand him. I really wanted to "focus on his good side." But this cruelty made no sense to me. His bad side covered up the good like an eclipse of the sun so that I couldn't see the good through the darkness.

I could not understand how Paul could be the cool guy who took me cross-country in a tricked-out van to Haight-Ashbury and Chinatown; who took me to Disneyland, where I got to reclaim a moment of childhood; who bought me the Mamas & the Papas album; who bought us a go-cart to ride around and around on a circular dirt track in the yard. But he was the same guy who tore down the Christmas tree, raged at me violently—with or without alcohol—and who beat poor Tawny and let him attack and maul an innocent pig.

Tossing and turning in bed that night, exhausted from trying to make sense of Paul's good and bad sides, I finally focused on thinking back to our trip to San Francisco: Salty wind on my face and ocean waves crashing on the rocks and shore. Winding, hilly, narrow San Francisco streets. The clean smell of eucalyptus trees. Fog in the mornings. Pretty, pastel-painted Victorian houses. Jumping on and off cable cars. Sourdough bread and clam chowder at Fisherman's Wharf. Crazy sights and sounds and smells and herbs in Chinatown. And that dreamy hippie boy in Haight-Ashbury.

I remembered these beautiful moments, planning the details of my escape, until I finally fell into a deep California dreamin'.

MOON CHILD

By the summer of 1968, the war in Vietnam was raging on, with death tolls growing daily. Life was a series of the evening news flashing horrific reminders of war and death in Vietnam and Black people fighting for their lives in America. I could not erase the grisly and shocking image broadcast on national TV of the Viet Cong prisoner being executed by the South Vietnamese General. The whole world felt so hateful, so violent, so unpredictable and unsafe. In less than five years, my father had died, and JFK, Dr. Martin Luther King, and Bobby Kennedy had all been assassinated. Death seemed to be the only constant; I dreamed of a time when humans would stop hurting each other, and I wondered if this was what life was always going to be like.

During that year, I continued to steer clear of Paul on his moody days and learned to tiptoe around him. It felt like the entire nation was tiptoeing too. I felt helpless, voiceless, both in my own home and in a world that was spinning out of control around me.

Mark had left home the previous fall to attend a Baptist college in the South, and when he did come home, he spent his time at church or in his room. I had eschewed religion since I was accidentally baptized, but Mark had continued full force and was now in college to become a minister.

I wanted to understand why my brother felt so drawn to being a Baptist, but I couldn't quite make sense of it. I sometimes envied

Mark's certainty about his faith, but I knew that I would have to find another way to find God—find my own path toward life's purpose and meaning.

That spring, Mom and Paul bought their first house together. I was happy to leave behind the rental house with the sad memories of the torn-down Christmas tree, the threat of being killed, the mauled pig, and the locked screen door. I held hope lightly that a new home and a new start at junior high school would also mean a new beginning for our little family.

The new house was a small, rectangular three-bedroom, one bath, with fancy dark wood beams on the bedroom ceilings that made my small room feel expansive. All the houses on the street were built the same way, just painted different colors.

I had read in a teen magazine about a girl who had a swinging bed, and I thought that sounded like the coolest thing ever.

"Paul, do you think you could turn my twin bed into a swing?" I gingerly asked him.

"Why certainly," he said, apparently eager for the challenge.

He came into my room with his tools and measuring tape, drill, and tall ladder and measured the distance from the beam to my bed.

"Okay," he said, "let's go to the hardware store for sturdy rope, two-by-fours, and clamps."

I had no idea what a two-by-four was, but I jumped up, keen to be helpful. Busy as he always seemed to be, I was surprised, and grateful, that he'd agreed to do this for me.

It didn't take long to get the supplies we needed, and once we got back home, he got to work. First, he climbed a ladder and drilled a large hole in one of the beams on my bedroom ceiling to accommodate the rope. Then he pushed the rope through the hole and slid a clamp over both pieces of the rope to secure it. I stood in awe as he pulled on the rope to ensure the clamp held.

"How do you know how to do this?" I asked, amazed.

"Oh, you know, I've picked things up along the way," he replied as he drew his lower lip in and blew on it, something I noticed he did when he needed to focus.

He then pulled my mattress off my box spring and, with one hand, flipped the box spring over.

"Help me hold this two-by-four in place," he instructed, and he set the board on the bottom of the box spring and hammered it into place while I held the other end. He quickly attached the other board to the box spring while I awkwardly tried to be helpful, and then he drilled four holes in each corner where the other end of the four ropes hanging from the beams were attached with clamps.

Within a few hours, I had a swinging bed. I was impressed by Paul's skills and touched that he'd taken the time on a Saturday, when he usually worked, to do this for me. This kind gesture made it easy to see his good side, and I even started to love him a little bit that day.

Mom and Paul liked the idea of the swinging bed so much that Paul soon made their full-size bed into a swing too. When he completed the project, Mom plopped on the bed and Paul gently pushed it.

Giggling with glee, she yelled out, "Whee!" like a little kid.

I loved to see her so happy and alive.

The previous year, Sharon had married, and on her twenty-third birthday she'd had a baby girl, Casey. She was busy being a new mother, so we didn't see her often, but when we did see her, I loved the opportunity to hold the baby and talk to her and count her fingers and toes. While my mom and sister were busy in the kitchen, talking and making coffee, I sat on the couch, holding and feeding my innocent baby niece.

"Hi, sweet Casey," I'd croon, "welcome to the world. I hope you grow up to have a wonderful life. I hope your daddy doesn't die when you are little, so you don't have to have a stepdad. I hope all your dreams come true and make you happy. I love you."

"Roll down the window and stick your head out to tell me if we're about to go off the edge," Paul gruffly commanded.

It was July. I'd just turned twelve, and Mom, Paul, and I were on another cross-country trip. I was thrilled to be out in the open landscape, where time seemed to stand still with hope and happiness and we got to escape from the sadness of the world, if only for a little while.

But right then, I was a little nervous.

A few minutes earlier, Paul had turned off Highway 40 onto a dirt road that climbed up a red rock mountain covered with what he said were ponderosa pines and pinyon juniper. The dirt road was marred with deep gullies and potholes, and we'd lurched from side to side the whole way up.

Now, at the top of the mountain, our van barely fit on the narrow road. We were boxed in by the sheer granite wall on Paul's side and a steep drop-off down the mountain on my side.

As we made a turn on the switchback, the wheels of the van perched precariously on the edge of the narrow dirt road, all I could see out my window was blue sky—meaning there were no trees to stop us from going over the edge. Looking down into the precipice, terrified, I hoped Paul would decide that this was not a good idea, put the van in reverse, and get us the heck out of there.

Instead, Paul did that funny thing he did when he was serious and wanted to be listened to: He pulled his bottom lip in and exhaled in short bursts.

"Pooh, keep your eyes on the road. How we doin'?" He yelled this, but his volume was softened by him calling me by the nickname he had given me after we went to Disneyland the previous year: making a play on Winnie the Pooh, he'd started calling me "Wendy the Pooh," which he'd since shortened to just "Pooh."

My heart pounded with fear, terrified to have that much responsibility. To be the one in charge of whether we lived or tumbled down the mountain.

"We're on the edge! We're on the edge! Are we gonna be okay?" I yelled, repeating it to make sure he heard me.

"Lord willin' and the crick don't rise! So long as we're on the edge and not going off." He laughed as he slowly made his way around the dangerous switchback to a wider part of the road.

I turned around to see Mom holding tightly to the grab handle, swaying back and forth, looking a bit green. "Mom, are you okay?" I asked protectively.

"I'm fine, Wendy Beth, just hanging on! I'll be glad to be off this mountain though," she said with a laugh.

Mom was a trooper. She didn't complain. She was happy to just be along for the ride and the adventure.

Paul was an excellent driver. I always felt safe when he was behind the wheel, even on this crazy mountain dirt switchback that was only meant for four-wheel-drive Jeeps. I wished I trusted him not to get angry and violent as much as I trusted his driving.

We made it to Horsethief Canyon campground in one piece, where Mom and Paul cooked steaks and potatoes on a grill over the open fire. The desert air smelled sweet with the sage and sweetgrass and juniper, and my love for the West and mountains and the outdoors grew stronger.

That night, I stared into the flickering flames of the campfire Paul had built and dreamed of a life filled with wholesomeness and love at home with him and my mom. In that moment, as we sat around the crackling fire, our meditative faces illuminated by the blazing light, each of us quiet in our thoughts, everything was perfect. I wished I could stay there forever.

At school, popular and pretty cheerleader Becca—with her perfectly curled, long blonde hair and braces—befriended me and invited me to her house for a few dinners and sleepovers. Her family became my fantasy family, and I often wondered what it would be like to live with them.

"Tell us about your family, Wendy," Becca's soft-spoken Norwegian dad prompted me one night while we were all gathered at their table for dinner. He owned a small family grocery store, and Becca's mom, who didn't work, was very involved in the school and the cheerleading program, their Lutheran church, and the community.

Feeling self-conscious and awkward, I said, "Well, I have a big sister who is married and a big brother who's in college. I have a mom . . ." I paused, unsure what to say next. "My father died when I was seven, but my mom has a . . . um . . . boyfriend, and they own a machine shop together." My face flushed and my heart raced. But when I looked up, I only saw their kind and compassionate faces recognizing how uncomfortable I was.

"Well, it's wonderful to have you as our guest, and you are welcome anytime," Becca's father replied softly.

His gentle nature touched me deeply, and I wondered what it would be like to have a father who was always peaceful and kind.

"Yes, absolutely. And you are welcome to go to church with us tomorrow morning too," Becca's mom added.

I loved to go to Becca's house for sleepovers and observe what a normal, nondrinking, loving family looked like. I did go with them to their Lutheran church on Sundays when I slept over. I was skeptical of the church but loved her family anyway.

"Mom, why are you so dressed up? You look so pretty!"

She was dressed in her long sleeve, tufted yellow dress and hat trimmed in matching yellow fabric flowers. I'd always thought she could be Lucille Ball's blonde sister.

Usually when I left for school, Mom was dressed for work—old jeans and ratty sweatshirts, clothes that she didn't mind getting greasy and dirty at the machine shop. So her being dressed up was out of the ordinary.

Paul walked into the kitchen then, looking handsome: clean-shaven, with a fresh crew cut, and looking sharp in his white shirt, black suit, and thin black tie. I could smell his signature Brut aftershave.

"Paul and I are getting married today," Mom finally replied matter-of-factly, her voice devoid of emotion, as she applied some fresh lipstick. She blotted her lips on a tissue and then gave her wrists a spritz of Youth Dew perfume.

"What? I didn't know this! Why didn't you tell me before? Can I go with you?" I asked excitedly. I was confused why she hadn't told me that this long-awaited event would be taking place. I had been a bridesmaid in my sister's wedding the year before; wouldn't Mom want someone to be there with her too?

"No, honey," she said. "It's no big deal. You need to go to school. We're just going to the courthouse and then we're going to the shop to work."

I didn't understand why Mom wasn't treating this as a joyous event and including me. She was getting married! I was so happy and relieved for her—but underneath those good feelings ran a current of ambivalence.

Now Paul really would be my stepfather.

After they married, I contemplated calling Paul "Dad." Now that he was legally married to my mom, after all, he was technically my stepdad.

Mom never said anything either way about what I should call Paul, and neither did he—although he now referred to me all the time as "his daughter."

Not that this meant he had legally adopted me. "Why on earth would I pay a bunch of lawyers to tell me she is my daughter?" he demanded when it came up in a conversation with my mom. "She's my daughter because I say so, and I don't need any goddamn lawyers telling me what I already know, goddammit."

I felt conflicted about calling Paul "Dad" because I thought it betrayed my "real" dad, Burt; but I thought that since my dad was dead and was never coming back, maybe it would be okay. I really wanted to have a dad, and since Mom was now married to him, I decided I would really "focus on his good side" and all the cool places we went on vacations.

I tried calling him "Dad" a few times—but it felt awkward, so usually I just kept calling him "Paul."

I still didn't understand why he seemed mad so often over little things and sometimes acted like he didn't even like me. But when he was in his happy-go-lucky, upbeat mood, he was affectionate and loving toward Mom, which made me feel secure.

"Hi, Dolly," he would say, calling her his pet name for her in a sugar-coated tone, before giving her a big, sloppy kiss. "How was your day today, dumplin'?"

My mom had married him, I reasoned, so she must be happy. She certainly seemed happy. She sang along to the radio and danced around the living room. She hummed while she cooked dinner. She smiled and hugged me and patted my arm with affection like her whole family did and kissed my cheeks.

Mom being happy meant I didn't have to work so hard to make sure she was happy, and I felt relieved.

Most Saturday nights Mom and Paul got dressed up to go out for dinner, and they often took me with them to what became my favorite family-outing destination: the Mayflower.

The first time we went, I looked around as we were being seated at our table and noticed that there were very few children my age. I felt proud that my mom and Paul thought that I was mature enough to go to a fancy restaurant with them.

Once we were seated at the table with the white tablecloth, cloth napkins, and intricately carved silverware, Mom flashed a smile at me. "Wendy Beth, would you like a Shirley Temple with a cherry?"

I didn't know what that was but said, "Yes, please, Mom," and smiled and sat up straighter.

"My wife will have a Grasshopper, and my daughter will have

a Shirley Temple, and I will have a schnapps on the rocks, please," Paul stated to the attentive waiter.

When the waiter returned with the drinks, he served my mom a yummy-looking green blended drink in a fancy round glass with a stem. Then he placed the tall glass of 7UP with grenadine syrup swirling around the ice cubes, complete with a small paper umbrella toothpick skewering a maraschino cherry.

I had never had such a treat. I felt so special and loved. Mom and Paul were surprised to see me eat and enjoy the same dinner they ordered: Lake Superior whitefish cooked in lemon and butter and topped with sliced almonds, baked potato with sour cream and chives, and an iceberg lettuce salad with shredded carrots and Roquefort dressing.

"You have quite an adult palate, Wendy Beth," Paul said admiringly.

"And I'm very proud of your table manners." Mom beamed. "You're very mature."

They made being an adult and drinking look very inviting, but I remembered how sick I had felt when I got drunk at my sleepover and decided it wasn't as good as it looked. Mom usually only had one drink, and I never saw her even a little bit tipsy. She always completed her meal with a hot cup of black coffee, and I knew not to get antsy about wanting to leave until she was finished drinking it.

The three of us together felt like a nice, happy little family sometimes. I hoped it would last.

Early in the summer of 1969, we took a vacation through Southern Canada to Banff via Mackinaw Island, Michigan.

Driving cross-country, I felt happy to once again be out of boring Forestville. It was easier to pretend that we were a wholesome family on our long journeys, since when we traveled Paul didn't drink as much.

He had started to teach me to drive when I was eleven, and now that I was almost thirteen, he let me drive on long stretches of desolate highway with pillows propping me up. While I drove, I asked Paul to tell me about his first job in his Swiss family's cheese factory, and then I asked Mom to tell me about her first kiss. I wanted to hear stories about who they were and what they thought about when they were my age; I wanted to know who they were. Who were these people who were my parents, and how had they gotten to be the people they now were?

After we got home from that trip, on Sunday, July 20, I turned thirteen. That day, we watched astronauts walk on the moon for the very first time.

CBS News blasted all day long with ongoing reports and updates and interviews. After a long day and much suspense, Edwin Aldrin finally landed the module that afternoon, and Neil Armstrong announced, "The Eagle has landed."

It amazed me that the grainy images of the Apollo 11 lunar module touching down on the moon's surface was somehow broadcast two hundred and forty thousand miles to our TV set in Forestville, Illinois. After so many years of horrible and sad world events since my father died, the news coverage about the moon landing felt hopeful and exciting. I began to cry, overwhelmed with emotion, wanting to believe that things might now change for the better in the world and in my home.

I'd started to read my daily horoscope in the newspaper recently, so the astronauts landing on the moon on my birthday was the best present. I'd learned that I was a Moon Child and was amazed that the astrologer's Moon Child characteristics described me accurately: nurturing, sensitive, compassionate, loving, intuitive, home-loving. It felt particularly auspicious that the astronauts were landing on the moon in 1969—the number sixty-nine being the symbol of Moon Children.

After watching the news coverage for most of the day, I was getting ready for bed when my mom yelled, "Wendy Beth, come watch!"

I ran to the living room and got there just in time to see Neil Armstrong take his first step on the moon.

I squinted at the grainy images on the TV. The surface of the moon was so stark and desolate and cold-looking. As exciting as it was that NASA and the astronauts had accomplished this remarkable feat, I was happy and grateful to be on Earth with its oceans and rivers and lakes and seas, its snow-capped mountains, jungles, forests, grasslands, and deserts—not to mention plenty of oxygen.

"That's one small step for man, one giant leap for mankind," Neil Armstrong said after taking his first step.

I hoped with all my heart and with my thirteenth birthday wish that men and women and children alike were in fact really going to take giant steps to be better humans to each other right here, at home, on our little blue planet.

HEAVEN'S RENEGADES

After the historic moon landing on my thirteenth birthday, I spent the summer days and nights of 1969 with my friends Sherrie, Angela, Jan, and Fella, hanging out at the pool hall at the end of my street. All the neighborhood kids hung out at the pool hall playing pool or pinball; my favorite machine was called *Aquarius*, and my friends and I collected Coke bottles to exchange for quarters at the liquor store to play. But mostly I loved going there because my neighbor, Milo—a boy with dark, thick hair and big brown doe eyes that reminded me of the hippie boy in Haight-Ashbury and made me swoon—worked there.

Suddenly, my world had expanded beyond my swinging bed, radio, and bedroom.

One day Milo invited me to Pine Lake in Rockland State Park. I watched him put his boat on the trailer and attach the trailer to his Jeep and was impressed by his maturity and responsible nature.

At the lake, Milo rowed us all the way across to the other side and then motored through some swamps. We had a great time—so much so that the next week we spent almost every day together, hiking through the woods, going out in the boat, and hanging out in his bedroom listening to music. I felt so fresh and outdoorsy with Milo that I thought I might just marry him when I was older.

Milo took time to notice things more than any other boy I knew. One day as we sat on his bed, listening to Steppenwolf's

"Magic Carpet Ride" and other songs on his very own jukebox, he pushed the hair out of my eyes and asked, "Tell me about your right eye. How did that happen?"

Most people didn't notice my eye despite the filmy white cataract that was beginning to cover my pupil. I felt self-conscious that he'd noticed but also pleased that he cared enough to ask.

I told him the story: "One summer morning when I was four years old, I woke up with a pounding headache. I stumbled out of bed and into the living room. My sister took one look at me and let out a long scream. My head was swollen and mushy like a water balloon. My face and eyes were so swollen and puffy I could barely see through the slits. My mom came running and scooped me up in her arms and ran to the car and my sister drove us straight to the doctor. In the car I felt so sleepy, but Mom kept shaking me to wake me up. The doctor said I had been bitten by a black widow spider on my temple, and it was probably a baby spider, or I would be dead."

"So, you didn't feel the spider bite you or see the spider?" Milo asked, eyes wide. "Is that what blinded you?"

"No, I didn't see the spider, but it wasn't the bite that blinded me," I explained. "When the doctor examined me, he noticed that my right eye wandered a little bit, so he suggested to my mom that he bandage my left eye to strengthen the right eye. But once he put the bandage on, I couldn't see. I stepped forward and stumbled, my hands extended out in front of me so I wouldn't run into the wall. 'Oh my God, she's blind!' my mom yelled, and she jumped up to wrap her arms around me."

Milo shook his head with amazement. "So then what happened?"

"For years I saw specialists in St. Louis, in Chicago, and at the University of Michigan." I shrugged. "Most of them agreed I had been born blind in my right eye, and that the optic nerve was congenitally deformed. Their explanations never really made sense to me—they seemed incomplete. But no one ever gave me a different answer that did make sense."

Milo smiled, brushed my long blonde hair from my face, and kissed me. "It doesn't matter, your eye is beautiful. You are beautiful. And what really makes you beautiful is that you don't even know how beautiful you are. I know that even when you're an old woman, you'll still be beautiful."

No boy or man had ever told me I was beautiful. He was so sincere as he said the words. I felt embarrassed and flustered. I didn't know how to accept such praise. He seemed so mature for his age.

He studied me carefully. "When I die, I'm going to leave my eyes to you."

He said it so sweetly. I'd never heard anyone talk like this before. I looked into his eyes—the biggest brown eyes I had ever seen—and laughed. "Thank you," I said, "but I don't think they'll fit!"

Max pulled out a bag of marijuana and some Zig-Zag rolling papers from his coat pocket. I had never seen marijuana before, so I watched intently as he removed the seeds and stems from the bag and then crumbled a little bud into the mix.

Max was one of my favorite new friends that I'd met at the pool hall. His hazel eyes twinkled as he stroked his thin, scruffy beard, and his southern-twinged voice was still changing, so it cracked when he spoke. He always wore an Australian bush hat and green US Army jacket.

He deftly rolled the paper around the marijuana and licked the glue to close it. He flicked open his Zippo lighter, lit the end of the joint, and inhaled deeply. Holding the smoke in his lungs, he squeezed out a raspy, "Here, take a hit," and handed me the joint.

I hesitated, unsure I should smoke marijuana.

He exhaled a stream of smoke. "Go ahead," he said. "It's just pot. No big deal."

He laughed and patted me on the back as I inhaled and immediately choked on the smoke, tears running down my cheeks.

Max introduced everyone in our group to the newest rock bands and talked to us about sex and drugs like it was his job to educate us. He'd show up at whoever's house we were hanging out at that day with a stack of the newest albums by the Beatles, Jimi Hendrix, Janis Joplin, the Doors, Pink Floyd, and Led Zeppelin. We spent hours in someone's garage or basement, usually while parents were out, listening to his albums, studying the album cover artwork, and scouring the liner notes and lyrics while we drank beers and smoked cigarettes and pot. I thought of him as my big brother, since I wasn't close to my own brother, and he said he'd look after me.

On May 4, 1970, I was sitting at the kitchen table doing my homework while Mom cooked dinner and watched the CBS Evening News when Walter Cronkite's tone suddenly caught my attention. I ran to the television and froze as I watched footage from Ohio's Kent State University that day.

I was horrified to learn that four college students had been killed and nine others had been wounded by the Ohio National Guard that day for protesting the war. The national guard was supposed to protect Americans, wasn't it? I'd learned in school and felt proud to believe that as an American in a democratic society, I could disagree with my country. I'd been taught that in the US I could protest without being imprisoned, unlike in many other countries. But now I felt tricked and lied to. In just five years, I could be one of those college students protesting—and it was now clear to me that I could get killed for voicing my disagreement with my government's actions.

Paul, who happened to be at home that night, walked by and callously blurted something like, "Serves them right, goddamn hippies. They had it coming."

I felt a surge of bile rise in my throat. His words felt personal. A wave of heat pulsed up my body from my feet and slid across my scalp. My face and ears burned with anger. I had never hated anyone as much as I hated him in that moment. How could he say such a terrible thing? What could he have against these students?

There was no use asking him why he would say such a horrible thing. That would only turn his rage toward me. Who was he, really? Why was he so angry? Why had Mom chosen him to be my father?

I ran to my bedroom and sat alone, overwhelmed by my disappointment with Paul and my country.

Around this time, one of the guys from the pool hall, Jim, announced that he was starting a gang called Heaven's Renegades. Jim was nicknamed Tiny because he weighed three-hundred-plus pounds. His curly, greasy, black hair always seemed to be wet with sweat. Since he was so big and tough, he was the president of Heaven's Renegades, and he convinced another one of the guys—Gary—to become his vice president.

Soon almost everyone who hung out at the pool hall wore Heaven's Renegades patches on their jackets—except for Milo, who wasn't interested in joining the gang and had joined ROTC at school.

Although I still had a huge crush on Milo and thought that someday we might get married, Wade became my boyfriend. Part Cherokee, he had beautiful, tanned skin; long, dark brown hair; and blue eyes. He didn't have much of a butt—his blue jeans hung low, and the frayed cuffs dragged on the ground—but he was adorable.

Wade only wore cowboy boots and black T-shirts and jeans. He played the drums and smoked unfiltered Camel cigarettes that he kept in his rolled-up shirtsleeve. I liked him because he was cute and a drummer and not as serious as Milo.

Wade joined Heaven's Renegades and was given the nickname Stud. I had no idea what that meant, except that it was some kind of compliment.

All my friends had now joined Heaven's Renegades. My girlfriend Jan was with Max, Fella was with Ben, and Angela was with

Dan. We were all together, we were cool, and nobody could fuck with us. I proudly wore my jean vest emblazoned with PROPERTY OF STUD, HEAVEN'S RENEGADES, RIVERSIDE, ILLINOIS.

I belonged. I had a gang. They were family.

That summer of 1970 after I turned fourteen, Mom, Paul and I went "out west" again on vacation and took back roads to Wounded Knee, South Dakota. I read the inscription on the small memorial and learned that the spot where I stood was the site of the 1890 massacre of nearly three hundred Lakota men, women, and children by soldiers of the US Army.

How could soldiers kill innocent people? I wondered. But then I remembered the Mai Lai massacre, which had occurred in Vietnam in 1968, and the truth was not revealed until the fall of 1969. And then there was the killing of the four students at Kent State University just a few months earlier. Why had I never heard about Wounded Knee and other atrocities against Native Americans in school?

After visiting the memorial and gravesite, we drove to an old ramshackle bar in Scenic. Above the door were cow head skeletons and horns and a sign that said NO INDIANS ALLOWED, but with the NO crossed out. I was beginning to understand that Native Americans were discriminated against just like Black people in the US.

Inside the bar, pairs of shoes and boots hung from the ceiling. The white bartender told us they had been traded for alcohol. I wondered if Paul had ever felt that desperate for alcohol—but then I realized he always had money and always had his beer.

When I went to the restroom in the back of the bar, I peeked out the back door and saw an older disheveled Lakota man sprawled out in the dirt—passed-out drunk.

That's what desperation looks like, I thought.

Until that experience, I had only learned in school about the generous and welcoming Wampanoag people who'd shared "Thanksgiving" with the surviving Pilgrims after their first harvest. But now I'd seen with my own eyes the poverty, disease, and alcoholism that had befallen the Native people of America. They had been forced off their lands and stripped of their language and traditional ways by us "good" Americans with the help of the Catholic church and forced boarding schools separating children from their families.

Witnessing what the Native people were subjected to on the reservations made me question the choices me and my friends had made about being in a gang. Suddenly it seemed trivial and stupid to me.

I appreciated that my parents took me on vacations across the West, not just to the tourist attractions but also off the beaten path to places where real people lived. I wondered if they were affected by what they witnessed. We never discussed these issues in any depth—we didn't have authentic conversations about any serious worldly issues, in fact, though I wished we did—so I didn't know. And ever since Paul had angrily voiced his hateful opinion about the Kent State kids, I was afraid to voice my opinion on anything.

Neither Mom nor Paul had a word to say about my Heaven's Renegades jean jacket declaring that I was the "Property of Stud," even though I was only fourteen. There was no discussion with me about what it meant or if that was how I wanted to present myself. No discussion with me about how I was developing as a young woman. No discussions of what desires and goals in life I might have. Mom had graduated high school, but Paul hadn't even completed grade school. Did they feel that because of their lack of education they weren't qualified to speak on social and political issues?

I could only speculate. But because they didn't share their humanity and outrage with me by responding to the atrocities we witnessed on the news and on our travels, I felt alone and separate from them. I also often wondered why I felt everything so deeply and was so utterly disappointed and perplexed by human beings. Was I the only one?

ORANGE SUNSHINE

Since I was nine, my senses had increasingly sharpened to detect Paul's anger and moods. I knew to retreat to my room when he was in a bad mood—brooding, cursing, huffing and puffing, and drinking.

I imagined that my heightened sense was a pet wolf who lay on the floor of my bedroom. When I heard Paul angrily stomp around, my wolf would start to pace the floor and sniff the air. Sometimes, the hair would stand up on his haunches, his nostrils would flare, and he would bare his teeth.

One day in the spring of 1971, I noticed that my legs were getting hairy. Having watched my sister and mom shave their legs, I decided to do the same with a razor I found on the bathroom sink. I carefully soaped my legs like I had seen them do and drew the razor up each leg, leaving them nice and smooth and shiny. It was a step toward feeling more grown up.

When I finished, I left the bathroom feeling satisfied with myself and my new smooth legs and went back into my room to change into shorts.

Suddenly, I smelled the acrid scent of anger and danger. The temperature in my bedroom seemed to drop and goose bumps covered my arms. My wolf jumped up and pressed his nose onto the crack of my bedroom door, sniffed the air, bared his teeth, and raised his hackles.

Paul's ranting began as a low rumble in the hallway just outside my bedroom door. "Who used my goddamn razor?!"

The low rumble became a louder and louder boom that shook the walls. My wolf growled and bared his teeth and gave me a look that said, *Get the fuck out of here! Now! Run! Run!*

"Goddamn it, who the hell used my goddamn razor? Goddamn it, I'm going to kill her!"

I froze on the word *kill*. He might *kill* me. Because I used his razor? I didn't know it was his razor. How did he even know someone had used it?

As Paul cursed and yelled and stomped around, I started shaking, feeling trapped and fearing he would barge into my room and kill me.

The door opened, and I froze. When I realized it was my mom and not Paul, I yelped in relief.

Calmly and slowly, she said, "Wendy, pack some clothes, pajamas, and your toothbrush. Paul is in the backyard, so do it quickly. When you're done, take your bag, go to the neighbors', and call Dorothy's husband to come pick you up." Dorothy was my grade-school friend who was now married and pregnant at sixteen and lived nearby. "I want you to stay at Dorothy's house for a few days until Paul calms down."

Terrified, I did exactly as I was told, and I made it out the front door before Paul came back inside.

That night I lay on Dorothy's couch and wondered what was wrong with Paul that he would threaten to kill me because I'd used his razor. What had made him so angry and crazy? Was I really such a horrible person? How could he say I'm his daughter and then want to hurt me?

He seemed to be getting worse instead of better.

Mom called me at Dorothy's a few days later and said I could come home. She said she had told Paul to calm down and that having that kind of a reaction over a razor was silly.

Paul usually acted like nothing happened when I saw him again after an episode. Still, when I went home, I tiptoed around the house until I felt sure no retribution was coming.

There would be plenty more nights when Mom would cheerfully say, "Wendy, why don't you go to Dorothy's for the night."

I knew she was trying to protect me from Paul, and I'd go without complaint, grateful to be out of the line of fire. But why was I the one who had to leave?

Fair or not, a pattern had been set, and my protective wolf was now always on duty.

"You guys should try LSD," Max said. "I've had some amazing experiences. It's a trip, man. Did you know that it gives you a deeper understanding of yourself and the world and makes you feel connected to the whole universe?"

Whoa. Connected to the whole universe? That was the opposite of how I usually felt. It sounded amazing to me.

It was the summer of 1971. I'd just turned fifteen, and home life around Paul had become so unbearable that I'd decided not to go with him and Mom on our beloved summer vacation, this time to Florida. Mom had said she thought that it would be okay since Mark was home from college for the summer. However, he was never around, so I was on my own with my friends.

Max and his girlfriend, Jan, had come over to my house to hang out—and now Max had presented us with the opportunity to try Orange Sunshine LSD, a.k.a. acid, for the first time.

I'd heard stories from other friends who'd tried LSD and said it was amazing. I also thought some friends took too much and too often.

"Isn't it dangerous if you take too much?" I asked. "I don't want to OD. And I don't want to take so much that it makes me crazy." I was anxious about how this stuff was going to make me feel.

"Okay," Max said protectively. "I'll cut the pill in half. You'll be okay."

We decided to spend the night in my parents' van—which, since they weren't going to be camping, they'd left parked in the yard and took Paul's other car on their trip.

We climbed into the van, opened the small folded square of paper Max had given us, and placed half the Orange Sunshine pill under our tongues.

As we waited for the acid to take effect, Jan and I rolled down the windows to blow our cigarette smoke into the warm summer air so Paul wouldn't know we had smoked in the van. After a while, I got chills, and my spine tingled up to my head and over my scalp. A deep sense of peace came over me; I sensed that everything was going to eventually be okay with my life.

We talked and giggled and then giggled more as the acid took over. We reclined the car seats and watched the tree limbs, laden with leaves, sway gently in the breeze. My skin vibrated, and I felt like I'd outgrown my body. I sensed that my soul was larger than my small life in Forestville, and with this thought I became even more calm and relaxed.

For fear we'd drain the battery and earn the wrath of Paul, we didn't turn on the radio. Instead, we sang every song from *Hair*, the rock musical, a cappella at the top of our lungs.

By now I was floating and tripping. I felt my body drifting among the stars and felt connected to God as we sang "Walking in Space." Singing the lyrics to "LBJ," I thought of the Vietnam war and wondered why anyone would want to kill another human being when there was so much beauty and joy in the world to see and experience. I knew that I belonged with the young people in the world who wanted the same things I did: peace and love, and connection to the bounty of planet Earth and the vast universe.

As I gazed into the tree above me, I began to hallucinate and saw colorful images form in the bustling leaves. I blinked my eyes and suddenly I was watching a technicolor Disney parade of Pooh Bear and all his friends—Eeyore, Rabbit, Piglet, Roo, Kanga, and Owl—marching in a parade, singing, twirling batons, carrying signs and banners, and smiling and waving.

I blinked hard again and reopened my eyes, but the images were still there. I started laughing. "Do you see what I see?" I asked Jan.

She laughed. "Yes! Do you mean the skulls and skeletons and witches?"

"What?" I shook my head. "Wow, no! Don't you see Pooh Bear smiling and waving and the Disney parade?"

"No," she said, "just skulls and skeletons and witches."

I wondered what it meant that we saw such different things.

"I'm going to do a train with the gang," announced a teen girl who lived in the neighborhood.

It was a beautiful summer day, and I was hanging out with the Heaven's Renegades in someone's attic that had been converted to a living space.

"What are you thinking?" I asked, horrified at the idea. "Do you even know what you're doing? You know what a train means? You're going to have sex with all the guys in the gang who want to?"

"Yes, I know what I'm doing," she said. "But you can't tell anyone. If my parents find out, they'll kill me." She was already moving toward the door of the bedroom.

Tiny walked over to me and gave me a hard look. "Promise you won't tell," he said.

I caught the girl's eye and shook my head to say, *No, don't do this*, but she turned away.

The guys who didn't have girlfriends started to line up. I gave them the evil eye and tried to decide what to do. I wanted to run right over to her house and tell her mom, but I wasn't sure if I should. Was it my place?

After the first guy went into that room, I walked out of the attic feeling sick to my stomach. As I walked home, I chastised myself for hanging out with these kids, especially these guys. "These are not the kinds of people I want to be around," I said aloud. "They are disgusting. I hate them."

I started to cry.

The whole idea of these guys being in a street gang seemed absurd to me now: Their gang initiation rites and cocksure bravado threats of violence, their disrespect of us girls, the rule that we wore PROPERTY OF patches, their consumption of drugs and alcohol—I hated all of it. From what I knew, real street gangs were in poor inner cities where kids might really need protection. But these kids in Heaven's Renegades lived in tree-lined cul-de-sac suburbs, in nice safe homes with warm beds and full refrigerators. What were they doing calling themselves a gang? Did they think they were tough guys in a Hollywood movie?

I decided that belonging to a street gang was no different than being in a Charles Manson cult.

Life felt so confusing. I had sewn an embroidered patch on my torn Levi jeans that spelled out CONFUSED ONE, because I was indeed confused. People seemed so complicated. My family was confusing. I felt like I didn't even know my sister or my brother. My mom seemed helpless to do anything about Paul's violent outbursts except to remind me to "focus on his good side" and send me away until the good side reemerged.

Paul was driving me away from my home. But I realized that at least he'd shown me where to go. I thought of California—the sunshine, the hippie boy, and the ocean. And Colorado—the mountains, fresh air, and roaring rivers.

I loved them both, but California was as far west as I could go, so I thought I'd go there first.

I just wanted to be with people who were gentle and honest and interesting and uncomplicated. I'd had enough of living my life on high alert, walking on eggshells.

As I walked along, I became determined to get out of suffocating, depressing, dead-end Forestville, where none of my friends planned to go to college or do anything to learn and improve their lives and challenge their minds, who instead spent their paychecks on drugs and alcohol. As soon as I could, I would get as far away as possible from these misguided kids, this crumbling town, my complicated family, and especially my stepdad's crazy.

CALIFORNIA DREAMIN'

"Wendy, I heard a rumor that one of the neighbor dads was accused of molesting a boy."

Mom kept unloading groceries from the car as she said this but seemed very agitated and looked as if she was in pain just saying the words.

I, meanwhile, was stunned. *Which dad?* I wondered.

She took a deep breath and exhaled loudly. "If anyone ever touches you—anyone, even if it was Paul—you have to tell me."

I swallowed hard and considered what she'd just said as we carried the groceries into the house. I hadn't told her about the sleepover when my friend's older brother touched me in my sleep, and I hadn't told her about my other friend's stepdad kissing me in my sleep and then fleeing the room. Why hadn't I run home and told her after each of those incidents? Was I too afraid? Or did I think that if I didn't say anything, maybe I could just forget it? At the time, I'd simply decided I just wouldn't go to any more sleepovers. But perhaps I'd gotten an unspoken message that some secrets, we keep to ourselves.

Maybe some things we shouldn't discuss, I thought. *Especially if they are ugly. Why is Mom having this talk with me now?*

She smiled at me as she unloaded the food into the refrigerator, looking more at peace. It seemed she felt her job was done.

I went to my room, where I thought about what Mom had said and all the things she didn't know about me. She didn't know that I had been having sex with my boyfriend, Wade, for two years already. I'd lost my virginity to him when I was almost fourteen, in the grass in his backyard during a stunning summer golden hour. We'd been going steady for almost a year before it happened, and it had been a beautiful experience for me. I'd felt safe and loved, and it had felt normal and natural to have sex with him. By this point, I felt grown-up about sex. It was no big deal. I'd recently learned on the news that Illinois had passed a law that allowed minors to get birth control, and a clinic had opened in Riverside. I planned to go there now that I had my license and a car.

It had never occurred to me that Paul would ever do anything like that to me. Then again, he was weird sometimes. He never talked to me about going to college or what I would do with my life, but he had told me that I could be a Playboy Bunny in Lake Geneva, Wisconsin, and could make a lot of money as a cocktail waitress. I wondered if other dads suggested that their daughters become Playboy Bunnies. Also, I didn't like it when he got too close and friendly with me or my girlfriends. He may not have meant any harm, but when he put his arm around our waists and rested his hand on the front of our hips in a seemingly "friendly" way, it made me cringe. He didn't seem to know how to be affectionate in a fatherly way, the way I saw some other fathers hug their daughters, so his physical closeness made me feel awkward and uncomfortable.

But he would never cross the line—would he?

The very next day after Mom mentioned the molestation gossip, Paul started one of his "wrestling" joking behaviors with me in the kitchen—something he'd been doing with me since I was a little kid. But this time, in his "wrestling" he pressed me up against the wall with his whole bulldozer body and grabbed my tiny wrists and held down my arms.

I felt trapped and alarmed by his aggression. It was not right. He should not be pressing his body against mine. *Is this what Mom meant?*

For a moment I thought I'd leave my body like I had at my dad's funeral, but instead a voice inside me said, *Get away!*

Paul was laughing as if this was a big joke, funny as hell. His beer breath on my face, he taunted, "Okay, smarty pants. What are you going to do now?"

Filled with a surge of adrenaline, I broke away from him, grabbed an old ashtray from the kitchen table, and raised it over my head. I was only pretending that I planned to throw it—but the force of my mock-gesture broke the old glued-together thing apart, and a piece of it flew toward Paul and hit his hand.

His looked at his hand and his face transformed into bloated purple rage and clenched gnashing teeth.

I looked down and saw that I still had half of the ashtray in my hand. I couldn't make sense of what had just happened. I just wanted him to stop touching me. I hadn't even thrown it at him. I'd just waved it over my head.

Even as my mind was saying, *But I still have half the ashtray in my hand*, Paul balled up his calloused fist and back handed me across the face.

I felt the blow to my face and then my feet left the floor—I was airborne. All ninety-five pounds of me flew head-first over the kitchen table and toward the wall. My head and then my body hit the wall with a thud, and then I fell to the floor.

Crumpled into a ball behind a chair, I felt warmth in my crotch. *Am I bleeding?* I wondered hazily. *Did I just get my period?* Then I realized I had peed my pants. The shock and fear of being punched by Paul had literally scared the piss out of me. I was afraid for my life.

Mom rushed into the kitchen, her beautiful face anguished. She yelled at Paul, but I couldn't hear anything. My head hummed as if filled with angry wasps, my limbs felt like my bones had transformed into rubber hose, and I was wet.

Like a zombie, I rose from the floor, sleepwalked to my room, and packed a bag.

This time, I stayed at Dorothy's for a whole week.

When I walked into the kitchen a week later, Mom was standing at the stove making dinner, but all I saw was Paul's fist coming at me. My legs buckled underneath me as I relived the experience—flying across the table, hitting the wall—in a flash.

I started to cry. "I wish I was eighteen so I could just leave," I blurted out. "Why am I always the one who is forced to leave when Paul does something wrong? I hate it here, anyway. What's wrong with him?"

"I told him if he ever laid another hand on you that I will leave with you," Mom said, her face tearstained and puffy. "He will never touch you again, I promise. But in the meantime, I also thought you might like to spend the summer with Sherrie in California. I already asked her parents; they said yes, and Paul has agreed to drive you there."

"Really?" I asked, eyes wide.

Sherrie had recently moved to Concord, California. I was so over the moon about the idea of visiting her and getting out of Forestville for the summer that I almost forgot how upset I was.

Paul walked into the kitchen then, head hung low, unable to meet my eyes. I could see that he felt sorry, but instead of saying he was sorry, he acted sugary sweet, like everything was okay, and called me by my childhood nickname.

"Hey, Pooh, Mom says you'd like to go visit your friend Sherrie in California. If you want to go, Mom and I will take you there."

Mom stopped stirring the pot on the stove and glanced at me with that pained "See there, he has a good side" expression. But I wasn't buying it this time. I wondered how I could ever trust him again. There was something wrong with him deep inside; he had been hurt, and now he had a rage inside him that was an uncontrollable monster. He was a real-life Dr. Jekyll and

Mr. Hyde. But he was too much of a tough guy to admit to his own pain.

Still, I couldn't be mad at Mom. It was also beyond my capability—too painful, too unacceptable—to think that she was also responsible for subjecting me to his violence. I saw her as a fellow victim who was struggling with what to do about him.

I just wanted the love of my parents. I hoped that the peace we always seemed to find on our vacations would wash away this last episode as we drove cross-country.

The farther we got from Illinois, the calmer and happier Paul and Mom were. We listened to the radio and sang along and, as usual, I asked Paul to tell me the story of his daughter Betty in the makeshift drawer/cradle by the fire—something I only ever did on vacation. He obliged, and as he finished his story, John Denver's "Rocky Mountain High" came on the radio. I sang every word, with Mom and Paul humming along and singing the chorus.

"You know that song isn't about getting high on drugs, about smoking marijuana, right?" Doing that thing where he blew on his lip, Paul glanced over at me as I sat in the front passenger seat.

In a flash, I knew he must care about me, but he didn't know how to show it when he was out of control.

"Yes, I know it's not about getting high on pot," I said. "It's about nature and how happy it makes John Denver feel. I feel the same way. You and Mom do too." I smiled at Paul with compassion, and I suddenly felt tender toward him. It struck me that he was the only father I would ever know, and that it was okay to love him and let him love me back. I wanted him to be my father.

But I wondered if he could ever be the father that I'd always dreamed of having, and if I could ever really let my guard down around him.

We left beloved Colorado and drove west to Reno. As we drove on the Nevada Scenic Byway, also called Mount Rose Highway, I gasped in awe at the sight of aquamarine Lake Tahoe below us; its beauty filled my eyes with tears.

We found our way to a campground in south Lake Tahoe, where we slept in the van surrounded by pine trees that smelled like vanilla. While Mom and Paul went to the casinos, I wandered on the busy, touristy sidewalks and met a bunch of kids my age, some of whom were runaways. One of the girls said she lived near the Bay Area and gave me her phone number so we could get together when I was at Sherrie's.

One day in California, and I was already making friends.

When we arrived in Concord, Sherrie's mom and stepdad, whom I called Mama San and Papa San, gave me a warm welcome. Sherrie wouldn't be home for a week—she was on vacation with her boyfriend and his family—but they said it was okay for me to stay even though she wasn't there.

I said goodbye to Mom and Paul and wished them a good time in Las Vegas, where they were headed next. As I waved goodbye, I was relieved to be left alone with Mama San and Papa San.

After a few days of sunbathing by Sherrie's kidney-shaped backyard pool and fully stocked koi pond, I called the girl I'd met in Tahoe, who said she was heading back up there and asked if I could go. Sherrie's parents said it was fine.

When the girl arrived, she introduced her older brother, who was driving us to south Lake Tahoe. When we pulled away from the house, she told me that he was not in fact her brother but a guy who'd picked her up hitchhiking. I felt terrible that I had unwittingly misled Mama San and Papa San and was relieved when we arrived safely in Tahoe.

We found a few of the kids on the strip and then were reunited with the rest of the group, who'd taken up residence in an empty cabin.

Here I was, on my own, with no parents! I hung out on the strip and slept in the empty cabin with my new friends, and after a few days one of the kids convinced me to panhandle money to get food and beer. I sat on the low cement wall of Harrah's casino and asked passing tourists for money "to get a bus ticket to go home to the Midwest." Many of them took pity on me—a sweet-faced, blue-eyed, blonde-haired, all-American girl just wanting to go home to her family—and gave me what they could. I was thrilled about the money but felt guilty that I was lying about why I wanted it.

The next thing I knew, two men in black suits and ties were standing in front of me, flashing their gold badges in my face. I had some pot in my purse; I quickly and surreptitiously tucked it into the bushes behind me as the officers asked me questions about why I was asking people for money and if I was a runaway.

"Panhandling is illegal in Nevada," one officer said. "Since you're a minor, you'll have to come with us to the police station, and we'll call your parents to come pick you up."

In a flash I considered my choices. Could I outrun them? Should I try?

Paralyzed by indecision and fear, all I could do was stand and follow directions. The two officers walked on either side of me as they escorted me to the jail. The kids I had been hanging out with watched as I walked, grateful dodged-a-bullet looks on their faces. I started to cry and felt so ashamed that I was arrested. I was the kid who got great grades in school, who loved her teachers and never gave them a hard time, who had gotten herself out of a street gang. I couldn't believe I had gotten myself arrested.

I'm a good kid, I wanted to tell the officers. *I just did something stupid that I didn't even know was illegal.*

The police were kind and sympathetic to me; I probably looked like their own daughters. They bought me a McDonald's hamburger and fries and a Coke for dinner—not exactly jail food—before calling my parents.

Paul told them to put my ass on a plane or a bus so he could beat it when I got home and that I was going to be "in a world of hurt," as he liked to say. Mom, however, insisted that she did not want me to come home and asked the police to call Mama San and Papa San.

They agreed to pick me up, but I had to spend the night in jail because Papa San couldn't come until the next day after work.

Thankfully I was all alone in my cell, which included a steel toilet, a metal-framed bed with a thin mattress, and a thin wool blanket. I wore scratchy, baggy gray pants and a matching V-neck top. I had nothing with me but my agonizing thoughts of shame, embarrassment, and guilt . . . and my voice.

Since my main source of comfort besides drugs and alcohol was music, I started singing "The Derelict" by Fleetwood Mac, the song I had sung in my high school talent show.

I'd been petrified to perform in that talent show—had no confidence—but a friend of mine had convinced me to do it and had played the guitar to accompany me. I'd long dreamed of being Christine McVie, the lead singer of Fleetwood Mac. She sang like a bird, and to be able to sing like her seemed like the most powerful thing in the world to do.

As I finished the first verse of "The Derelict," the police officer on duty said, "Hey, keep it down in there." His tone was kind, but firm.

I didn't want to defy him, but I needed to sing so badly—I started sobbing and singing under my breath. I knew I had fucked up and punishment was waiting for me.

After a long night of crying and trying to sleep in the cold cement cell under that thin, itchy wool blanket, in the morning the kindly police officer served me runny scrambled eggs and dry toast for breakfast with a hot cup of black coffee.

Finally, Papa San and Sherrie's sister came to get me. They tenderly smiled at me from the waiting area as they watched the police hand me a plastic bag filled with my belongings. I was so grateful and relieved to see them, I couldn't wait to get in the car. I hugged them both and as I climbed into the back seat, I began to cry.

"Papa San, I'm so sorry for making you drive all this way to come get me," I said plaintively. "I made a mistake. I thought I was going to Tahoe with her parents. I should have come right back when I realized we were hitchhiking. And then they convinced me to panhandle, and I didn't know that was illegal. Please ground me or whatever so I can make up for it."

He looked back and smiled at me kindly. "Don't worry about it, Wendy. People make mistakes. I know you'll learn from this mistake. We just worry that you could get hurt. Just promise me you'll make better choices from now on. I bet you never want to get thrown in jail ever again, do you?" He laughed, his kind eyes crinkling at me in the rearview mirror.

I couldn't believe his compassion and kindness. Why couldn't Papa San be my dad?

With that question repeating in my mind, I fell into a deep sleep. The California sun shone on my face all the way back to Concord.

"With the money we both get from Social Security and veterans' benefits, we could get an apartment together and go to college after we graduate from high school," I proposed as I lay next to Sherrie in our bed in the RV. Both of our fathers had died when we were young, so we were entitled to those benefits if we went to college.

We'd loaded up the RV and driven to Carmel-by-the-Sea for a week of beach walking after I was arrested. I kept waiting to be reminded about my arrest or punished for it, as I would have been at home, but Mama San and Papa San hadn't said another word about it. Instead, they'd both been encouraging me to think about my future.

"Wendy, did you know that if you were a California resident, you could go to state college here for free?" a smiling Mama San had informed me the previous day.

I had grown very close to her and Papa San, and the idea of living close to them felt right. It turned out that if I stayed in Illinois the junior college in Riverside would be more expensive than if I moved to California and paid out-of-state tuition for a year while establishing residency. That sealed the deal for me. Knowing that I only had two more years left of high school and then I could leave Riverside and Forestville forever made the idea of going home to Illinois at the end of the summer more bearable.

After that week in Carmel-by-the-Sea with Sherrie, I was in a California dream for sure. We spent the week walking on the sandy beach, collecting colorful seashells, and watching the sun melt into the horizon in the evenings, the sky engulfed in sunset colors I had only ever dreamed of. I loved the ocean breeze on my face and the way the salt air felt on my skin and hair. We walked around the adorable, cottagey seaside village and popped into art galleries, something I had never experienced before. I couldn't believe that people got to live there, and soon I would too.

I flew back home at the end of the summer armed with my plan.

I thought that by the end of the summer Paul would have forgotten about me getting arrested, or at least forgiven me—but he hadn't. He was stiff and unfriendly toward me when he spoke to me; usually, he just ignored me. Mom told me that while I was gone, she'd reminded him that she would leave him if he ever touched me again.

Luckily, since he worked two jobs and was gone so much, it was easy to avoid him and his moods.

In November that fall my sister had another baby girl, Jessica Marie, to join five-year-old Casey Ann. I loved those little girls, and in my plans to leave Illinois the only thing I really worried about was that I wouldn't get to watch my nieces grow up.

In a moment when Paul was home and more friendly, I told him and Mom we should move to a more rural area. I dreamed about living on a farm or in the mountains in a cabin. I thought that what my family needed was tranquility and wholesomeness. Mom and Paul somehow agreed, and we moved to Biscoe, a small, rural village north of Forestville.

The house was on a one-acre lot with huge mature oak and sycamore trees overlooking the Rock River—a beautiful place just like I had dreamed of. Although I was happy for this move, there was still always an underlying tension at home, depending on Paul's mood and drinking.

In the evenings I gazed west out the living room window at the land—the stately trees and the rainbows of color on the river as the sun set—and sang along to my favorite Led Zeppelin album, thinking about going to college in California. I was afraid to stay in Illinois, and I was afraid to leave. And I knew I would be going with an aching in my heart.

FREE BIRD

The Hamilton High School gymnasium brimmed with a sea of blue caps and gowns. I found my seat amidst four hundred of my peers—the graduating class of 1974—and smiled at the familiar faces around me as I sat down on the hard metal folding chair. The cacophony of excited voices was a low roar in my head as students and their families streamed in and greeted each other and finally sat down.

I anxiously looked through the seated crowd for my mom, who'd gotten dropped off by Paul on his way to his night job. I found her several rows behind me and waved, heartened to see her big smile and the bouquet of flowers in her lap for me.

She was the only member of my family who'd come to my graduation. As the speakers droned on, I tried to brush off the reality that no one else was there with some facts: Paul was working that night, Mark had converted to the Methodist Church and was now a pastor in Indiana, and Sharon was home, busy with two little kids.

At the end of the ceremony, Mom grabbed me and squeezed me hard. "I am so proud of you, Wendy Beth," she exclaimed, thrusting the bouquet of flowers into my hands. "You're going to do great things with your life!" She threw her arms around me and hugged me some more.

As she hugged me and patted me on the back, I saw Becca nearby, her big smile showing off her straightened teeth, having just gotten her braces removed and surrounded by her family. *All her family*: her mom and dad, siblings, grandparents, cousins. But the real fact was that my mom was the only person in my family who cared about and loved me enough to celebrate the milestone of my high school graduation, and that fact squeezed my heart with a twinge of sadness.

I quickly dismissed that sadness and puffed up my chest, however, because I was so exuberant to have graduated with great grades—all A's. Now, I was free to leave Forestville, Illinois. But I loved Illinois. I loved the rich, thick oak and pine forests and all the rivers that flowed into the great Mississippi River. I loved the landscape dotted with farmhouses and red barns and grazing cows and horses surrounded by green and yellow fields of corn. My blood, heart, and soul were the limbs of my family tree that grew from the deep roots planted here by my ancestor's and their connection to this land. But it was the people surrounding me that I knew I had to leave so that I could save myself.

"Mom, are you going to be okay when I leave?"

I'd thought that moving to the new house in the country would make us all happy—Paul always seemed happier in nature on our road trips, after all—but I could see that not all was well with them. He was often sullen and ignored me when I was at home. I worried about my mom and just wanted her to be content and safe. After brooding over her situation for months, I'd finally found a good moment to talk to her about my concern.

"Seriously," I said, "do you think Paul will get better when I'm gone? I'm so glad you're going to get your driver's license, so you aren't so dependent on him."

At fifty-five years old, at my urging, my mother was finally learning to drive. But she was still subject to Paul's moods and whims, and I hated that.

She looked at me as if she wondered whether she should share her next thought or not. "I heard that he was flirting with someone at his night job," she said, "so I told him he better straighten up. I told him I wanted him to cut down on his drinking too. He agreed to drink less, and he's quitting his night job, so we'll have more time together."

I was relieved to hear this, but I still wondered why she put up with him. And he was still so cold toward me that he wouldn't even cosign for me to buy a used car to drive to California. My uncle did instead.

I awoke to the happy smell of mom's signature breakfast: over-easy eggs, crispy bacon, slightly burned toast, and black coffee. It was the morning of my departure; I was finally California-bound.

"Where's Paul?" I asked when I walked into the kitchen, yawning.

"He left early to go to the shop," Mom said, "but he'll come back to get me in a little while."

I tried to put on a happy face and smiled at Mom over my eggs, but the emotion was rising in my throat. I was going to miss her terribly.

She handed me a small box.

"What's this?" I asked.

"A gift from Paul," she said with a shrug. "Open it!"

In the box was a collectable Jonathan Livingston Seagull silver pendant on a chain engraved with the words: YOU HAVE THE FREEDOM TO BE YOURSELF HERE AND NOW. I loved it, but it broke my heart that it seemed so difficult for him to be so thoughtful. In all the years we'd lived together, he hadn't given me many personal gifts: the Mamas & the Papas LP when I was ten and a Suzuki 50 motorcycle when I was thirteen that I rode in circles in the backyard were the only others I could think of, in fact. And why couldn't he stay home to see me off and watch me open his gift?

Mom handed me a notecard with a seagull on it. Inside, I found cash for my trip and a note from her:

Dear daughter,
Please take good care of yourself wherever you are. Be careful, honey. Just remember I'm here when you need me. I know there have been times when you feel I let you down. If I did, I never meant to. I'm very proud of you, you know that? As you spread your wings and fly off into the sunset, may God be ever with you. I envy you your spirit and courage to do the things you want to do. My beautiful daughter, please be as beautiful spiritually as you are in the flesh always. I love you very, very much. Good luck in whatever you undertake.

Mom

As I read the card, tears spilled down my face. I stood up and hugged my mom tighter than I ever had and, choking on my words, said, "Mom, I'm going to miss you. You're the best mom in the world. I love you so much. Maybe I shouldn't go."

She pulled me away from her and, tears streaming down her face, said, "Now you listen to me, Wendy Beth. You're doing the right thing. You have to go to California. You have to spread your wings and fly. You are going to do great things. I'm so proud of you and your courage. And I am going to live vicariously through your adventures."

Hesitatingly, I put one foot in front of the other and walked out of the house as Mom stood in the doorway, watching me go. I felt my heart break into a million pieces as I drove away, already missing her warm, soft hugs and sweet voice.

I cried all the way out of town, not feeling one bit of the courage that my mom said I had.

Except for attending two years of community college, Concord had not been a good experience for me. From the day I arrived, it had been apparent that Sherrie had no intention of going to college. She was running with a rough bunch of kids called the Gilmore Gang, and I'd gotten sucked right into their drugs and drama—until I decided I'd had enough. Now, at only nineteen, I felt broken, unworthy, and unsure of myself, and I was tired of covering all that up with partying, sex, and languishing with other people who were just as lost.

I needed to find a way to heal myself, and I wasn't going to do it in Concord. So, I was glad when I was accepted to transfer from Diablo Valley College—where, despite the turmoil in Concord, I'd managed to earn an associate degree in psychology—to Humboldt State University in Arcata, California, in the fall of 1976.

I went home to Illinois for a quick visit before moving to Arcata and spent most of my time with my gay self-taught artist friend Norm, whom I'd known since the third grade. He introduced me to the world of visual art, Broadway musicals, and the singers Joan Baez, Judy Collins, and Joni Mitchell.

I'd had a fake ID since I was sixteen, and since then almost every weekend, I had crossed the Illinois border into Beloit, Wisconsin, where the drinking age was eighteen. There, I typically drank fifty-cent shots of tequila and smoked Marlboro Reds in dingy bars that reeked of stale beer, cigarettes, and—frequently—vomit. Saturday nights I would head to the Waverly Beach in Beloit to dance to the hometown heroes Cheap Trick who hadn't quite yet had their big breakthrough. On this visit home, though, Norm and I disco-danced in the only gay bar in Riverside (which also didn't card us) and pirouetted on the dance floor to sultry Donna Summer under a spinning disco ball that shot shards of sparkling light across everyone's beaming faces.

As usual, music was a dependable source of catharsis and comfort for me.

Winded from climbing rocks and trying not to slip, I scrambled up on the huge boulder and inhaled the fresh, earthy oxygen infused with the emerald-green forest of Douglas fir and giant sequoias.

"As living timelines, many of these redwoods have been standing for more than twenty-five hundred years," Steve, an environmental science major, said reverently. "The Native people called these sequoias the Ancient Ones and considered them to be relatives."

I liked what he said—it inspired me, and hearing it, I felt I'd made the right choice transferring to Humboldt. I settled onto a flat spot on the boulder and pulled my jacket closer to stave off the foggy chill, realizing I'd arrived in a magical place. Except for the wind in the distant trees and the sound of the little critters cracking twigs, there was only a peaceful stillness that touched me deeply. In the silence of pristine beauty, with each deep inhalation and exhalation, I knew I'd found the place where I would begin to find myself and begin to heal from my painful childhood.

Here, I would find the wholesomeness I so needed and craved.

I gazed in awe at the magnificent sequoias, each sip of apricot liqueur from the bottle my new friend Ned had provided warmed and relaxed my body and spirit. Locals referred to living in Humboldt County as living behind the Redwood Curtain, both because of the densely forested land, which was comprised of a large percentage of all the remaining old-growth redwood forests on Earth, and because on a spiritual level, it offered a respite from the outside world.

In this moment, the name resonated for me on every level.

I'd only been at my new school for a week, and yet I'd already connected with my dorm suitemates, many of whom were from California. Since I was new to town and already a junior, they'd decided it was their duty to introduce me to all things Humboldt. Tonight, that entailed taking me on my first moonlit hike to a secret rock hidden by dense brush off the logging road up the steep hill behind the dorms.

The moon glow illuminated the faces of my new friends as we traded stories about where we'd grown up, what we were studying at Humboldt, and what we hoped to make of our lives. I was amazed by my new friends' stories, and by my own journey and what it had taken to get me there.

We talked about the fact that of all the human beings in the world, how we had come to be sitting here together in this very moment, in this sacred place.

"The Wiyot, a local indigenous tribe, called this place Jaroujiji, meaning 'here is where you sit and rest,'" Steve said.

This resonated with me. I felt safe here. I could sit and rest here. My shoulder muscles softened and relaxed, my breathing was deep and even. I hadn't felt this relaxed in many years—perhaps not since before my father died.

I was in heaven on earth. I was home.

"Look at this," Ned whispered as he pulled a chair to the middle of his dorm room. He climbed up on the chair, pushed on a rectangular drop ceiling panel, and pulled the panel aside, revealing grow lights rigged in the ceiling and an impressive crop of thriving marijuana plants.

"Oh my God, Ned, aren't you afraid you'll get caught?" I asked, nervously.

"Nah," he said, "they won't ever find it—besides, it's only a few plants. It would just be a slap on the wrist."

All I could think of were the dire warnings in the Midwest about threats of long jail terms for growing or dealing marijuana, and that horrible time I'd gone to jail for panhandling in Tahoe. What a different world I was in now.

Ned explained the history of pot in Humboldt. During the 1960s and 1970s, hippies from Haight-Ashbury had gotten into the back-to-the-land movement and flocked to Humboldt. They'd bought cheap land and built homes off the grid. At the time, most of America's weed supply had come from Mexico. Then the US government had started spraying the Mexican marijuana with a poisonous herbicide called paraquat that made it unsafe to smoke. So, the Humboldt hippies had started growing marijuana for themselves and their friends in the Bay Area. Using the sinsemilla, or seedless growing technique, they'd created a very strong and therefore highly prized and expensive strain of marijuana eventually dubbed Humboldt Homegrown.

I was astounded to hear this history and find out that, despite weed being illegal, these young people had taken a chance to create their own strain and learn how to farm and produce it in bulk.

"So that's what I'm growing for myself and my friends." Ned grinned. "You'll find out when I harvest it!"

Ned had quickly become a major influence in my life. From Los Angeles, he was highly intelligent, adventurous, and was majoring in geology at Humboldt State. He played guitar, backpacked to many of California's highest peaks, rode a motorcycle, and was constantly introducing me to amazing things in Humboldt.

I loved him in a sisterly way and hoped he would be content to stay platonic.

Ned's Honda Gold Wing growled underneath me as we rode down a rural farm road. Suddenly, he pulled over next to a marshy cow pasture that sat high on a hill, with a fabulous view of the ocean in the distance.

I inhaled the visual beauty and the scent of the breeze, which offered a mixture of impending rain and salty ocean air. I took off my helmet and pushed my fingers into my ears to retrieve my hearing from the vibration and wind. "What are we doing here?"

Waving his hands with the flourish of a professor, Ned exclaimed, "We are in search of *psilocybe semilanceata*!"

"What's that?" I asked, impressed with his scientific pronunciation but clueless about what it meant.

He pulled a small field guide to mushrooms from his pocket and began to read: "The *psilocybe semilanceata*, a.k.a. liberty cap, is likely the most popular magic mushroom in the world. The penile glans-shaped cap—"

"Oh, so we're looking for penises here?" I couldn't help but interrupt.

Ned smirked at me like I was a naughty adolescent and continued. "The penile glans-shaped cap is a dark chestnut brown when moist and dries to a light tan or yellow. Bluish stains emerge when it is bruised. It grows in fields and on dung patties where cattle graze from fall to early winter in the temperate climate of the Pacific Northwest." He flashed an impish smile and motioned toward the field. "And we just happen to be in the Pacific Northwest, where cattle graze, in the fall."

We ducked under the barbed-wire fence that corralled the cows and began walking into the pasture. We'd just come out of a few days of good rain, and the soggy earth grabbed my shoes; each step squelched as I pulled my foot free of the mud.

"I might have worn different shoes if I knew we were doing this," I said, scraping off some of the mud.

Good-natured, philosophical, and playful, Ned responded, "Ah, but then it would not have been spontaneous and serendipitous!"

We quickly found our prize in cow dung patties and tufts of grass, some solitary and some in clusters. It was a liberty cap gold mine. As we walked closer to a group of cows, they lifted their heads and gazed quizzically at us with their watery brown eyes, as if to ask, *What are you doing in our pasture?*

I nervously looked around for any mamas with babies, figuring that they would be protective and grumpy. Then I grew nervous about other dangers. "Ned, could we get arrested for trespassing?" I asked, looking down the road for the farmer's truck. "You know, I've already been to jail once, and I didn't like it."

"Don't worry," Ned assured me. "The farmer is used to people 'shrooming.' He'd probably just tell us to move along." He handed me a few of the bluish caps. "Here, I cleaned these off, eat them."

At first, I hesitated. I had never tried mushrooms before. But I trusted Ned, and I knew he was knowledgeable and experienced with shrooming, so I shoved the caps in my mouth and began to chew. The smooth texture felt like button mushrooms in my mouth but tasted strange, both earthy and metallic.

We continued gathering and eating the mushrooms, keeping an eye on the cows, an eye on the road, until the effects set in. I lost time, and the absurdity of it all hit me. The sky and grass and trees were a vibrant technicolor, and the cows smiled at me with giant teeth like the Cheshire Cat. Feeling peaceful and happy, I realized that I should strive to feel that way all the time.

Giggling uncontrollably, I looked over at Ned, who was also doubled over with big belly laughs. The *psylocibe* mushrooms were indeed magic.

The Center was sparse, with only coed twin and bunk beds, toilets and showers, a kitchen/dining hall, and meditation room. The Zendo, or meditation room, was a large, open room, painted white. Around the perimeter of the room were raised platforms, covered with cushions. The Zen Master and his helper monks from the San Francisco Zen Center sat on an elevated stage facing the lay students.

Entering the room, we each performed *gassho*, a bow of gratitude, with palms together at our chest. New to all of this, I simply followed along with what everyone else was doing.

I'd signed myself up for this Zen Buddhism retreat a few weeks earlier, after seeing a flier on the bulletin board at my member-owned health food co-op in Arcata. I had read Chogyam Trungpa's *Meditation in Action* a few years prior; I'd found it very academic and difficult to understand, but it had made me want to learn how to meditate. I wanted to learn how to calm and feel connected to myself without using drugs—even plant-based ones. This three-day intensive felt like a good way to start.

Once we were settled and seated on our round cushions, the Zen Master—seated at the front of the room and dressed in a traditional black monastic robe—addressed the room.

"Hello, earnest students, and welcome," he began. "We will begin the day with seated meditation. Please turn around to face the white wall. Now gaze at the wall with your eyes partially open, relaxed, and softly focused. Bring your attention to your breath. The meditation practice instruction is to inhale to a silent count of one, exhale one, inhale two, exhale two, and so forth to ten, then start again with one."

It was very disconcerting to realize that I didn't know how to breathe, something most humans do automatically without thinking about it. I discovered that I'd developed a habit of holding my breath as I waited for Paul's next outburst. When I tried to breathe as instructed, my inhale was short and grasping. I held my breath and then exhaled in a short burst.

Inhaling without holding my breath, I found, made me dizzy. My mind wandered, and I kept finding myself counting past ten, lost in thought. When that happened, the Zen Master had said, "one should gently bring the attention back to the breath and begin again with 'one.'"

Learning how to breathe and staying focused on counting my breath was exhausting.

When thoughts arose from what the instructors called "monkey mind chatter," we were told to simply acknowledge that we were *thinking* and gently move the mind back to the breath. Of all the challenges I was encountering today, this was the most calming, exhilarating, and difficult.

I sat with my legs tucked back alongside my cushion, but they kept falling asleep and tingling. Sitting up straight caused my back to ache. I became bored focusing on counting my breath. I wasn't doing this new task very well. I felt discouraged and thought maybe I couldn't meditate after all.

This is only day one, I reminded myself. *Be patient.*

Whack!

My eyes flew open; suddenly, I was wide awake.

It was the second day of the retreat, and after a night of little sleep and hours of meditation, I'd begun to doze off, so I'd raised my hand—and a monk had come over and whacked me on the back with the *kyosaku*, the bamboo wake-up stick.

Although the *kyosaku* is not used for punishment and I'd asked for it, I only asked for it that one time. Although it didn't hurt, it did feel like punishment, and I didn't enjoy that feeling.

What I did love was the chanting. At every gathering I would chant loud and strong, and it made me feel alive and powerful. *"Gate, gate, paragate, parasam gate, bodhi svaha!"* Singing the Heart Sutra, I felt my heart and throat soften, as if burdens were being lifted from my body and soul, and emotional tears filled my eyes.

The Zen Master informed us that the Heart Sutra had many translations but generally was translated as: "heart of the perfection of wisdom and insight." I didn't understand what that meant, but I knew that chanting made me feel strong and happy, soothed my anxiety, and filled me with a warm sense of love. After a lifetime of having no voice at home, the chanting awakened and freed me.

After each evening meal, the Zen Master gave a talk on the Buddha and the philosophy of Buddhism. I was like a dry sponge, eager to absorb everything. The story of Buddha's life and how he gave up his family and cushy life in the palace to search for an end to human suffering amazed me. It sounded so simple—such an easy answer to all of life's questions, challenges, and pain. But the Zen Master also said that was why Buddhism or any spiritual practice must be a *daily practice*—although we were meant to be happy in our lives, navigating life's difficulties, even with the best resources, was not always easy.

On the final day, a few people took vows, making a serious commitment to the Zen tradition. The ceremony was elegant, and the students recited the vows and explained to the community what each vow meant to them personally.

I sat in awe of these practitioners, thinking how lucky they were to feel so deeply committed, so certain that they were Buddhists. Considering my childhood experiences with the Evangelical church and my fear of anything cultish, however, I wasn't ready for that kind of commitment. I wanted to participate in Zen and practice meditation—but I wouldn't take any vows until I felt sure that Buddhism was right for me.

"Wanna go for a ride?" Ned asked with a grin.

He'd just picked me up from the retreat on his motorcycle. It was a typical, cold, foggy Humboldt day, and I was wearing only a thin jacket and cotton pants, not nearly enough to stay warm on a motorcycle ride. But I loved riding up into the hills with the wind in my face.

"Let's do it," I said.

The wind blasted my face and body as we drove down a rural road, and I tensed up against the cold. *Brrr!* I thought immediately. *Why didn't I wear a better jacket? Why don't we go right back to the dorm instead of taking a ride?*

But then I remembered to practice what I had learned in the retreat. I inhaled one, exhaled one, and my body began to relax. I thought of the teaching about letting go of attachment and accepting what is. I tasted a bit of *kensho*—what the Zen Master said was an awakening experience, a glimpse into one's own nature and the true nature of reality. I stopped resisting and felt the cold—as deeply as I could—and the resulting feeling was ecstatic. Alive. I was breathing deeper and exhaling longer than I ever had.

Gazing at the blur of majestic redwoods rising toward the hawks circling overhead, a deep peace came over me—a deep joy in simply being alive and breathing. The more I relaxed, the more I melted into the full experience of the cold and the windblown ride and the gorgeous landscape all around me, the more ecstasy I experienced. The cold forced me to be in the moment, to completely enjoy and embrace the present and allow it to be what it was.

This moment is all I have, I thought. *This moment and the next and the next.*

The Zen Master had talked about how focusing on being alive one moment at a time was like threading translucent pearls onto a silk cord, creating a necklace of mindfulness, and that each breath, each moment, was also an opportunity to focus on loving-kindness, or *metta*, toward myself. To contemplate my Buddha nature. My own goodness. He'd said that I was good, that I was lovable.

Buddhist meditation and wisdom made me feel like I was wrapped in a warm blanket of love. Gratitude welled up inside of me, and warm tears streamed down my windblown, frozen face as Ned and I wove our way home.

Part II
BECOMING

BRAVE NEW WORLD

In Humboldt, the world seemed to become more accessible to me. Since I had been raised in a cultural and educational vacuum growing up, I piled on the courses. I wanted to learn everything—experience everything—that I'd missed growing up.

Although my mom had always said she loved to read, I'd only ever seen her read the newspaper and *Reader's Digest*. She'd named me Wendy Beth for two children's book characters, but I'd never read either *Peter Pan* or *Little Women*. No one had read to me as a child, and I'd never owned a book or visited a public library. And yet I had always loved school and learning and, despite my family trauma and troubles, had never had problems at school.

Even though I had found some peace and happiness in Humboldt, I still felt troubled by my memories of what had happened in my family as I was growing up. I decided to major in psychology to better understand my family and myself; for fun and my own interest, I also took many theater and Native American studies classes.

"Hello, Wendy. Welcome. Have a seat," my academic advisor said, waving me into his office.

I was now in my senior year of college, and when I'd gotten a notice that my advisor wanted to see me, I'd worried that I was in trouble. But as I walked into his cluttered, paper-strewn office, he was all smiles.

"Let me begin by saying, congratulations!" he said, beaming. "You have been performing tremendously here at Humboldt. Are you aware that since you have been taking more than the required credits each semester, you could, if you want to, study one additional year and graduate with *two* bachelor's degrees? One in psychology and one in theater arts, as well as a minor in Native American studies. Also, I did check with Social Security and Veterans Affairs. You can continue to receive your benefits for another year if you choose to stay!"

My jaw dropped. I wanted nothing more than to stay in college and continue living in Humboldt, but I'd had no idea that I was eligible for another year of Veterans and Social Security benefits. This was incredible news.

Tears welled up in my eyes. "Yes, sir," I said gratefully. "I would like that very much."

Through my Native American studies courses, I met several students and professors who were working with some of the Northern California tribes—the Yurok, Hupa, Karuk, and Wiyot. Together, we initiated the Yurok Customs and Rights Support Group to help the tribe fight against the Forest Service's plans to construct the Gasquet–Orleans (G–O) logging road, which would desecrate sacred ceremonial land and negatively impact the area environmentally. We were all earnest college students, newly formed environmentalists who genuinely cared about the Native peoples and their plight to protect their culture and the environment. I believed that indigenous people were the first environmentalists, the caretakers of Earth. Now that I was aware of what was happening to our environment and to the indigenous people of the US, I'd decided I had to contribute whatever I could to right these wrongs.

In 1978, an Aztec dance troupe of the Nahua indigenous people from Mexico called Four Arrows came to Humboldt to perform in schools and colleges throughout Northern California, and I was invited to join them on their tour for several days. We were housed in private homes, and I was assigned to sleep in a bed with Yetlanizi, an elder female dancer and spiritual leader. Most of the dancers spoke Spanish in addition to their indigenous language, Nahuatl, but even my Spanish was sketchy.

After dinner at our hosts home, Yetlanizi motioned for me to help her wash the dishes. I quickly jumped up and began running the water from the faucet on the dishes. Yetlanizi shut off the water and said no, shaking her head. Then she showed me how to do it correctly: She filled a bowl with warm water and soap and began scrubbing the dishes with a soapy cloth, and only when the sink was filled with clean, soapy dishes did she turn on the water.

I smiled at her and nodded, happy to be receiving a lesson on the sanctity of water.

The next day, we went to a high school gymnasium for a performance. Watching the Four Arrows dancers gather in their traditional costumes, I realized that I had never seen anything so spectacular in my life. Each dancer had a unique, elaborately beaded costume and a crown of ornate and colorful feathered headdresses. They were barelegged and barefoot, with ankle rattles made from tree nuts that created a *shooshing* sound as they walked and danced.

The lead dancer blew a conch shell trumpet, and another dancer burned a resin called copal in an abalone shell to commence the sacred dance. Once the drumming, ankle rattles, flute playing, and percussion began, everyone in the gymnasium fell silent and was as mesmerized and in awe as I was.

As we traveled on the Four Arrows bus to the next few towns, I seriously considered moving to Mexico after graduation—to study Spanish and to live among my new Nahua friends. But when I discussed the idea with a Shoshone friend back home, he challenged me.

"In what capacity would you go there?" he asked. "As an anthropologist? To *study* your friends? As a *cultural tourist*?"

In the Yurok Customs and Rights Support Group, we often discussed the delicate learning curve of working with tribe members and elders correctly and respectfully, without acting like cultural tourists. We were committed to learning how to be helpful leaders without appropriating the culture and how to build bridges while maintaining good boundaries. We spent countless hours researching, making phone calls, writing letters, and attending Environmental Impact Statement (EIS) hearings on behalf of environmental and cultural concerns.

Challenged by my friend to think more deeply about my motivations, I ultimately decided that going to Mexico was not what I should do.

The Humboldt Homegrown pot harvest was completed, and my roommates and I were hosting a potluck hoedown to celebrate—lots of casserole dishes and salads as well as pot-infused brownies, cakes, muffins, and corn bread in celebration of the harvest.

I now lived in a cute two-bedroom house and compound with three friends: Ned, Robert, and James. My room was an add-on attached to the garage with its own woodburning stove and a built-in redwood bed and desk. The walls were covered with rough-hewn redwood and the room smelled delightful—even more so when I fired up the stove. I loved our home.

Ned and Robert were fabulous guitar players, and that night the Beatles, Grateful Dead, Old and In the Way, and bluegrass tunes were on the playlist. I loved to watch Robert's long blond hair fall onto his clean-shaven baby face as he played, smiling ear to ear, face flushed, lit up from the pot and high on the music. I smiled at how Ned's John Lennon-esque glasses slid down his nose as he anticipated Robert's rifts. Like a game of tag, they played off each other, taking turns with their improvisation.

Friends kept streaming in and setting their potluck dishes on the dining table. I looked around the room at my fabulous new friends—gathering, chatting, and tuning up their instruments—and felt a wave of gratitude.

Juniper, who was studying with the famous herbalist teacher Rosemary Gladstar and lived on a goat farm up the mountain east of Arcata, walked over just then, and I said, "Hi."

"Hey, Wendy!" she said brightly. "Guess what? I concocted a new herbal tea blend for Humboldt Crud."

Humboldt Crud was the cold/flu that everyone in Humboldt seemed to get every winter. I was learning about herbs too, and I loved that she shared recipes with me. I looked at her eagerly. "What's in it?"

"It's a mixture of echinacea, ginger, peppermint, rosemary, yarrow, and thyme," she explained. "And it really works."

I couldn't wait to make my own blend and have it on hand the next time I got the Humboldt Crud. Juniper had also taught me to smooth pennyroyal oil on my abdomen and lower back for menstrual cramps, and I'd discovered that the warming oil soothed the cramps immediately—a godsend, since mine were often debilitatingly painful.

Then there was Melody, who had taken two of her horses for a month-long trek on the Pacific Crest Trail. What bravery and self-reliance! She was like a tough cowgirl.

"Weren't you afraid to be all by yourself on the PCT for a whole month?" I asked her. The very thought was intimidating to me.

"Oh, but I wasn't alone. I had my horses." She smiled and winked at me.

She was being humble; I knew she was a tough, self-confident woman, and I aspired to be like her.

Ned and Robert, meanwhile, discussed and debated complicated physics concepts like quantum physics and the philosophies of Plato and Nietzsche while passing a joint back and forth; I couldn't follow a word they said.

Absorbing the energy of everyone gathered in our living room, I was profoundly impressed by these young adults who modeled for me how to live life fully, fearlessly, and adventurously. My new friends were so intelligent, creative, and inspiring, and I cherished these gatherings, where I experienced wholesomeness that I'd so long desired.

In this space, embraced and comforted, I was no longer the Illinois girl who'd arrived in Humboldt angry, frightened, and on edge.

DO YOU GET IT?

"Oh my gosh, Wendy Beth, I am so happy for you! Not only did you graduate from college, but you earned *two* bachelor's degrees. Oh my, I just couldn't be any prouder of you."

My mom smiled at me radiantly as I clutched my two diplomas. But as I observed how many family members surrounded my college friends, I once again felt a pang of sadness and wondered why my family wasn't like that.

It was June 1979, the day of my college graduation, and my mom was the only family member who'd come to California for the ceremony. This fact was easier to brush off than when no one else attended my high school graduation though, since this one was halfway across the country.

"I'm so glad you're here with me, Mom," I exclaimed, trying to put on a good face. "Thank you for coming!" I said as the emotion filled my lungs.

"Why, I wouldn't miss it for the world!" she beamed.

This only made me think again about those who *were* missing it.

Seeing my sad look, Mom pulled me in for a warm hug.

It almost made me feel better.

Back at my house, Mom pulled a few things from her luggage.

"You know, since we own our own business, it's just too hard for Paul to get away," she said. "But he sent you this."

She handed me a graduation card with some cash in it. All he'd written on the card was, "*Congratulations, show Mom a good time.*"

"And you know Sharon is just so busy with the girls with their school and all their activities," she went on. "But she sent you this." She handed me a box.

Surprised, I opened the box and found a Pentax camera inside. It was the first special and thoughtful gift I'd ever received from my sister, and it touched me.

"And you know Mark just got a new job as a minister in Indiana, and he's on a very meager salary . . ." Here she trailed off, since she had nothing from him to give me.

"Oh, Mom, this is all great," I said, wanting to shake off the sadness. "We're going to have a great time together. I can't wait to introduce you to all my friends. They're going to love you."

"I see the red, ripe strawberry moving toward my mouth. I see its red heart shape and green, pointy cap . . ."

I'd attended San Francisco's American Conservatory Theater summer program on a scholarship the summer after graduating from Humboldt, and although being on stage made me anxious, I'd fallen in love with theater and film acting. I'd decided to move to Hollywood with my theater-college friend, Misha, to continue my studies. We were in the middle of a sense memory exercise, a tool of the Method school of acting, in a class we were taking with the well-known and respected Hollywood acting teacher Pierrino Mascarino, and it was my turn in front of the group.

"I feel the coolness and the texture of the soft strawberry on my tongue." I shifted uncomfortably on the metal folding chair on the stage, peering out at my classmates and teacher. "I feel the heat of the sun on my arms and on my forehead."

For this exercise, Pierrino had asked us to choose a childhood memory and try to recall all the senses associated with that memory. Our warm-up exercises had included lying on a mattress on the floor and rolling from side to side, first slowly flailing our arms and emitting a deep, guttural, open-mouthed moan/hum and then, as our flailing became faster and more frantic, our voices shot to a high-pitched, terrifying wail. This exercise, Pierrino said, broke down our inhibitions—our shell, the mask that held our true selves back—and allowed us to connect with the deepest parts of our psyche, where the raw, deep-seated emotions would bring to life the characters we hoped to embody.

At first this experience felt weird, but then it began to be physically and mentally freeing. I liked the guttural yet controlled way we yelled during the exercise, and how it made those stuck places in my body begin to shake loose and melt. Eventually it came to me, the perfect sense memory: A hot summer's day in 1960, just before my fifth birthday, when I followed my dad out into the yard—his domain—as I often did. He went straight to his strawberry patch and plucked the reddest, ripest one he could find, brushed it off, and popped it into my mouth. The juicy sweetness exploded in my mouth, and his thoughtful gesture made me feel so loved.

"I feel my teeth connect as I bite down," I continued. "I taste the sweet juice released from the strawberry. I hear the robins chirping in the trees. I am content and happy and loved."

I described the taste of the succulent, juicy strawberry as if it were the first strawberry ever eaten. I continued to describe the scene with microscopic sensory details—following my father around the yard to peruse his mini-orchard of peaches, and pears; the smell of the fresh, fragrant persimmon fruit that had fallen to the ground, heavy with its own ripeness; the texture and shape of the bark of that stately old persimmon tree.

"As I move through the garden, I see a beautiful white lattice archway heaving with the most delectably fragrant white honeysuckle," I said.

This was the pinnacle of my sense memory: holding my daddy's hand, squinting up into the bright July sunshine, happy and safe. I described how my dad stopped to take in the moment fully—how he closed his eyes and inhaled, as if he were consuming the very elixir of life. It was one of the most vivid memories I had of him.

Wonderful.

But then Pierrino said, "Speak to him."

I paused. I didn't know how to speak out loud to my dead father. My mouth didn't know how to form the words; my brain couldn't access them.

"Speak to him," Pierrino insisted, louder this time.

A volcano of emotions rumbled in my chest, and I gasped and snuffled. I couldn't grasp what emotion was bubbling up. Sadness? Grief? Confusion? It felt like the same twisted emotions I'd felt when the neighbors asked me how my dad was doing just after he had died. They did not match this deeply touching memory of him, which I clung to as if it, too, could be taken away from me.

"Wendy, what do you want to say to him?" Pierrino prodded and implored.

I sensed that he knew something I didn't. I squirmed in my chair and choked on words that refused to leave my body. I felt a tension rise and consume my chest and throat, but I couldn't explain what it was. I thought I might explode and then—

"I'm mad at you!"

The words shot out of my body like water from a firehose that had been kinked, then suddenly released. Tears burst from my eyes along with the words from my mouth.

"Why are you mad at him? Tell him why. Tell him *why*!" Pierrino yelled.

"I'm mad at you for dying," I blurted. "I'm mad at you for not taking better care of yourself and leaving me—why did you leave me?"

Tears flooded my face, and my body began to shake with the release.

What a shock. I had no idea I was mad at him. I knew that I missed him. I knew I was sad that he died. I'd grown up imagining what my life would have been like had he lived, and I'd spent years fantasizing wonderful scenarios. But mad at him?

What a revelation. Had I buried the anger, sadness, and grief that I'd never dealt with for all these years? Who at that time, after all, had known they should help a seven-year-old child deal with the death of her father? Who would have even thought to consider her feelings or known how to talk about such difficult things?

As the layer of anger lifted, unresolved grief and sadness were revealed and laid bare for me to freshly feel. I was surprised and astounded by the power of this exercise.

Pierrino came to my chair, hugged me tightly, wiped the tears from my face gently, and thanked me for my courage.

"You have to take baby steps here," he said. "This is new information that has been buried deep inside you. You need to be gentle with yourself over the next few days as this revelation settles in. The death of a parent at such a young age is a deep wound that sometimes never heals."

I hugged him back. "Thank you, Pierrino. I had no idea that was all deep inside me."

As I went about the rest of my day, I felt lighter. The heavy feelings that had weighed on my heart for so many years had broken open. Was this what healing felt like?

The only color in the cavernous, stark white ballroom where the Erhard Seminar Training (a.k.a., est—the early precursor of Landmark Forum) was about to begin was a gray-blue carpet with hypnotic white swirls. I stared at it from my padded seat, mesmerized, as the chairs around me filled and the facilitators kicked things off.

I'd learned about est from the actor Anthony Zerbe when he came to Humboldt with Michael Learned to perform a staged reading of *Dear Liar: A Comedy of Letters*. Afterward, we theater students had gotten to mingle and chat with them. I'd approached Anthony and asked him if I should move to Los Angeles or New

York to study acting. He'd smiled warmly, held my hand, and said, "It doesn't matter. LA or New York. Both great places. The most important thing is that you continue to learn about yourself and get to know yourself deeply, to become a fully developed person. And then you need to learn how to draw from that knowledge as you develop characters as an actor. What I would encourage you to do, if you ever get a chance, is do this thing called est."

Now I was acting on his advice.

"Welcome, everyone," a female facilitator dressed in a navy blue pantsuit said into a microphone at the front of the room as the large crowd settled into their chairs. "Congratulations for showing up for yourselves and for choosing to prioritize your own life. I am thrilled for you to be here to learn new tools that will help you to connect with your authentic selves, to be real and honest about how you feel and what you think, and to take complete responsibility for your own lives, for your own happiness and success. This will be a life-changing experience for you!"

I resonated with the strong message of taking responsibility for our own lives with integrity; that was what I wanted to do, after all. I listened intently to the speakers and found that the est message relied heavily on the Zen message of transformation through being present in the moment without trying to push anything away.

Zen meditation and est both promised to enhance the fullness of life, and that was exactly what I craved.

The following weekend, on the final day, after many grueling late-night hours and in the final minutes of the est training, I sat in the ballroom surrounded by a couple hundred other people. Many were smiling and jubilant, some were crying tears of joy, others appeared content and quiet, and a few looked confused and forlorn.

The lead male trainer took to the microphone, and I sat on the edge of my seat in anticipation of his final words.

"You are perfect just the way you are," he called out, like a preacher delivering a sermon. "Do you understand that? You are perfect the way you are, even with all your imperfections." He paused, letting his words settle. "Please raise your hand if you believe this and if you know it. Please, a show of hands to acknowledge that you've Got It!"

"Got It" was the message to be responsible for your own life, to be your authentic and honest self. To know that life occurs in this moment with the circumstances you have.

People looked around and meekly and slowly raised their hands. I raised my hand to confirm that for my $400, I, too, "Got It." Like the Zen meditation experience, it seemed so simple. I wanted to believe that I really did get "It." I wanted to believe that no matter what I was faced with, I could hold on to these principles.

I inhaled one, exhaled one, to seal my intention to take responsibility for my own life, for my own happiness and success, and to assure myself that I was indeed worthy of all that my heart desired: love, wholesomeness, happiness, and healing.

PRETTY BABY

"Hey, Wendy, do you want to go to the ashram in Santa Monica to see Swami Muktananda with me?" a friend asked casually one day.

She and I often discussed spirituality, and I had told her about my Zen meditation and est experiences.

I was curious about Swami Muktananda, the world-renowned leader of the Siddha Yoga spiritual path. I had recently learned that est founder Werner Erhard and psychologist Richard Alpert, a.k.a. Ram Dass, had both sponsored him to come to the United States. I had read Ram Dass's book, *Be Here Now*, which informed me deeply.

"Yes, I would love to go. Thank you for inviting me!"

I had settled into life in LA by this point: I'd found a job as a cocktail waitress at the Comedy Store on the Sunset Strip where Robin Williams, Howie Mandel, and Richard Pryor regularly performed. (I made good tips there, but even better tips when I found rolled-up $100 bills on the floor, dusted with cocaine.) Misha and I now lived on Las Palmas, down the street from Francis Ford Coppola's Zoetrope Studios, and she'd recently been cast in a film at the studio. I had also found my way into the Screen Extras Guild and worked as an extra on many of the most popular TV shows: *Love Boat* (girl roller skating on Venice Beach—even though I still didn't know how to roller skate), *Hill Street Blues* (hooker in Downtown LA, Skid Row), and my favorite, *Brett*

Maverick (saloon girl who spins the roulette wheel). I was happy to be making an income with my new career as an extra and to spend time on locations and on the Paramount, 20th Century Fox, and Warner Brothers movie lots.

I was thrilled when I was awarded my Screen Actors Guild card on the film *Mommie Dearest* by being prompted to speak by Faye Dunaway who portrayed Joan Crawford, and the kind director Frank Perry approved it. I was happy about my accomplishments but longed to find inner peace and contentment. I was still searching to find meaning and belonging and a connection to—God? A higher wisdom?

I wasn't sure what to call it. But I did feel sure I would know it when I found it.

The day of the opening ceremony, I drove to Santa Monica, where a huge white "satsang" hall (community tent) that accommodated thousands of people had been erected. The temporary ashram would host the Swami and his entourage for the entirety of his six-month stay.

Carrying the blanket my friend had suggested I take, I picked my way through the crowd until I finally managed to find a spot on the packed floor.

In the front of the room, on the elevated stage, Swami Muktananda found his seat on a throne, adorned with a garland of carnations and surrounded by vases of colorful flowers, burning candles, and several helpers. Behind and above him on the wall were giant poster-sized photos of both him and his guru, Swami Nityananda.

The mayor of Santa Monica approached the microphone and addressed the crowd: "Welcome, esteemed guests. As mayor of the beautiful city of Santa Monica, California, it is my honor to welcome the renowned spiritual leader Swami Baba Muktananda on this historic third world tour. For the next six months, the residents of the cities of Santa Monica and Los Angeles will be enriched with the teachings, blessings, and festivities that the Swami will bestow upon all of us."

After numerous accolades and introductions of his vast disciple staff, Swami Muktananda spoke as an assistant interpreted: "I welcome you all with love and respect. Let me begin by saying that meditation is not a religion. Because you meditate on yourself, you don't have to give up your religion to meditate. You can be Hindu, Jewish, Muslim, Christian, or Buddhist and reap the benefits of the Siddha Yoga meditation without giving up your religious beliefs. God dwells within you as you."

This message, that God dwelled within me, resonated deeply for me. As I sat on my blanket, I studied Swami Muktananda—taking in his yellow knit cap, yellow jacket, orange shirt, and baggy pants—and felt drawn to learn more about his mission to bestow grace and awaken people to their own divinity, beauty, and self-worth. He said we were all conscious spiritual beings having human experiences—we were all precious jewels. I thought if everyone believed this, the world would be a very different, more peaceful, place.

Even though the est trainers and my Zen Buddhist teacher had assured me that I was perfect just as I was with all my flaws, I didn't always believe it and still struggled with feeling okay about myself. But Swami Muktananda made me feel like it might really be true. I felt nourished by his words and felt that in his presence I, too, was precious.

Muktananda was known as the *shaktipat* guru. *Shaktipat*, I had learned, was energy transmitted from the guru or teacher to the seeker to awaken the seeker's own spiritual energy. Through continued meditation and yoga practice, one could maintain this awakening.

Although sitting still in meditation for long periods of time was still very difficult for me, I had continued practicing the Iyengar yoga I'd learned at the summer acting program I'd attended at American Conservatory Theater in San Francisco. To me it felt like a moving meditation, and it worked for me.

With Muktananda's help, would I find my own awakening?

I signed up for the special two-day *shaktipat* initiation weekend, hoping to find out.

On the first day of the initiation weekend, I joined thousands under that big white tent. Many people wore loose-fitting, colorfully embroidered, white cotton clothing from India, and several others were dressed like hippies, but there were also business types in suits and people dressed in jeans and T-shirts like me. All kinds of people were there, young and old alike.

The first day was filled with intensive meditation and chanting. I enjoyed the chanting and time in silence and sensed that there was something special about the teachings of Siddha yoga. But I also observed the culture of the ashram with some skepticism. I noticed how the disciples revered and adored Swami Muktananda as he sat on his throne. The devotees dashing about in their flowing orange robes made me feel uncomfortable. I had been leery of anything that smelled of a cult since I had become aware of Manson and his followers when I was thirteen.

I'd had one up close and personal experience with cult members before, during my time at my community college in Concord. I was sitting in the quad one spring day when three clean-cut, conservative-looking, business-type men approached me. One of them, smiling broadly, handed me a flower and a piece of candy. At first, I was touched, but then he asked for a donation for his church. Suddenly, I recognized them as the Moonies I had seen on the news. I handed back the candy and the flower and said, "No thank you!" I'd been horrified to learn how the ex-members had to be deprogrammed. Thinking about cults gave me the shivers and made me queasy.

I hoped Siddha was different, but I would stay on my guard until I was sure that was true.

On the second day of the initiation, one of the disciples announced that we would receive *shaktipat*, the energy transmission, and that Swami Muktananda would bestow a spiritual name upon each of us.

In that moment, I made an arbitrary decision: *If he gives me a name beginning with the letter* S, *perhaps I'll believe that he's a true guru.*

The tent was vibrating with people murmuring softly to each other; everyone was full of anxious anticipation. Sandalwood incense smoke filled the tent, and music from an organ-like instrument called a harmonium wafted through the air. Sitting close together on our individual blankets before Muktananda, who was sitting on his lavish throne surrounded by vases of freshly cut lush flowers, we began to chant "Om Nama Shivaya," a Hindu healing chant to Lord Shiva, or Universal Consciousness. It was a beautiful and powerful chant, and I loved how vocalizing made my body vibrate with energy and joy just as the chants of the Zen Buddhist retreat had done.

Eventually, the initiation began. I took a yoga child's pose with my forehead and arms on the floor, my knees bent under me and spread apart. A few times I looked up to see what Muktananda was doing. As he methodically walked down the aisles of people, he swatted them with a large plume of peacock feathers. I put my head back down on the floor and hoped I'd feel something special today.

When Muktananda reached me, the heavy peacock plume struck my lower back at my coccyx, and I saw and felt a white light wave shoot up from my coccyx, up my spine, and out the top of my head. An electrical tingling traveled up my spine, and every hair on my body stood up on end.

I blinked, trying to decipher how I'd seen the white light—visually or mentally? I decided it was both. I'd "seen" the light move through my body, and then I'd truly seen it as it shot out the crown of my head.

Wow, I thought. *That was amazing. It was real.*

It had really happened. Filled with a sense of peace and calm, well-being, and joy, I experienced a sense of my own divinity and a connection with God and the Universe.

As Muktananda moved to the next person, I continued to breathe deeply and absorb the experience.

After we had all received *shaktipat*, we were instructed by one of the lead helpers to line up one row at a time to lay our offering of flowers or incense, or whatever we'd like to let go of, at Muktananda's feet.

"When you arrive at the front of the line, a helper will gesture for you to move to the pillow in front of Baba," she explained. "There you will bow and place your offering at his feet. He will then give you a spiritual name."

When it was my turn, I nervously placed a packet of incense and a pack of Marlboro cigarettes at his feet. Gazing into his eyes, I begged him silently to take away my desire for cigarettes.

He returned my gaze with kind, adoring dark eyes and a sweet smile, as if he read my mind. He paused for a moment and then simply said, "Shankara." He bowed to me and placed his palms together in prayer pose at his chest.

Joyful tears filled my eyes, and I burst into a smile as I slowly walked back to my spot.

I'd challenged the universe to prove to me that he was authentic, and now I was in awe. He named me Shankara, a name that not only started with the letter *S* but also meant "lucky" or "auspicious" in Sanskrit. I felt very lucky indeed.

Whatever else I felt about the culture of the Siddha Yoga tradition, I knew that my experience that day was authentic.

Still, I wasn't interested in packing up, donning orange robes, and joining an ashram like some people I had met had decided to do. I would continue to study, meditate, and chant at home—and, hopefully, quit smoking.

That summer of 1981, at twenty-five years old, I decided it was time to visit my family. I hadn't been home in several years, and I was thinking the visit would be a good chance to catch up—I especially wanted to see my adorable nieces, who wrote to me often. I was hopeful that my newfound skills would help me to feel less bothered and more peaceful around my family, no matter how they decided to act.

I may have been overly optimistic.

"Casey, this room is a mess." Sharon yelled shrilly. "I want you to clean it up right now."

Sharon was now married to her second husband, a doctor twenty-five years her senior, and led a lifestyle I envied. She was seeing a psychotherapist, and she enjoyed frequent visits to Chicago's Miracle Mile to shop for expensive designer clothes and hair stylists.

Still, she didn't seem happy.

"I'll do it later, Mom!" thirteen-year-old Casey protested.

"I said *right now*, or you're grounded!" Sharon roared.

Feeling that Sharon was being overly harsh, I spoke up for my niece. "Sharon, why are you being so overreactive?"

Sharon's face twisted with rage, and she paced back and forth, her hands on her hips. "Oh, you think you're so perfect," she spat. "You're not perfect. You're just like Mom. You're not perfect. Come down off your pedestal!"

All I could do was gape at her. She'd always been combative and easily agitated, and I had heard her angrily talk to and about Mom this way before, but not so much toward me. *Aren't people who go to therapy supposed to be calmer and more in tune with themselves?* I thought. But Sharon seemed angrier than I'd ever seen her. Her words were particularly hurtful since I had just confided in her how I had been working so hard to feel better about myself, and how hard it was to believe that I was worthy and special despite what my Zen teachers, est trainer, and Muktananda had told me. Now she was making the idea of thinking of yourself as perfect despite human imperfections as shameful and self-centered—using the information I'd trusted her with against me.

"I don't think I'm perfect. I know I have faults," I said defensively. "I've never said I was perfect. I was just sticking up for Casey, that's all. And what does Mom have to do with this anyway?"

"Ha," she scoffed, crossing her arms and glaring at me with cold eyes. "Do you know what Mom said to me, a twelve-year-old girl, when she brought you home from the hospital?"

"No, of course not, I was a newborn," I replied. What did my birth have to do with what was happening now?

"What she said was that she finally got her 'pretty baby'! That's what she said to me, an insecure twelve-year-old girl." She exhaled angrily and waited for me to respond.

"What? Why would she say that?" I asked, genuinely confused and concerned.

Sharon picked up a sweater from Casey's bed and threw it back down. "She said to me, 'You were born premature and looked like a drowned rat in the incubator, and Mark wasn't very pretty either, but now I have my pretty baby.'"

Stunned into silence, I stood there trying to absorb and make sense of this story. It was hurtful to think that Mom would say such a thing. Not wanting to believe it, I grasped at straws. "Sharon, that was twenty-five years ago. Are you sure you're remembering this correctly? Maybe you misunderstood. Have you asked Mom about this?"

My questions just infuriated her more.

"You think you're so perfect. You're just like Mom," she hissed. "You need to get out of my house."

I stared at her, sure she couldn't mean it, but her face was red with anger.

"Well," she added as a parting shot, "you're Mr. Lee's daughter anyway."

I was reeling from her anger toward me, but this was something new, and my attention caught on her words. "What? What are you talking about? Who is Mr. Lee?"

She waved her hand and turned away. "Oh nothing. Never mind. I'm just angry."

"But—"

"Please," she said through clenched teeth, "get out of my house."

I stumbled out of the house, tears spilling down my face, and climbed into my mom's car, which I'd borrowed for the visit.

Why did my sister hate me? How could she blame me for something Mom had said when I was a newborn infant?

As I drove back to my parents' house, I went over the conversation again. This was the first time I'd ever heard this "pretty baby" story.

I was twenty-five years old, and Sharon was thirty-seven. She was married to a wonderful man, she had two beautiful daughters, a beautiful home, and a privileged life. She should be happy and grateful. It sounded like she was just digging for something bad to say about Mom. *But where did she come up with this "Mr. Lee" story?*

I brushed it off as Sharon just being mean. She could cut deeply with her hurtful words. She had blurted out in anger a few times in the past that I was the milkman's daughter; this was just a different version of the same old venom, I supposed.

Having a violent stepdad who I wanted to think of as my dad was bad enough. But I also had an absent and indifferent brother and an angry and spiteful sister, and I didn't know which of those was worse. What was wrong with my family?

Of everyone in my family, Mom was the only one I'd always been able to count on. She was consistently kind and loving and affectionate with me, and I'd always assumed she was the same way with my older siblings too. But I'd come along almost twelve years after my sister and seven years after my brother. Were there secrets, lies, and dysfunction in my family that predated my birth? What else did I not know?

"Mom, Sharon and I had a fight, and she said that when you brought me home from the hospital that you told her that you finally got your 'pretty baby.' Did you really say that?"

I was still in shock from my fight with Sharon, and I wanted to hear from Mom if this story was true.

"Oh, Wendy, I didn't say that." She pursed her lips. "I might have said you were my *best* baby, because Sharon was a tiny, premature baby who had to be in an incubator for a month, and Mark was skinny and colicky and cried all the time. But you were born healthy and happy and chubby, with dimples in your arms and legs. You were my *best* baby."

I felt a little sorry for Sharon, despite what had happened. "Oh, but Mom, still. You shouldn't have said that to a twelve-year-old girl. She is still hurt by that twenty-five years later."

"Wendy, I didn't mean anything by it," she said, sounding irritated. "I love all my kids equally." Then, sighing, she added, "I don't know why Sharon wants to bring up something that happened so long ago." Her voice choked with a mixture of sadness and hurt on those last words, and she turned away, rattling pots and pans on the stove as she started dinner.

"It's okay, Mom," I said quickly. "I know you didn't mean it."

But privately, I began to see that what my mom had said to Sharon twenty-five years before had been the beginning of the wedge—a wound that had festered into deep-seated primal anger, competition, and jealousy in my relationship with my sister. It was a wound that might sometimes scab over temporarily but was easily torn open again.

So much for all the "healing" I'd done. With my family, none of it seemed to make any difference.

I wished that I could simply change my name to Shankara, the name given to me by Swami Muktananda, and everything else would change too. Shankara, the great male Indian philosopher, writer, yogi, and teacher who had renounced the world and became an ascetic. Perhaps if I lived in another time, in another place, and as a man, I, too, would renounce the world. But in

1981 America, changing my name would not change my family members or how they treated me.

Would I ever to be able to fully embody and put into practice what I was learning through retreats and studying and meditating? How was meditation going to help me face the pain and hurt inflicted upon me by my family and the world?

I thought of the words of Baba Ram Dass: "If you think you are enlightened, go spend a week with your family."

Now there was a man who knew what he was talking about.

FLESH AND BLOOD

A few days had passed since the "pretty baby" incident with Sharon, and Paul's entire Swiss–American family were at our house for an afternoon Sunday potluck: his ninety-five-year-old grandfather who barely spoke English, his elderly mother, his two elderly aunts, his brother with his wife and three kids, and his sister with her husband and three kids. The women brought their mandarin and pineapple whipped cream Jell-O desserts and their casserole dishes swimming in cheese and set them on Mom's stainless-steel island in the kitchen. Mom made her signature Thanksgiving dinner spread with all the trimmings, even though it was August. She was famous for her perfectly butter-browned turkey, sage dressing, giblet gravy, cooked-to-hell green beans, and—my favorite dessert—homemade lemon meringue pie, with its stiff waves of perfectly browned meringue.

Paul had built a huge sunroom extension to the house that overlooked their acre of land on the Rock River; we all gathered there to eat. As everyone sat around the numerous café-style tables Mom had set up for the party, eating and chatting, I resumed my fantasy about what it might have been like to grow up in a large, close-knit family. Family who would be there to celebrate milestones together: birthdays, holidays, graduations, weddings, baby showers. Mom and her siblings had been close-knit growing up, but as adults, half of them had moved away from St. Louis. Since then, the gatherings had all been mostly for funerals, with only the occasional family reunion.

After dinner, the adults gathered around a large round table in the sunroom to drink beer and play the card game euchre. I had never learned to play, and I wasn't invited to join, only to watch. I sat and studied their faces as they seriously scrutinized their cards and gulped beer from iced glasses.

Looking around at everyone amiably chatting and drinking and laughing, I thought back to when I first learned anything about Paul's family—the spring after that horrible Christmas when I was nine and he'd torn down the Christmas tree.

Mom, Paul, and I were driving through downtown Riverside, and we came to a stoplight.

Paul looked over at the car next to us and nonchalantly remarked, "That's my brother."

"Oh," Mom said gently. "Wouldn't you like to say hello?"

Paul looked at Mom with a pained expression and hesitated, but then beeped his horn.

At first, Paul's brother and his wife and kids looked over at us quizzically. Then Paul's brother recognized him and nodded, and Paul waved for him to pull over.

We pulled over behind them, and Paul got out of the car and went to speak to him. It was clear to me that he hadn't seen his brother for a while, maybe years.

While waiting for him, Mom studied the brothers talking on the side of the road and whispered to me, "Paul finally told me that his mother and sister live in Freeport, near Riverside, and that his crazy father already died. He didn't know where his brother lived."

I sat up and rested my arms on the front seat, straining to see the people in the car in front of me. Knots formed in my stomach, and I wondered why Paul hadn't seen his family for so long.

"Mom, if his mean father is dead, why doesn't he see the rest of his family? Especially his own mother?" I couldn't imagine not seeing my mom for many years; I shuddered to think of it.

A few minutes later, Paul's brother drove off, and Paul got back into the car to drive home.

"How crazy is that, running into my brother at a stoplight?" he said, laughing—and that was it. Conversation over.

It wasn't until three years after the stoplight run-in that we finally met Paul's entire family at a gathering at his sister's house. After that, we saw them for holidays for the next five or so years, but once I went off to college, I only saw them occasionally.

I never did learn what had caused Paul to be estranged from his family for so many years before that chance run-in.

I returned to Illinois four months later to spend Thanksgiving at Sharon's tastefully decorated French Country-style home in a tony section of town on the Rock River. It was the largest Thanksgiving family gathering I had ever attended. Paul's whole family joined us again, and even Mark drove up from Indiana. Sharon's cook, Mrs. Sledge, helped with the cooking, and Mom brought her famous lemon meringue pie. It was the picture-perfect Norman Rockwell gathering. Everyone was warm and agreeable and smiled a lot and nodded and talked about the weather.

I found a seat in the living room and observed the large crowd. Sharon was smiling and moving around the room, offering her guests cocktails. After the "pretty baby" episode with her that previous summer, we hadn't spoken about it again, but a nagging whisper deep inside me told me that I shouldn't trust my sister. I felt I had to be guarded and protect myself from any further attacks.

After seven years of living on my own, I had spent time with quite a few of my friends' families—families who were close and loving—and I'd found people like Misha, who had become like family to me, yet I still yearned for warmth, closeness, and authenticity in my own family. It made me sad that I didn't feel like I belonged in my own family and didn't feel close to anyone in it except for Mom.

Sitting there, I thought of my dad, as I often did on holidays. Watching Sharon as she attended to her guests, I noticed that I didn't look like him like she did. She looked exactly like him, in fact, with her auburn hair and brown eyes and even his receding chin, which she hated.

I looked across the room at Mark and wondered who he looked like. He didn't look like any of us—me, Sharon, Mom, or Dad Burt. I looked over at Mom, smiling and chatting with Paul's sister, with her fair skin, green eyes, and blonde hair and decided that I looked a lot like her. But I wondered where my nose came from. Mom had a cute, upturned little nose, not a hook nose or "Roman nose," as people liked to call mine. *And why do I have these short little legs?* That was the one thing that Sharon and I seemed to share. Why hadn't I gotten Mom's long, lean, beautiful legs? She sported short-shorts like nobody else.

I felt like all I had was questions, with no answers in sight.

After dinner I moved to sit next to Mom on Sharon's exquisitely upholstered designer couch. I held her warm "little hand" in mine, and asked, "Mom, where did my nose come from? This is not your nose or Burt's nose. Do you remember anyone in the family with a nose shaped like mine?"

I'd asked her these kinds of questions before, when I was younger, but I'd never gotten a satisfactory answer back then. Maybe I would now.

"Oh, Wendy, I don't know," she said. "You ask so many questions." Laughing uneasily, she added, "I've never known anyone who asks so many questions about their birth and where they came from."

I smiled and squeezed her hand but felt a tingling in my stomach. Something didn't feel quite right. Something didn't quite add up. I remembered Sharon's comments about the milkman, about Mr. Lee.

I had a crazy thought: *Was I adopted?*

Then I had an even crazier thought: *Sharon is twelve years older than me. Is it possible she is really my mother, and Mom only raised me as her daughter?*

That might explain why Sharon acted like she hated me and loved me in the same breath.

I shook my head, chastised myself for my crazy thoughts, and laughed it off. *That is ridiculous thinking, Wendy. Just drop it*, I told myself. But the weird feeling about not fitting in with my family stayed with me.

I looked around the living room at Paul's huge family and once again allowed myself to wonder for a moment what it might have been like to be a member of their family. When I was younger, I'd fantasized that they were the big, loving, wholesome, tight-knit family I had longed for and that they would fill the gaping hole my dad's death had left. One member of the family was kind to me: Dad's sister-in-law, who decades later would confide in me that she understood my outsider feeling since she, too, had struggled for many years to feel accepted by her husband's family. But as I sat in my sister's living room on that Thanksgiving Day in 1981, it finally sank in: While these people were pleasant enough toward me when they saw me, they were never going to include me in *their* family. I was not their flesh and blood—never had been, never would be. They were barely more than strangers.

I sat with a forced smile on my face, uneasy from the realization that I was an outsider in my own family and in Paul's family too. *Why did I ever think they could possibly care about me or claim me as one of their own?*

It was time to move on from that childish dream.

Riding the bus to O'Hare airport the next day, I dreamily gazed out the window at the white farmhouses and red barns that I had seen every time I made the ninety-minute bus trip to Riverside and again back to the airport. But this time I understood what they had meant to me for so long. I now saw that these red barns had always sparked my Hollywood movie idealized version of family and home. Seeing them had filled me with hope and nostalgia for the wholesome home I dreamed of and hoped I would find when I got there.

But I was homesick for a family and home that didn't exist. I was filled with longing for something I had never had.

Now I understood that what I longed for would have to be something that I created. I wasn't ready to let go of the fantasy of fixing my family and making us whole, but I was ready to start looking for a family that would love and support me in a way my family couldn't. To survive, I needed to belong—and since I didn't belong in my family, I needed to look elsewhere.

My people were out there somewhere. I just needed to find them.

PEACE SUNDAY

I woke up from a sweaty fever dream, pajamas drenched. I lay still in bed, breathing to calm my pounding heart, grateful that it was just another crazy nightmare.

Once my heartbeat slowed, I leaned over and pushed open my bedroom window to let in Venice Beach's salty ocean breeze.

Every day that passed, nuclear war between the United States and the Soviet Union seemed more and more likely, and it terrified me. It was January in 1982, and I was having near-nightly post-apocalyptic nightmares in which every person in the world was assigned a specific job to contribute to human survival, but I didn't know what my job was and felt useless. Every time I had this dream, I woke up shaking and wondering what my contribution would be in a postapocalyptic world. What was the most important job I could do? Would my degrees in psychology and theater be worthless in a world where survival was the real question?

I wasn't going to wait to find out. Even if I could only minimally contribute to the prevention of nuclear annihilation, I needed to do something.

That week, I signed up for civil disobedience trainings, attended lectures on the proposed Bilateral Nuclear Weapons Freeze Initiative, and started helping gather signatures to get California Proposition 12 on the November ballot. We rehearsed planting ourselves on the ground with linked arms, an action that would make it more difficult for police to move us en masse during a demonstration. We practiced nonviolent communication to learn how to disagree with people without the conversation escalating into violence by role-playing opposing positions and using the four pillars of nonviolent communication: observation, feelings, needs, and requests.

As the last day of the training was ending, my nonviolent communication supervisor approached me. “I noticed that you attended all the trainings and did very well in the nonviolent communication role-playing,” he said, smiling. “There is going to be an historic concert at the Rose Bowl in Pasadena in June—we’re calling it Peace Sunday. We’re hoping it will bring even more attention to Proposition 12. Would you be available to help with security detail?”

“Yes!” I responded immediately, excited to be asked.

When I found out that many of the most famous rock and folk musicians of the moment would be performing at the concert and over a hundred thousand people would be attending, my excitement grew even more.

Three years earlier, three weeks after the near disaster at Three Mile Island in Harrisburg, PA, there had been a “No Nukes” protest concert in Washington, DC. Joni Mitchell, Jackson Browne, and Graham Nash had performed there, and speakers had included California Governor Jerry Brown, actress Jane Fonda, and her husband, California State Assemblyman Tom Hayden. This Peace Sunday event promised to be just as big.

I decided I had a new passion: political activism.

It was a crystal blue, not-a-cloud-in-the-sky Pasadena day. Dozens of people scurried around the Rose Bowl, setting up the stage to prepare for soundcheck, moving heavy speakers and equipment into place, unloading boxes of food, setting up craft services, and loading in trailers for the musicians' backstage comfort.

I found my way to Marie, the volunteer coordinator, who was seated at a folding table in front of the stage. After checking for my name on a list, she handed me a lanyard with my laminated SECURITY backstage pass attached to it, and I excitedly hung it around my neck. She rifled through a stack of papers on the folding table, then looked me squarely in the face and said, "Okay, you're going to be backstage, looking after Gracie Browne, Jackson's sister."

She could have knocked me over with a feather. My jaw dropped. *She said Jackson Browne!* For a second, I couldn't speak, but I quickly pulled myself together and pretended that it was no big deal—tried to project the image of a trustworthy professional who would do a good job of looking after my charge. No one had to know that I was secretly in love with Jackson, just like countless other girls he didn't know existed.

"Oh, here's Jackson now, let me introduce you," she exclaimed.

Please stay cool, Wendy. Please stay cool. I repeated this to myself on loop in my head.

Standing with Jackson was Jesse Colin Young, the singer of the iconic 1960s song "Get Together," whom I had briefly met when he had performed at Humboldt State a few years earlier. Marie quickly introduced us all.

"Do you want a photo?" she asked, gesturing to the Pentax camera hanging around my neck.

"Yes, please!" I handed the camera over eagerly.

She snapped a few photos of me with my arms around Jackson and Jesse. I smiled like the Cheshire Cat the whole time, wondering how a girl from the Midwest got to be in this place, with these incredible musicians. I thought Jackson was much more handsome in person than he'd been in all the album cover photos I'd spent hours drooling over since I was a teen.

Photos done, Marie led me to the ARTISTS ONLY bleachers behind the stage, where a teen Gracie was sitting.

"Gracie, this is Wendy," Marie said. "She is your escort for the day. Jackson prefers that she hang out with you and walk with you to craft services and the bathroom. And when you are ready to go home, Wendy will get your driver."

Fourteen-year-old Gracie was a shy, pretty girl with dark brown hair like her brother and dark, almond-shaped eyes. She sat with her elbow on her knee and her hand on her chin, biting her fingernails like she was bored—or, perhaps, felt out of place.

"Wow, this is going to be an incredible concert," I said cheerfully, trying to break the ice.

No response.

"But you must get to go to a lot of concerts with your big brother, huh?" I asked. "What's that like?" I sincerely wanted to know.

"It's okay." She shrugged.

I didn't want to continue to pry or make her uncomfortable, so I dropped that line of questioning and changed the subject. "Hey, are you hungry? Shall we go see what craft services has?"

I got Gracie a hamburger and fries at craft services—I didn't get anything; I was much too nervous to eat—and by the time we were back to our seats in the bleachers, she had come out of her shell a bit. Holding her food in a paper boat on her lap, she began telling me about her favorite subjects in school.

Soon, the concert started, and Stevie Wonder led the masses in a "We Demand World Peace Today" chant. I encouraged Gracie to join me in standing and chanting, and she did.

"Can we go backstage?" she asked when the chanting was done.

Hang out with the folk and rock icons I idolize? Yes, please.

"Of course!" I said, smiling, and I led the way from our seats in the bleachers and walked down the metal bleacher stairs to the backstage area.

We stood on stage as Joan Baez and Bob Dylan sang "Blowin' in the Wind," and Dan Fogelberg performed several songs with Jackson and Graham Nash backing him on guitar. Stevie Nicks, with her long blonde hair and flowy bohemian dress, performed next.

These were people whose songs and lyrics educated me, comforted me, inspired me, made me want to fulfill my highest potential. I couldn't believe my luck to be standing so close to them.

After several hours of walking back and forth to craft services, watching performances from backstage, sitting in the bleachers, and making trips to the porta-potty, Gracie told me she was ready to go home. Once I found a staff security driver to take her home and said goodbye, I was free to hang out backstage and watch performances by my idols for the rest of the night.

I pinched myself at the thought that I was there on the stage for this powerful, historic, star-studded event. A feeling of deep gratitude and hope filled me. I observed how it wasn't just celebrities who could make an impact with their voice; everyday humans, too, could be a force to be reckoned with when they joined together in grassroots efforts. The whole stadium hummed with the energy of people who had a united purpose. I hoped people like those here tonight would continue to fight to save themselves and the planet for future generations.

Stevie Wonder and Civil Rights leader Jesse Jackson joined the crowded backstage as Jackson Browne sang some of his most popular songs. The entire stadium sang along to the bouncy "Doctor My Eyes" before Jackson ended with the tender and heartfelt "The Pretender."

"This is pretty incredible, isn't it?" a woman said to me.

It was Margot Kidder, the actress who had played Lois Lane opposite Christopher Reeve in *Superman*. She was standing on my blind side, and I hadn't even realized she was there until she spoke.

"Yes, it is!" I exclaimed.

"I'm Margot." She warmly extended her hand to shake mine.

"I'm Wendy," I responded, and we held hands for a moment and smiled at each other.

Margot and I continued to chat between songs. She appeared to be at the concert alone, and she asked me a lot of questions, showing genuine interest in my life. I marveled at how comfortable and familiar our conversation was, as if we were old friends.

After ten hours of speeches and music, the concert was winding down, and I was exhausted and overwhelmed with emotion. After Tom Petty performed two songs, the roadies hurriedly shuffled to bring out a half-dozen microphones, lining them up along the front edge of the stage. Suddenly, Jackson, Dan Fogelberg, Crosby, Stills and Nash, Bonnie Raitt, Linda Ronstadt, Stevie Wonder, Stevie Nicks, Joan Baez, Bob Dylan, the Eagles, Bette Midler, and the entire rest of the cast of celebrities and musicians and politicians present gathered around the microphones, three or four together at each one, and broke into Graham Nash's "Teach Your Children."

The crowd roared, the music I loved swept over me, and everyone gathered seemed as one entity.

Margot was supposed to be joining in on a microphone, but she didn't move.

"Margot, you can go on up to the microphone and join the singing with everyone," I encouraged her.

"Oh no, I couldn't. I'm too nervous. I'm too scared," she replied with her signature raspy voice.

Her insecurity surprised me. How could this beautiful, famous actress—beloved for her many film roles, a movie veteran who had worked with some of the top actors and directors in the business—be afraid and insecure?

"Oh, you'll be fine," I cheered her on. "No one can really hear you anyway, with all the people on stage and a hundred thousand people in the crowd singing too. Just go have fun!"

"I'll go if you'll go with me!" Her dark eyes flashed as she challenged me.

I laughed. "No, Margot, I'm not a celebrity or singer! I'm just security. I'm not supposed to do that." But there was nothing I'd rather do, of course.

"It doesn't matter. I won't go unless you go with me," she said firmly, gazing into my eyes.

As the first notes of "Give Peace a Chance," the grand finale, rang out, Margot linked her arm around mine and pulled me toward the microphone. I tried to hang back, but she swept me along with her. For a moment I looked around to see if the volunteer coordinator was watching, fearing I would get in trouble—but this was a chance of a lifetime, and I didn't want to miss out on it.

"Oh, fuck it!" I said, grinning. "Okay, Margot, if that's what you want!"

Timothy B. Schmidt from the Eagles, my other teen crush, was on my left, and he smiled at me as our lips came close together on the microphone. Margot was on my right, and I pulled her in close and smiled at her as she sang loud and strong.

I looked down the line of the rock 'n' roll legends that filled the stage and then out at the huge crowd of cheering people, and I felt the high—the rush—I realized performers must get every time they played in front of an enthusiastic audience. In awe of my own kismet luck, I felt the energy of all of us connecting as we sang "Give Peace a Chance." I sang my heart out and tears welled in my eyes to hear the thundering sound of so many voices, everyone swaying side to side and waving the peace sign in the air.

As the song ended, I hugged Margot. "Thank you for a once-in-a-lifetime experience!" I said, beaming.

Smiling, she hugged me back. "Thank you for getting me up there too."

I had found my kindred people. My admiration for them didn't stem just from the fact that they were famous musicians whose music inspired millions of fans around the planet. It was also inspired by their activism, the fact that they used their status to speak out for the environment and human rights causes.

I felt in my bones that I had to find a way into the music industry. Although I wasn't a musician myself, music had raised me. I had grown up nurtured and soothed by contemporary blues, R&B, and rock music, and I believed that music was one of the highest forms of human expression and connection to others. I wanted to work with artists who used their celebrity voices to speak out. I wanted to be a part of making that happen.

My high from the concert lasted for weeks. I was so elated to feel that I had found where I belonged. People I admired had opened their arms to me, and I was sure it could happen again.

Somehow, I would become a part of that family.

BIG TOOTHY WRITER

I smiled proudly as I greeted supporters and VIPs and checked off names on the backstage list, enjoying feeling valued and important in my VIP Security role. Six months had passed since the Peace Sunday concert, and the results of the California Proposition 12 campaign would be known tonight. Supporters were gathering at this downtown LA ballroom to watch the election night coverage, and I was honored to be a part of it.

Standing at my position at the door, I heard the cheers and hurrahs indicating that Proposition 12 had passed. This ensured that Governor Jerry Brown would implore President Reagan to reach out to the Soviet Union to negotiate a bilateral nuclear weapons freeze agreement. Some might think that was just a drop in the bucket, but it was important. I was thrilled to have been a part of this effort.

I didn't have to look at the VIP list to check off the name when Paul Newman, with his million-dollar smile and crystal blue eyes, walked up. The next person to arrive at the door was a guy with classically preppy handsome features: chiseled jawline, thick black hair, and piercingly green eyes.

He looked me up and down, and his eyes penetrated my flesh like laser beams. With a big, toothy grin, he said, "I am not leaving here until you give me your phone number and promise to go out to dinner with me tomorrow night."

I thought I might be swallowed whole by the power of his overwhelming attention. I was instantly swept off my feet.

"Well, I wouldn't want you to have to sleep here, so I guess I have no choice but to agree to have dinner with you," I teased and smiled, unmoored by his gaze.

I met Big Toothy Writer at a traditional Thai restaurant on Venice Beach the next evening. He requested a private curtained booth covered with colorful silk embroidered cushions and pillows.

My stomach fluttered as we slid into the booth opposite each other.

"Here's to destiny." He smiled, eyes intent on me, as we clinked our wineglasses together and I attempted to catch my breath.

He took an orchid from the plate of chicken satay appetizer and placed it behind my ear as he slid his bare foot up my leg to my crotch under the table.

"I can't wait any longer to kiss you," he said, and he leaned across the table, grabbed the back of my head, and kissed me passionately. He wrapped his fingers around my long blonde hair and gave it a gentle but firm tug, then took a breath and kissed me again, this time gently biting my lip and then my neck.

Feeling chosen by this Hollywood A-lister with a magnetic, laser-beam focus on me, I succumbed immediately.

That night was the start of a whirlwind romance. Within a week I moved in with Big Toothy Writer at his Santa Monica beach condo, certain that this was the love of my life. He asked me to stop working so we could spend all our time together traveling and playing on the beach, and offered to pay the rent on my small West Hollywood studio apartment so I wouldn't have to let it go.

I was ecstatic to go along with these over-the-top, romantic-whirlwind plans. I thought it was a good idea to keep my apartment "just in case," but I hoped a "just in case" scenario would never present itself. Our connection was so deep—physically, emotionally, and spiritually—that I was sure it was the real thing. I believed he was my knight in shining armor.

"Tell us about your family. Where are your parents? How many siblings do you have?"

My sister jumped in with a barrage of questions as we—my mom, Paul, Sharon's husband, my nieces, and Sharon—sat on the stiff couches and upholstered high-backed chairs in Sharon's classically decorated living room.

My niece, Casey, had collapsed a month earlier while watching a soccer game at school, only to be diagnosed with a heart condition called Long QT syndrome—a condition most likely inherited from her father. I adored Casey and wanted to offer her my support, so I'd decided to visit the family, and Big Toothy Writer had offered to come with me to Illinois to meet everyone. I'd readily agreed. We'd been together less than a month, but I was sure it was true love. Meeting the family was the next step, I figured, and I was curious about how everyone would react to him.

"We saw your movie," offered my adorable younger niece, Jessica. "It was really good."

"Oh, yes, congratulations," everyone piped in simultaneously, smiling and clearly impressed with my handsome and successful writer boyfriend. Everyone was on their very best behavior, including Paul, who matched Big Toothy Writer's charm with his own.

"I think the real congratulations should go to Mom!" Big Toothy Writer announced to surprised looks all around. "You did a great job raising you-know-who. Thank you for bringing her into the world!"

"Thank you. I agree, she is a fabulous woman." Mom beamed shyly, not accustomed to being so lavishly praised.

I was bowled over by his declarations of love for me to my family. Finally, at twenty-six, I'd met the right person. I watched how easily my new boyfriend joked and laughed with my family, thrilled that they seemed to genuinely enjoy each other's company.

With this relationship, I imagined that now the bad things that had happened with Sharon and Paul could be left in the past. Although my relationship with Sharon had been distant and strained since the "pretty baby" incident, she warmed up to me and my new boyfriend on this visit and hosted us in her beautiful home.

With Big Toothy Writer, I thought perhaps I, too, would make a beautiful home soon.

Since Casey had been released from the hospital after a month's stay and was taking medication for her heart, Sharon thought that a family trip to Jamaica was in order. Big Toothy Writer suggested that we join them, and I was thrilled to get to spend more time with my nieces, ever the bright spot in my family. Since I'd left home for college when they were two and seven, they'd been the ones, besides my mom, I'd missed the most. Casey wrote letters to me in California, and now that Jessica had learned to write, she too had started sending me letters replete with lots of hearts, rainbows, and flowers.

Young and innocent and darling, they had adapted well to Sharon's divorce from their father and to their new home with their stepdad, Dr. Bill.

In Jamaica, after dinner every evening, Casey and Jessica would erect a makeshift stage and regale us with their rendition of "Tomorrow" and other songs from the hit musical *Annie*, complete with hats, scarves, and costume changes.

"Future stars for your movies," I leaned over to whisper to Big Toothy Writer, who was more than game to watch them put on a show, and I meant it. I adored my nieces and felt they were the glue that held my loose-knit family together.

As the months passed, my exciting adventures and travel with Big Toothy Writer were nonstop. We flew first-class to Hawaii and stayed at the lavish Mauna Kea resort beach hotel. We traveled to Washington, DC, where we stayed at the infamous Watergate Hotel and had a private tour of the White House, stopping for lunch in the exclusive Senate Dining Room. We stayed in his Upper East Side Manhattan apartment and attended numerous Broadway shows. He had a play bound for Broadway in early rehearsal, and I pinched myself as I sat at the table reading with the actors cast in his play—stage and screen legends.

I also accompanied him to film screenings and events, which was always thrilling. When we arrived in Westwood, California, for the premiere of the film *Sophie's Choice* in Big Toothy Writer's gleaming Jaguar, an attendant opened my door, and as I stepped out of the car, I was bombarded and blinded by paparazzi flashing lights in my face. I barely remember the film, as I couldn't get over the fact that I was sitting next to the incomparable Gregory Peck, still as handsome as ever, and his beautiful philanthropist wife, Veronique.

During the winter we spent forty days at Big Toothy Writer's condo in Tahoe, where he bought me ski equipment and ski bunny outfits. I had never skied before—I'd always thought it was only for very rich people. Dr. Bill kind of rich. But now *I* was living that rich life, and my handsome boyfriend was teaching me to ski.

One afternoon, Big Toothy Writer told me how pleased he was with my persistence to learn and declared, "We should just go down to that little chapel in town and get married—today!"

Laughing off his statement, I responded with something silly, like, "But first we need to get groceries."

I was filled with love and hope and trepidation. I wanted to believe him. I wanted to believe in us. But I was beginning to wonder where *I* was in this relationship. Who was *I*?

Intuitive whispers told me I should be careful. But I didn't listen to them. I hoped the tiny cracks I sometimes perceived in this perfect relationship were just that—tiny, insignificant—and I could simply overlook them.

I was on top of the world. I could hardly believe my life.

A few days after that burst of enthusiasm and almost-proposal, Big Toothy Writer asked me to read a manuscript he was working on and give him some creative feedback.

When I questioned a few minor things, he balled up his fist in my face. "Why are you criticizing me?" he yelled and then smashed the medicine chest mirror. "See what you made me do?" he roared, holding up his bleeding hand.

His hand was cut so badly that I had to take him to urgent care for sutures. He lied to the doctor and said he cut it doing a household chore.

I knew something must have triggered him, and I wanted to find out what it was.

"Does this have something to do with your childhood?" I asked gently after we got home. There had to be a reason for that violent overreaction. "I want to help you get to the bottom of your anger and fears so that you can understand it and repair it."

"Yes, I guess so. I didn't feel very loved or supported by my family," he confided for the first time. "I'm sorry, I just couldn't control myself. I know I asked you for feedback, but I didn't expect you to tell me it wasn't perfect."

I was grateful that he had confided in me some of his insecurities and wounds and hoped his vulnerability would bring us closer, but still I worried about his violent overreaction. It reminded me too much of someone else I knew.

"Before we eat," Big Toothy Writer said, "we have to write each other a love poem."

He'd surprised me with a trip to San Francisco for my birthday, complete with a day adventure to Angel Island. After disembarking from the ferry, the two of us had hiked around until we found our perfect picnic spot.

I played along, though I was hungry. “Okay!” I agreed.

“Fifteen minutes,” he said. “Go!”

He went over to sit on a big rock to write; I stayed on the picnic blanket, pen in hand.

I meant to write a love poem, but in the moment, I felt inspired to write about a childhood memory, so I followed that spark.

When the fifteen minutes were up, he joined me on the blanket. We opened our sandwiches and took a few bites, then exchanged what we had written.

The bright sun reflected rainbows of light off the lapping waves on the shore. San Francisco skyscrapers and Coit Tower glowed like golden pyramids in the distance. It could not have been a more peaceful and stunning scene—a perfect moment to share with him the seeds of my writing.

I watched his face as I read, curious what he was thinking. A dark cloud seemed to cover his face, and then he began to scowl. I heard him grunt, and I felt a cold chill as my eyes landed on the stark prison perched on Alcatraz, the island looming in the distance.

Big Toothy Writer’s face was backlit by the sunlight, so I squinted to see his expression when he suddenly spit out his half-chewed sandwich bite and screamed, “You were supposed to write me a love poem! You didn’t write me a love poem! You didn’t write me a love poem!”

He stood up and stomped around, kicking sand at me. The sand stung my skin, and I ducked, trying to protect my face.

In a final fit, he threw the rest of his sandwich on the ground.

A familiar feeling of fear rose in my chest. Although no one else was around, I felt embarrassed for him, as if he was a petulant toddler in need of a nap. I held my breath and felt that out-of-body feeling that had always come over me when I was scared. I suddenly realized that I didn’t know this guy in front of me. Was he the same guy I was in love with, living with, and had contemplated marrying? It was as if a weird switch had flipped inside of him—without notice, without provocation—and it had happened in reaction to something so stupid. Just like Paul.

The Christmas tree, the screen door, the razor, the broken ashtray that sent me flying across the room . . . all of it was happening again, in slow motion, in my mind.

The cracks in the foundation of our perfect house had been expanding and mounting in recent weeks. He wanted to manage what I ate, how much I ate, and how often I exercised. *You shouldn't drink coffee. Are you sure you want that dessert? Maybe you're just thirsty. Drink water instead.* I'd shrugged it all off. But now, sitting on the sand on Angel Island, I had to admit that I'd turned a blind eye to his dangerous flaws, to his angry, Jekyll-and-Hyde moods. I'd learned well from Mom to "focus on his good side."

Big Toothy Writer had a reputation in Hollywood as being an arrogant asshole, but I'd thought I could turn him around. I'd convinced myself that I would be the one he loved so deeply that he would mend his ways. Was I just in love with the idea of him?

As I sat there wiping sand off my skin and pushing my hair out of my eyes, now filled with tears, I knew I didn't want my fantasy relationship to be blown up. Just like I didn't want to blow up my fantasy of having a loving, intact family of origin. Bad as his behavior was, I wasn't ready to let go of this man.

We argued all the way back to the ferry about how I should have written him a love poem.

On the ferry ride back to San Francisco, I stared out at the water, trying to understand what I was feeling. I wanted to be compassionate and understanding, to get to the bottom of what was so upsetting to him. But secretly I worried that I was in an abusive relationship and couldn't admit it.

Not long after that, back in LA, I found myself once again defending myself against one of Big Toothy Writer's verbal attacks. I walked away from him toward the bedroom—and he chased me down the hall of the condo and tackled me.

"Is this what you want?" he cried. "Is this the kind of relationship you want?" He stormed into our room.

I picked myself up off the floor, horrified by how unmoored he had become. Yet I still couldn't bear to lose the fantasy of what we'd had. Stunned, I limped toward the bedroom, following him.

"What's going on? Why did you tackle me like that? What the hell is wrong?" I asked, crying and shaking my head in disbelief, not wanting to accept what he had done.

As he grabbed a suitcase and started throwing clothes into it, he spat out between clenched teeth, "I'm going to New York for a few weeks. You need to be moved out by the time I get back."

I was too shocked to say anything else as I watched my relationship crumble into a puff of dust.

Without another word, he walked out the door.

I stood frozen, trying to figure out what had just happened. My whole body went into a spasm of horror and disbelief; my dream-come-true relationship had just burst into a ball of flames. Had I made everything up? Had I believed only what I wanted to believe? What about the deep love, the compatible companionship, the promises of marriage, the talk of children and how many there would be?

I called my mom, and when she answered, I began to sob loudly.

"It's over," I cried.

"What, honey? What's over?" She was now alarmed.

"My life—my life is over," I said, crying hysterically. "He walked out on me!"

Hearing that, Mom became resolute and firm. "Wendy Beth, you listen to me. Your life *is not* over. You are an incredible woman. You will meet someone else. Someone who is better for you. Better *to* you."

"I don't know, Mom—"

"Honey, listen to me. I am heartbroken for you—yes, I am—but in time you will heal. And I will always be here for you. I will always be a shoulder for you to cry on. But you know what else,

Wendy? I feel sorry for *him*. He didn't know a good thing when he had it. There is something broken in him. I could see it."

Somewhere deep down I knew that was true, but I felt like *I* was the one who was broken.

My skin and body looked intact, but inside I was filled with shattered glass. I believed I'd never find love again.

Big Toothy Writer arranged for his business manager to give me some money to get settled. They determined that a year of my life spent not working was worth $5,000. I moved out of his condo and my studio apartment and moved on to a boat in Marina Del Rey in exchange for teaching the dyslexic owner of the boat how to read.

I had quit smoking when I'd met Big Toothy Writer, but on the day of our breakup, I'd gone right back to my old habit. Night after night, I sat on the boat, smoked cigarettes, and made my way through the case of expensive Pouilly-Fuissé wine that I'd taken with me from his condo. As the waves gently rocked me on the boat, I cried and wrote morose poetry, my tears falling on my notebook and smearing the ink.

But during those days as I was recovering, I did a few other things too. I picked up more work in the Screen Extras Guild on TV shows and films; I enrolled in a master's program in clinical psychology at Antioch University in Venice. I worried that I had lost time while I was with Big Toothy Writer. I'd put my own career and life goals on hold to follow him around and support him emotionally. I still wanted to establish myself in a career that reflected my true purpose, intelligence, and passion—attempting to understand my fellow humans and, ideally, help them in some way.

In the wake of the breakup, it seemed that there were only two kinds of people in the world: destructive, hell-bent hurricanes and those in their path. The breakup triggered my deep-seated issues—abandonment, insecurity, and fears of being unlovable and unworthy—and I felt emotionally crippled. I wrote about Big Toothy Writer in my journal and cried, and then I got angry for wasting more of my precious time on him and ferociously read and studied for my college classes. But those negative thoughts inevitably crept back in. I believed that I didn't measure up to him or other people.

But why? Why did I think that everyone was better than me? That everyone else was smarter, prettier, richer, skinnier, luckier? Had he seen what members of my own family seemed to see? There had to be something wrong with me; why else would they all have rejected me?

A boat-neighbor guy visited me on my boat and brought over some cocaine. That, combined with my posh Pouilly-Fuissé wine and Canadian Export A cigarettes, pushed the bad feelings away and deep, deep down.

I felt as numb throughout my whole body as my nose and mouth did from snorting the lines of cocaine off the mirror. I just wanted the pain to go away.

JONI

"I can't sleep. I keep obsessing. I keep going over and over everything, trying to figure out what went wrong. He said he loved me and wanted to marry me, and we even talked about having kids. How do I stop obsessing about him?" I implored my therapist, Joanna.

Shocking me, Joanna replied, "I don't want you to stop obsessing. I want you to obsess and obsess until you're exhausted. Then I want you to take your drawing pad and chalk and obsess on the paper."

So at home, smoking and drinking and crying, I picked up the black chalk and drew a black spiral, like a black hole on top of a red heart, repeatedly, page after page.

Eventually I grew exhausted, just like Joanna had predicted, and instead of the spiral I drew a picture of a golden-haired goddess version of myself, dressed in a silk gown and peacefully sleeping on a chaise lounge, my hands crossed over my heart. Above me hovered layers of rainbow-colored auras.

I sighed, relieved and filled with peace.

The Antioch master's psychology program that I had begun attending required students to partake in psychotherapy as clients. I was grateful to have found Joanna. Over the next several months, she gently lifted the veil of ignorance I'd worn for so long, allowing me to look at my childhood wounds and the inner life of thoughts and beliefs it had created. She helped me to peel away layer upon layer of childhood grief, feelings of abandonment and unlovability, and the genesis of my lack of confidence and self-esteem.

It had been a few years since I'd done the sense memory exercise in my acting class when I'd recognized the unresolved impact of my dad's death and how that trauma had shaped me. Still, I was shocked when Joanna confirmed that childhood loss of a parent was a tremendous trauma with lifetime effects. She suggested, too, that it was natural for me to be terrified to lose my mom to death or to my stepfather after experiencing such a trauma. She confirmed that the experience of any kind of violence, whether it be verbal, emotional, or physical, was damaging to and traumatizing for a young child or teen. She then went a step further, illustrating how my feelings of abandonment when my father died were exacerbated by what I perceived as rejection by my stepdad and my siblings.

Together, Joanna said, all those experiences and emotions had shaped my thinking, personality, fears, and insecurities, and all my relationships. This was an eye-opening revelation. No one had ever spoken to me in such depth about how much my childhood and ongoing family story had affected me.

Joanna introduced me to my inner child and showed me how to be tender toward her and help her to heal the past. But she also cautioned me that healing would not happen overnight and that continued trauma, like my recent breakup with Big Toothy Writer, would set me back.

"Quitting heroin was easier than quitting smoking," the woman sitting next to me suddenly and matter-of-factly blurted out.

I had been showing her how to do an art-therapy project by dipping a string tied to a chopstick in India ink and using it like a brush on the paper to create Rorschach-esque images. At Antioch University, I had designed my own master's program to utilize creativity in therapy: writing, music, and art therapy. I had already spent months in an internship with an art therapist who worked with methadone patients who were attempting to kick heroin in a Venice methadone clinic.

"Really!" I said, and I sucked in my breath, alarmed.

Taking in what she'd just said, I shook in my boots. I knew how badly I needed to quit smoking, but I didn't know how. I looked at the clock on the wall, already anxious for the session to end so I could go get my nicotine fix. I had already tried acupuncture and hypnosis, to no avail.

Would I ever be able to kick this bad habit?

During one of our therapy sessions, Joanna suddenly asked, "Are you abusing any drugs?"

"No, no—I only do it when I have to write my school papers," I naively assured her. I'd been snorting cocaine regularly since my breakup with Big Toothy Writer.

She looked hard at me. "Wendy, any use is abuse."

That had never even occurred to me. I felt like a hypocrite, working with heroin addicts and going home to drink wine and do lines of cocaine. Although I wasn't a heroin addict, I was still an addict. I was using cocaine, nicotine, and alcohol to numb my feelings.

I needed to do better.

In my psychology program, I urgently wanted to reach kids who'd had tough childhoods like my own. I decided that with my family background, I had an empathetic understanding of what too many kids were going through.

For my second internship, I worked at a "last chance" high school, teaching journaling and poetry writing classes to kids who had been kicked out of every other LA school. I hadn't gotten to experience the arts, music, and literature as a child, but as an adult, I had experienced for myself what a powerful tool for therapy creativity could be. I hoped that poetry would help these kids—would engage and empower them.

It was a rewarding experience, but after working with me all week and showing a bit of progress by week's end, these kids would go home for the weekend and then come back on Monday at square one.

As was true in my own case, it was the parents—not so much the kids—who really needed therapy.

It was performance night at Gazzarri's on Sunset. A full band was setting up on stage for sound check, and the lighting and sound directors were already manning their booths. This would be a full-on, professional performance. Invitations had been sent out to friends, family, and music-industry types.

As people poured into the venue and sidled up to the bar for a drink, I peeked out from backstage and started sweating.

I'd recently found a creative outlet for my own healing: singing workshops. My classmates and I had spent the last few months singing in front of each other as our rehearsal to perform in front of a larger audience. The music director had accompanied us on keyboards. Our singing teacher had videotaped us and critiqued us on playback. Before we sang, he instructed us to stand at the microphone and shake and flail our arms and say things like, "I'm such a big idiot, I'm such a jerk," to let go of the self-conscious fear of looking like an idiot.

Now it was time to put all those lessons to good use.

When my turn came, the band played a few intro notes, and I nervously walked onto the stage to my microphone, set front and center, as my backup-singer classmates walked to their microphones on the side of the stage.

Everyone knew that I was terrified, but as I looked to the music director for my cue to jump in, he smiled and nodded, my teacher gave a thumbs up, and my classmates in the audience clapped.

Blinded by the hot, glaring lights, beads of sweat gathered on my face, and I belted out the lyrics to "You're Gonna Get What's Coming"—a Robert Palmer song also sung by one of my favorite female singers, Bonnie Raitt.

When the song was over, the crowd hooped and hollered. I flew down from the stage and hugged all my supportive friends, feeling confident, powerful, and strong.

Even if I wasn't the strongest singer in the bunch, I had a blast singing rock and blues songs in front of a captive audience. It was a great hobby and creative outlet. The experience of challenging myself to sing in front of an audience built up my self-esteem and confidence—even though I shook the entire time I was on stage and often felt like I had left my body during the performance, hardly remembering afterward what had just happened.

To pay the rent and put myself through school, I was working at a Malibu beach barbecue joint called the Jetty on the Pacific Coast Highway. Being beachy California casual, the floor was covered in sawdust and peanut shells from the trademark basket of peanuts on every table. Supposedly we were singing waiters, although we mostly just sang different versions of "Happy Birthday" to the guests.

I was just getting off work when my friend Boyd (Boyd Elder, the artist famous for creating iconic painted-skull album covers for the Eagles and other bands) showed up at the restaurant.

"Hey, Boyd, nice to see you. You here to get something to eat?" I asked, surprised to see him.

"No, I wanna take you up to Malibu to meet a good friend of mine," he said casually.

I had worked a busy shift; my hair was sweaty, my white bowling shirt was covered in barbecue sauce and sawdust, and I had no clean clothes to change into. But I was always game to meet any one of Boyd's interesting and artistic friends.

I jumped in his passenger seat, and he drove us up the Pacific Coast Highway.

It was only as we turned into a posh, gated Malibu enclave that I finally said, "Boyd, wait a minute! What friend are you introducing me to?"

"You'll see, you'll see." He laughed, mischievous eyes sparkling, as he parked the car.

Clearly, this was no ordinary friend.

As we walked toward the front door, I looked down at my stained bowling shirt and tried to smooth out my hair, feeling self-conscious. Grabbing his arm to stop him, I asked, "Do I have any makeup on? Or did I sweat it all off?"

He hugged me and said reassuringly, "You look fine. Don't worry. She doesn't care how you look." He stepped forward and rang the doorbell.

"Who is *she*, Boyd?" I asked, alarmed about how bad I looked. "Who is *she*?"

Just then the door opened—and there stood singing, song-writing legend Joni Mitchell.

Joni hugged Boyd, then gave me a warm smile and handshake as Boyd introduced us. I was stunned. I could not believe I was standing in the presence of one of my all-time favorite female musicians, the one and only Joni Mitchell.

It was apparent that she and Boyd had not seen each other in quite a while and were very close, so they had some catching up to do. As we moved into the living room, they kept discussing "Bobby" this and that. I had no idea who they were talking about until it finally dawned on me: Bobby was Bob Dylan.

My head went woozy; I felt like I was having an out-of-body experience.

Boyd got on the phone, presumably with Bobby, so Joni offered to give me a tour of her art collections.

Her home was a vision out of *Architecture Magazine*—breath-taking and beautifully, expensively decorated, but also warm and comfortable. As we moved through the house, she pointed out her own gorgeous paintings and her museum-worthy Native American artifact collection, most memorably an intricately beaded Plains

Indian cradleboard. As we talked about Native American spirituality and artifacts and about my psychology program at Antioch, I noted her Canadian accent and her beautiful teeth and smile.

I wondered why she seemed to like me so much—why she was being so gracious and friendly toward me. I was a stranger, and not a famous one at that. But something sweet passed between us, like we were loving sisters who simply knew each other without needing words.

As we moved back into the living room, she asked, "Are you familiar with the I Ching?"

"I am!" I said eagerly. In fact, I knew a lot about the I Ching, the ancient Chinese divination text.

"Fantastic!" she said. She grabbed her I Ching coins and book, and we sat on her gorgeous Persian living room rug and took turns asking questions quietly to ourselves and throwing the I Ching coins for the answer. It intrigued us both how accurately the oracle answered our questions; we marveled to each other how the I Ching provided deep insight into our questions as we read the interpretation of the text aloud to each other.

As Joni and I sat there talking, laughing, smoking cigarettes, and discussing the history of the I Ching, I could not help but think to myself, *I am sitting on Joni Mitchell's Persian carpet throwing the I Ching with her. How did I get to be so lucky? I must be doing something right. I must be a good person after all. I feel valued and important. I feel like I matter. What is it in me that Joni sees that members of my own family don't see? What Big Toothy Writer didn't see? Well, fuck them and anybody else who doesn't like me or see my value as a human. Boyd likes me, and Joni Mitchell likes me, and in just a few hours together, Joni seems to know me better than all of them.*

I sat up straighter, burdens from the past falling from my shoulders.

I didn't quite understand why Boyd and Joni liked me, but I was touched that they did. It seemed they saw something in me that I struggled to see—they mirrored back to me my worth and my value, even when I wasn't sure what it was.

Who was I? Who did I want to be? How could I measure up to these incredibly talented and famous people? I wasn't sure who I was becoming, but I knew I wanted to do something meaningful. I wanted to find my purpose. I wanted to contribute something. I not only wanted to surround myself with interesting, inspiring, creative, and authentic people, I wanted to *be* interesting, inspiring, authentic, and creative. All the people I had been meeting since my breakup—my Proposition 12 comrades, my graduate school friends, my therapist, coworkers at the Jetty, my singing friends, and Boyd and Joni—were examples I could look up to and learn from as I strived to become the whole me.

CASEY ANN

I had just begun the final semester of my two-year master's psychology program at Antioch University and was at my Venice Beach apartment where I had moved after living on the boat for six months. My friend Mo, who worked with me at the Jetty, and I were chatting in my kitchen on a mundane Monday evening when the phone rang.

"Hello," I answered casually.

"Wendy, it's your sister," Sharon said, crying. "I have terrible news."

"What, what? Sharon, what is it?" My heart was in my throat; I was frozen with fear.

"Wendy, I'm sorry to tell you that Casey died. She died. She was on the phone with her boyfriend when she died. I can't talk anymore right now." Sharon sobbed between every word she said. "You just need to come home."

"Sharon, no!" My body caved in on itself. "Oh my god, no. I am so, so sorry. I'll get a flight as soon as I can."

My beautiful seventeen-year-old niece, my sister's oldest daughter, was gone. How was that possible?

Ever since Casey's diagnosis with Long QT syndrome, Sharon had sought out the best possible medical care for her. But despite that care, my beloved niece had just died at home, without warning.

I didn't know how Sharon had the strength to call me. The trauma, the agony of losing a child, was incomprehensible to me. I had no idea how she, now divorced from her second husband, Dr. Bill, would survive such a loss. And how would twelve-year-old Jessica survive losing her only sibling, the big sister she loved and looked up to?

As I hung up the phone from the briefest and most devastating call I had ever received, a guttural wail left my body that I didn't even recognize as coming from me.

I fell on the floor, weak and stunned; the grief filled my body like helium gas in a balloon and squeezed all my organs numb. My lungs were so tight I could barely take sips of air. Not wanting to be a part of what was happening, my mind floated somewhere else. The shock of it—the utter shock of it—took away my ability to stand, to talk, to think. I thought my organs might shut down and that I, too, might die.

"The finality, the finality, no, no, no," I cried aloud, wailing like a wounded animal. "I don't want this. I don't want this." I shook my head as if I could just reject the notion that she'd died.

Mo sat on the floor next to me, reached out to touch my shoulder, and let me cry.

I sobbed and spewed words nonstop to her. "How can it be that sweet Casey is no more? She will never go to her senior prom, her high school graduation. She will not go to college. She won't get married. She won't have children. She won't be a grandmother. She will not grow old and wrinkled. She is gone at seventeen—in the prime of her life. Her life has been ripped from her."

When I was spent, Mo pulled me into her arms and hugged me. "I'm so sorry," she said gently, wiping away my tears. "I'll make you a cup of tea, okay?"

I nodded feebly and continued to lie on the floor, moaning. I felt that I might never be able to move from that spot. I was simply paralyzed with grief.

When I eventually fell into my bed that night, my face and eyes swollen, I was exhausted but couldn't sleep. All I could think about was how unfair life was. Talking out loud to a nebulous entity, I demanded, "How can there be a God who snatches the life from a child whose life was just beginning and who looked forward to fulfilling her dreams, while some people fritter away their lives, afraid to pursue their dreams? Those same people who make up excuses for their shortcomings and lack of motivation and complain about everything but do nothing about it, and yet they get to live to a ripe old age, mean and bitter? Fuck you, God—fuck you!"

And then a calm stillness overtook me, and as I lay under my warm covers, a response from deep inside me emerged: *"You are right, life isn't fair—but no one ever said it was. That is the beauty of life. Living creatures aren't guaranteed anything. Life is short. And maybe shorter than you know. Use your time well."*

Comforted by these words, I fell into a deep coma like sleep.

I flew to Illinois the next day to be with my family and attend Casey's heart-wrenching memorial. Holding Mom's hand as I sat next to her at the service, I could barely watch as Casey's grief-stricken boyfriend and all her devastated friends took turns reading poems and telling stories about Casey that paid a bittersweet tribute to her too-short life.

Every loss I had ever experienced in my life, including that of my father at seven years old, was eclipsed by the loss of our sweet Casey. My family was gutted. Sharon, my poor sister; Bill, her ex-husband and stepfather to the girls; Joe, the girls' father; and Jessica, Mom, Paul, Mark, and I all sat in stunned anguish, barely able to say a word between our stifled sobs. No words, no actions, no prayers, no stupid platitudes like, "Just be grateful for the time you had with her" or, the worst, "Everything happens for a reason," could relieve the pain. Nothing could save us from our suffocating grief, pain, and sorrow. I knew that the wound might eventually heal, but the pain of the scar would last forever.

"Here's a hit," Eccentric Singer-Songwriter said as he slid the razor blade across the mirror, forming lines.

I was back in LA, at my new famous boyfriend's Hollywood Hills bungalow, and I was numbing my grief with alcohol and cocaine and cigarettes.

I put the rolled-up dollar bill to my nose and inhaled deeply. As I swiped the leftover crumbs across my gums, I felt the euphoria kicking in.

He did the next line, then asked, "What movie do you want to watch?"

He had asked me this question every night for weeks; watching movies was our main activity, along with snorting cocaine all night, talking about nothing of interest or intellect, and listening to new music he was working on.

For a solid month, we fell asleep as the sun rose and slept all day. I was barely making it to my night classes. By the end of the month, my central nervous system was shot.

From my abnormal psychology classes, I knew what cocaine was doing to my body and brain. I knew that the euphoria cocaine produced in me was caused by the increased neurotransmitters serotonin and dopamine in my brain, and that once the drug wore off, those hormones crashed, causing my depression and other symptoms. I knew that every system in my body had become dysregulated, and the lack of sleep and proper nutrition only added to the ugly biochemical mess. I knew what I was doing, and I was disgusted with myself for doing it. Every afternoon I woke up feeling like I had aged a hundred years.

One day as the sun was rising, feeling sick and tired of feeling sick and tired, I asked myself, *Is this how I want to honor Casey's short life?* I had hit rock bottom with shame and disgust.

I drove home to my Venice Beach apartment, stopped seeing Eccentric Singer-Songwriter, and quit using cocaine that day—but

I kept on drinking and smoking cigarettes until I was good and numb almost every day.

I took a leave from the last semester of my master's program, fully intending to finish when I'd had enough time to grieve and reflect on what was important to me. It was all too clear to me that life was short—sometimes even shorter than we knew. Something I had learned when my daddy died when I was seven was now painfully reinforced.

Again, I asked, *What do I want to do? What is my purpose?*

I thought long and hard about this and wrote endlessly in my journal. I listed everything that I thought I wanted to do in my life. If my life were cut short, what would I wish I had done?

A single recurring dream swam up to my consciousness: a job in the music industry.

All my life, music had soothed, educated, and inspired me. I wasn't an artist myself, but I was organized and sharp. I decided I could work in the music industry supporting artists in some capacity, either in artist management or in a support team at a record company. Plus, my background in psychology might come in handy when dealing with unstable artists like Big Toothy Writer and Eccentric Singer-Songwriter.

With the help of a friend of a friend, I landed a job at a talent booking agency called Triad Artists. Soon, I was the booking agent assistant to two busy music agents who booked mostly college tours.

Triad Artists represented writers (including Big Toothy Writer), directors, producers, actors, and many of the most famous singers/musicians of that time—including Tina Turner, who, at the age of forty-five, was making an extraordinary solo comeback with her multiplatinum album and tour *Private Dancer*.

I'd loved Tina since I was ten years old and danced and sang along to "River Deep Mountain High" and "Proud Mary" in my living room back in Illinois. By now it was common knowledge that she'd endured terrible abuse in her marriage to Ike, but she had fought back. Spoken up. Stood her ground. Reinvented herself. And beyond being a resilient survivor, she was an extraordinary singer and performer with boundless energy. I was only one of millions of inspired fans who loved her.

For weeks after getting my new job, I danced around my apartment singing at the top of my lungs to "What's Love Got to Do with It?" with Big Toothy Writer in my mind.

Red lights flashed in my rearview mirror.

Oh shit, oh shit!

My friend Connie was traveling with the Thompson Twins on their Here's to Future Days tour, and she had invited me to join her and a bunch of the crew to have dinner and drinks at the celebrity-filled Sushi on Sunset. We were a raucous bunch, and I'd enjoyed many beers and sake and forgotten to eat dinner before leaving at 2:00 a.m. to drive home.

As I slowed down to pull over, I wished that I'd stayed with Connie in her hotel room at the Le Mondrian Hotel on the Sunset Strip.

A scowling LA police officer appeared at my window.

"Your driver's license and insurance card, ma'am," he said dryly.

After I handed them over, he went back to his cruiser to run my information, and I sat in my car, praying he would just give me a ticket for speeding.

But then he approached my window again, and this time his partner also went to the passenger side window.

"Ma'am, do you know why I pulled you over?" the officer asked like it was a quiz.

"No, sir, I don't. I'm sorry. Was I speeding?" I asked, still hoping it was just a speeding ticket.

"No, ma'am, you weren't speeding, but you were swerving. I'm going to have to ask you to get out of your vehicle."

This was not good.

I stood on the side of Venice Boulevard in my black leather miniskirt, fishnet stockings, high heels, and rabbit fur coat, hoping the police officers thought I looked rock 'n' roll cool, à la Tina, and not like a hooker.

"I need you to walk a straight line. Start here and walk toward the other officer."

It was dark but I squinted and focused on the officer, standing six feet away, and put one foot in front of the other.

No matter how hard I tried to walk a straight line, I stumbled and weaved. I started to panic.

"Ma'am, let me see you touch your nose."

I could not touch my nose. My finger kept hitting my cheek. I'd had no idea how drunk I was until this moment.

"You have the right to remain silent," the scowling officer stated and then finished reciting the Miranda Rights.

"Ma'am, please put your hands behind your back," the second officer instructed me before roughly snapping the handcuffs on my wrists.

Ouch. The scowling officer took my arm and guided me into the back of the cruiser, protecting the top of my head as he did.

As I slid onto the cold leather upholstery, I started crying. "Please no, please don't," I protested. "I'm not that drunk."

"We could just take you straight to the Sybil Brand Institute Women's Jail if you don't shut up," the scowling officer said, and frowned even harder at me in the rearview window.

Terror filled my body. Sybil Brand was no place for me or any woman. "I'm sorry, I'm really sorry," I said, and didn't say another word.

A few minutes later we arrived at the LA police precinct on Venice Boulevard. The scowling officer removed the handcuffs, and I rubbed my wrists, grateful to be free again. Mascara was running down my cheeks as he flashed the arrest photo. That done, he roughly took my hand, pressed my fingers into ink, and pressed them onto the arrest record, then emptied the contents of my purse on his desk and wrote down the inventory.

My one phone call was next: He placed a rotary phone on the counter for me to use. I called home, and luckily, my current roommate answered the phone. He told me he would come right way.

Limp with relief, I sat on a wooden bench and rested my head on the wall to stop the room from spinning.

I was startled into consciousness by the scowling officer an hour later.

"Hey, wake up. Your ride is here. Here are your discharge papers to sign."

The discharge papers listed the date, location, and time of my court date as well as information for mandatory counseling and mandatory Alcoholics Anonymous meetings.

I cried all the way home and apologized to my roommate repeatedly for the inconvenience of having to come get me in the middle of the night.

Finally, I crawled into bed and passed out.

In addition to my court-ordered appointments with a counselor and mandatory AA meetings, I had to pay a big fine for my DUI. For the next year, I would only be allowed to drive to and from work, the grocery store, and AA meetings.

I'd found a list of AA meetings specifically for musicians and people who worked in the music industry. When I arrived at the first meeting, I stood outside the door for a few minutes, gathering up my nerve, before walking inside.

As soon as I stepped through the door, a familiar-looking man with a big smile extended a welcoming hand. "Hello! Welcome!" he said. "My name is Richard. What's yours?"

I awkwardly smiled and stuttered out my name and shook his hand, but I wanted to blurt out, "Your name may be Richard, but it's also Ringo!"

His lovely wife, Barbara, also shook my hand and welcomed me, and I sat down in a daze. It was public knowledge that they were both sober. But to see Ringo Starr and Barbara Bach in the flesh, and to know that they, too, felt powerless over drugs and alcohol and could admit to that in public, made me feel better about myself and more willing to admit the same.

As I took my seat at the table in the middle of the room, facing the stage, my eyes finally adjusted to the purple haze lighting and swirling disco ball in the cavernous ballroom. The first thing I noticed was how elaborately the table was set: a stunning flower centerpiece accented with gold music notes set on the gold lamé tablecloth, white plates flecked with gold, on gold chargers, each one set with two knives, two forks, a bread plate with butter knife, a dessert spoon and knife, water, and a wine goblet. As I scanned the table, my eyes landed on the numerous bottles of wine, one set directly in front of me.

I'd left Triad Artists, and for a few months now, I'd been working at A&M Records, the world's largest independent record company, with artists such as Janet Jackson, Sting, and the Police. Tonight, I was attending a BMI/ASCAP songwriter awards dinner party.

I was sober over a year now and was still attending AA meetings, but as I looked around the table, my resolve wavered. As I watched everyone drink, loosen up, and enjoy themselves, I told myself that I could be a "normal person" and have "just one glass." I figured after a year of not drinking, I'd proved that I didn't *have* to drink.

One glass turned into two, which turned into three and maybe four. After that, the night was a blur.

When I woke up the next morning, my head pounding, I could not remember driving myself home but knew I must have done so. Feeling shaky and still drunk, I shuddered to think that I might have gone to jail for another DUI—or, far worse, killed someone else or myself. Lying in bed, I admitted that I was powerless over alcohol, that I was not a "normal person" who could have one drink and stop. I needed help and support to take my sobriety seriously.

I begged my higher power to help me one day at a time. Again.

And I went to an AA meeting right after work that day.

After one final slip-up (this time with pot) at the first SXSW Music Festival in Austin, I started the clock over again for the last time.

Now that I had given up pot, cocaine, and alcohol (of course), the only thing I had left to help push down my feelings and numb my pain was nicotine. Remembering what the methadone patient told me during my internship about how much easier it was to quit heroin than cigarettes, I couldn't even think about giving them up yet. Cigarettes were with me the moment I woke up, and cigarettes were the last thing I had before I went to sleep at night. They kept me company in my sadness and loneliness. They were always there for me, like a dear friend.

A little over two years had now passed since Casey's death. Big Toothy Writer had been gone over three years. Despite my losses and ongoing issues with my family, I had achieved my goal: I was now working in the music industry, and I'd met people who saw my value as a person. Now it was time, one day at a time, to love myself enough to take care of myself and make myself my number one priority. I had learned from Buddhism, AA and therapy that the only way to stop the pain was to allow, embrace, and feel it. I had to feel it all and face it all and sit with my grief and deep feelings of unlovability without using drugs and alcohol to numb my sorrow.

I wasn't sure who I was becoming or what I could expect on the other side, but I knew that Robert Frost had it right: "The only way out is through."

MITAKUYE OYASIN

I inhaled deeply, taking in the smell of salt from the ocean breeze drifting into my open window. It was an early summer evening in 1987, and I was sitting on my couch listening to Joni Mitchell's "Blue" in my Venice Beach apartment. I had been fully sober for a few months, and I was feeling good about taking things one day at a time.

The ringing phone jolted me out of my daydream, and a male voice asked for my roommate.

When I told him that she was not there but could I take a message, he said, "Sure, can you tell her that Daniel called to invite her to a sweat tomorrow?"

I had been a huge fan of saunas for years; my interest was piqued. "You mean like a sauna?"

"No," he said, "like a Native American sweat—a sweat lodge, a sacred ceremony."

Although I had minored in Native American studies in college, my studies had focused on the history of ongoing colonialism, genocide, and broken treaties. I had never attended any ceremonies, only powwows and prayer circles, so I was intrigued.

We continued to chat, and I learned that Daniel was a successful songwriter with a Billboard Top 40 hit song that was currently on heavy rotation on KROQ-FM. I told him that I worked for

A&M Records in music publishing, and we realized that we had numerous music industry friends in common.

"I minored in Native American studies in college, but I've never attended a sweat lodge. Would it be okay if I attended?" I asked sheepishly.

"Absolutely!" Daniel said immediately. He gave me the address and the time to show up the next day, Saturday. Then he filled me in on a few pertinent details and introduced me to my first words in the Lakota language. "The proper Lakota name for sweat lodge is *inipi*, and the ceremony will conclude with a *chanunpa*, or pipe ceremony, led by the Lakota elder, shaman, and spiritual teacher Wanbli Cikala, a.k.a. Grandpa Wallace Black Elk." Daniel enunciated the important words, making sure I heard them clearly.

Daniel explained that he had been participating in indigenous spirituality for many years and was trained and entrusted as a fire-keeper by the native teachers who ran the sweats he had attended.

"Is there anything else I should know?" I asked, suddenly a little anxious. This was a lot of information to take in.

"Don't worry," he said kindly. "You will be instructed on proper protocol when you arrive tomorrow!"

I thanked him for inviting me and looked forward to meeting him the next day. I hung up feeling incredibly lucky that I'd happened to be home and answered the phone when he called.

The next afternoon, I arrived at a beautiful suburban LA home rimmed with rose bushes bursting with fragrant red, pink, and yellow blooms. Even before ringing the doorbell, I had to investigate what other gorgeous aroma was clamoring for my attention and went to the side of the house, where I found orange trees full of intoxicating white blooms.

Inside, the rambling ranch-style house was already bustling with people who greeted each other as they placed their potluck contributions on a huge round oak dining table. I placed my dish on the table and followed people who were walking toward the backyard.

Nestled in a private corner among the Torrey pine and California bay trees was a dome-like structure covered in blankets and canvas tarps.

"You can't miss me," Daniel had quipped on the phone. "I'll be the skinny guy with long, straggly, brown hair building a fire."

He was right; I spotted him right away, preparing the fire pit in front of the dome.

Daniel introduced me to the people sitting at a picnic table nearby and asked one of them, Rachel, if she would teach me how to make my "prayer ties."

Rachel had a kind, welcoming smile, and soft blue eyes. She shook my hand firmly and motioned for me to sit, and as Daniel went back to his work, she began her instruction.

"Okay, so the first thing to know is that the *inipi* ceremony is meant to purify you physically, mentally, and spiritually, and is also an opportunity to pray for yourself and others. We are invited guests to this sacred ceremony. In many ways, the people who came to Turtle Island have lost their connection to the earth and to themselves. We are being honored with the gift of the wisdom of this indigenous ceremony to help heal our lost connection so that we can help to heal and protect our Mother Earth, our home, a beautiful, blue planet."

She lit a bundle of dried white sage and placed the redolent, smoking herbs in an abalone shell on the table. As the tip of the sage burned red, Rachel added a few sprigs of dried cedar, creating a popping and crackling flame that sent more fragrant smoke up into the air. The earthy aroma and the fire reminded me of those happy evenings sitting by a campfire with my parents when we camped across the West and Southwest.

Rachel pointed to what appeared to be a rope of braided dried grass. "The burning of sage and cedar and sweetgrass promotes wisdom and clarity and enhances healing. They are our helpers," she whispered as she lit the end of the sweetgrass. I inhaled its warm, hay-like aroma.

I felt a bit woozy from the mingling aromas, and I had to force myself to focus as she showed me how to cut out one-inch squares of white, black, blue, green, yellow, and red cotton cloth for the community attending the sweat lodge. For my prayers, she said, I would only be using red prayer ties.

"Symbolically, red is for the North or the Red Road of Life; yellow is for the East or wisdom; white is for the South or purification; black is for the Thunder Beings in the West or power; green is for our Mother Earth who provides us with sustenance; and blue is for Grandfather Sky or Tunkasila, the Great Spirit or God."

We placed the cotton squares in their respective color piles alongside the abalone shells with the smoking herbs and a large bowl filled with loose, fragrant tobacco and white cotton string.

"Now, take a little pinch of tobacco from the bowl and hold it in your palm as you pray," Rachel said, gently continuing her instruction. "Let your intuition guide your intention. Once that prayer is finished, place the tobacco onto the red cloth square, twist it into a small bundle, and tie it onto the long white cotton string. The tobacco will absorb your prayers now and while we are in the lodge. At the end of the ceremony, we'll place our prayers ties into the fire to release our prayers to Tunkasila, the Universe, God, or whatever name you prefer."

The freedom to choose how to refer to a personal spiritual connection struck a chord with me. It was like Alcoholics Anonymous, where many people used the term "higher power" because they preferred not to use a religious term that, because of prior experience, carried negative connotations for them.

I glanced around me as the other people present prayed and made their prayer ties. Many sat peacefully and meditated, gazing at the blazing fire Daniel had built.

I continued to make one prayer bundle at a time until I had a string of fifty red prayer ties to take with me into the lodge.

At sundown, when the stones were red hot and covered in white ash and everyone had completed their prayer ties, we gathered barefoot around the lodge, holding only our towels and prayer ties. The women stood in their bathing suits covered with cotton dresses, and the men in baggy trunks.

As we lined up, Rachel whispered, "We are invited into this circle, this lodge, by people who trust that we will go to a deeply spiritual and vulnerable place with them. When you get to the opening of the lodge, get down on your hands and knees and humbly crawl in, following me to your space. When you enter say, '*Mitakuye oyasin*,' which means, 'We are all related.' That Lakota phrase reminds us of our connectedness to everything. You will say it after your individual prayer spoken out loud and after smoking the *chanunpa* too."

I followed her into the lodge and did exactly as she had said with such reverence that I was on the verge of tears. Once we were inside, I placed my towel next to hers on the dirt floor.

Sitting on my thin towel, I could feel the cool, damp, solid earth beneath me. I felt connected to Mother Earth and connected to these people I'd never met before, gathered in the lodge. We were bonded by our sincerity, our humility, and our prayers.

After some introductory rituals, including a song, Grandpa Wallace said in his halting, accented English, "So tonight, we gather here to pray humbly and ask the sacred four directions and the Great Spirit, Tunkasila, our grandfather, to have pity on us. We come into this sacred womb of Mother Earth joined by the four elements: the fire, the water, the rock, and the green. The stone people remind us that we are part of the sacred web of life. The finned, the creepy crawlers, the winged, the four-legged, and the two-legged. The sacred mountains, the rivers and oceans, the sky and the trees and plants. We come to this sacred *inipi* to remember. We must remember our connection to each other and to Mother Earth. We need to work together so we can heal ourselves and our Mother Earth, our home." He looked around at our faces. "So, in this prayer round, you pray to the Great Spirit to ask for health and help in whatever it is you need for yourselves and your loved ones. We must help ourselves first so that we can help others." He raised his voice to Daniel, who was squatting by the flap opening, "Firekeeper, bring in six stones."

We sat quietly, watching Daniel bring in one big, sputtering basalt stone at a time on a shovel and place it into the round, foot-deep fire pit in front of us. Each glowing stone was adorned with dried cedar by a helper. The cedar crackled and filled the lodge with its sweet-smelling, smoky fragrance. The pyramid of stones created a red radiating light, illuminating everyone's solemn faces.

Grandpa Wallace called for the next song. As the drummer and lead singer began, he dipped a long-handled silver ladle into the bucket and poured cold water onto the red-hot stones, filling the lodge with hissing, aromatic steam.

After a few rounds of bringing in the stones, adding cedar, singing another song, and pouring water, we began the prayer round: Going around the circle, one person at a time, we each shared our prayers out loud.

I listened intently to what people were praying for, but I felt scared and self-conscious to share my deepest sorrows and desires. When it was my turn, I was so overcome with emotion I began to cry.

Comforting hands reached out to touch my arms.

"It's okay," Rachel whispered. "This is where you can let yourself feel whatever you are feeling."

I collected myself and began: "Ho, Tunkasila, thank you today for my sobriety. I pray that one day at a time I continue to stay sober and surround myself with others who are also sober. I pray today for healing for my family. I pray for their physical, mental, emotional, and spiritual health. I pray for good health for my mom, and sobriety for my stepdad. I pray for health and help for my brother and sister. I pray to heal the hurt my family has caused me. I pray to feel loved. I pray to belong. I pray for guidance and health and help for myself and my friends. Tunkasila, I pray for my life partner to come into my life, and I pray that you bless me with the gift of motherhood. *Ho, mitakuye oyasin*!"

Once I finished my prayers, I cried softly, relieved to have voiced out loud what I most desired and grateful that the people gathered with me in the lodge were willing to bear witness to my pain and vulnerability. Rachel slid her hand on to mine and squeezed my hand in support; her compassion touched me deeply.

When the ceremony was completed, we filed out as we had entered—humbly, on our hands and knees—saying, "*Ho, mitakuye oyasin*," as we exited the lodge.

Emerging from the lodge, I felt as if I was being birthed or reborn. I felt fresh and cleansed—physically, mentally, emotionally, and spiritually. I was a clean slate. I had a new beginning.

After we changed into our dry clothes, we gathered in the house around the big oak table. After a prayer was said for the food, helpers made a plate for our ancestors and one for Grandpa—our elder, our teacher—before we all filled our own plates.

As we all talked and laughed and got to know each other, Daniel walked up to me and gave me a hug. "So," he said, "how was your first sweat lodge?"

I reflected on my experience. "In the sweat lodge, I felt like I was coming home," I told him. "Not only symbolically, as if returning to the womb to be rebirthed, but in that circle of prayer. The humility of praying for my life and my loved ones with others who also prayed for their lives and loved ones was the first time I felt so included and safe in a group of people. Even in AA meetings I only share a little because I am so shy. But in the lodge—in the anonymity of the dark, in the sacred space—I felt freer to share my burdens and fears."

Daniel smiled at me knowingly. "Oh, you're a friend of Bill W. too, huh? Just so you know, each time that you participate in the sacred *inipi* ceremony to share your prayers, vulnerability, and gratitude, you strengthen the web of life—not just for yourself but for the whole community. So I hope you will come back next weekend."

"Oh, I will," I said quickly. "I definitely will."

I knew that everyone had struggles, but to hear people share theirs out loud, without shame, made me feel safe to do so too; it assured me that I was not a failure for struggling. The prayers we'd voiced that day had also included the gratitude each of us had for the good in our lives. Acknowledging that gratitude was comforting, healing, and hope about the future and my family returned to my heart.

I was in awe of everyone's profound honesty and vulnerability in this community and how each person was acknowledged for exposing their hearts. I could see how each time people participated in this ceremony they would be cleansed and wrung out over and over. With each sweat lodge I attended I was sure I would become more connected to my deepest, truest self—or, in AA terms, my higher power or highest wisdom.

The atmosphere was light and vibrant and friendly. Everyone smiled and hugged. I felt baptized, more so than when I was officially baptized at eight years old and didn't understand why or what was happening. I was home here, despite how new I was to the community. I'd found my spiritual family, and I belonged. I *belonged*.

In the tradition of many Native tribes, you *make* relations—you adopt people as family. It has nothing to do with flesh and blood. Nothing to do with lineage. It has nothing to do with your nationality, your race, or your gender—only with sincerity and heart and authenticity.

I was filled with gratitude to be connected to this little community in the great web of life. *Ho, mitakuye oyasin.*

YOU CAN HEAL YOUR LIFE

A year into my sobriety, in May 1988, I was hired at Geffen Records, an independent record company, as an artists and repertoire (A&R) assistant. The A&R executives were responsible for scouting, signing, and developing new artists and managing current artists. The company, founded by the savvy music industry genius David Geffen, boasted clients including Joni Mitchell, John Lennon and Yoko Ono, Elton John, Neil Young, Peter Gabriel, Aerosmith, and Guns N' Roses, whose album *Appetite for Destruction* was currently #1 on the Billboard 200 and would go on to sell over 30 million albums worldwide.

My A&R executive boss and I shared the bungalow next door to the main entrance at 9130 Sunset Boulevard with the A&R guy who had signed Guns N' Roses and his staff of three women. I shared the lobby space with Rose, and we had the pleasure of greeting many artists who came to meet with our bosses or as they passed through the lobby to head upstairs to publicity. Rose quickly nicknamed me "Face" because she said whatever I was thinking or feeling was prominently displayed on my face—something I had never been aware of, and which now embarrassed me.

I loved working in the music industry and the perks that came along with it—like my All-Access World Tour backstage pass to the Aerosmith shows with openers Guns N' Roses—despite the systemic and pervasive sexual harassment that also came with the territory. I spent most evenings at the Roxy, Whiskey, Lingerie, Troubadour, and other clubs seeing bands and networking with other music industry folks.

One night at one of those clubs, I chatted with a bearded executive from another record label. The next week he began calling me at work, harassing me with sexual come-ons.

One time when I answered the phone he taunted through heavy breathing, "Wendy, once you've had the beard between your legs, you'll never go back."

Disgusted, I slammed the receiver down as loudly as I could—I hoped I broke his eardrum—and then jumped up from my chair and stood in front of Rose's desk, shaking.

Rose stopped what she was doing and, registering the fury in my face, asked, "What the fuck happened, Face?"

I was so angry; tears filled my eyes. "He's so stuckin' fupid!" I finally shouted.

Rose paused to register what I had accidentally said and then burst into laughter, falling on the floor. When she got back into her chair, tears streamed down her face. "Oh my God, Face, you are so wonderful," she said, beaming at me.

We both burst out laughing as I realized what I'd said. From then on, we said "He's so stuckin fupid" every chance we got. And eventually, my phone harasser left me alone but not before bad mouthing me to my boss who told him where to go.

When Guns N' Roses came into the office, lead guitarist Slash liked to sit on the corner of my desk and glare at me from behind that dark, tangled mop of hair and those mirrored aviator sunglasses and blow cigarette smoke at me. I didn't know if that was his way of flirting with me, but I did know that Slash was one of those tantalizingly sexy bad-boy musicians who would be kryptonite to my sobriety.

Each time he sat on my desk, apparently wanting my attention, I felt a little tingle of excitement—but I made myself turn my back to him and focus on my work. I was determined not to be a groupie, or to fall for another musician who wasn't sober.

Around this time, Sharon and Jessica moved to LA. I hoped that the geographic closeness would contribute to a closer relationship, but we all still had our own lives, and I didn't see either of them very often.

That fall, Mark came to LA from Indiana for Thanksgiving. I had no idea what prompted his trip—he'd kept his distance for so long—but I was pleasantly surprised to see him. I hadn't seen him and had only rarely spoken to him since Casey's memorial three years earlier, and we hadn't spent a Thanksgiving together in seven years. I was pleased and surprised by his effort to connect with us again and felt that perhaps I had a family after all.

That weekend, Sharon, Mark, Jessica, and I all drove up the scenic Pacific Coast Highway to Monterey Bay and spent a lovely couple of days together, strolling around the aquarium and Hearst Castle.

"Orr orr orr," Mark yelled out to the seals sunning themselves on the pier at Monterey Aquarium and laughed.

"Oh, you speak their language too?" I laughed, realizing I *liked* my brother. He had a funny sense of humor when he wasn't so quiet and withdrawn. I felt achingly tender toward him and wished we were closer.

Seated in a leather banquette at a touristy seafood restaurant with views of the Pacific Ocean an hour later, I cut into my fresh Thanksgiving salmon dinner and realized it was the first time in my life that I wasn't having a traditional turkey meal. Even if I didn't go to Illinois, I often cooked the traditional meal myself for my "orphan" friends. Salmon for Thanksgiving was new and felt a bit odd, but looking around the table at my siblings and my niece, I realized that the four of us celebrating Thanksgiving together was even more out of the ordinary.

Because I went back to Illinois less often, Mom came out to visit me, and we always had entertaining, bonding adventures together. It was a fun romp to attend the first American tour of Cirque du Soleil at the Santa Monica pier with her. I had never been to a circus before. We were two little kids eating cotton candy, giddy with joy and wonder. When I was growing up, we hadn't had a mom-daughter tradition like some friends of mine who'd attended the ballet and high tea for the holidays with their moms. But now that I was an adult, I thought going to see Cirque du Soleil together could become a tradition for us.

"You know, Wendy, when I was a little girl with my deformed hand, I fantasized about being either a trapeze artist or a racecar driver," Mom leaned in to tell me as she gazed at the aerialist swooping through the air, adept and agile.

"Well, Mom, maybe the trapeze artist ship has sailed—but you did get your driver's license, so there is still hope to be a racecar driver!" I laughed and squeezed her little hand.

Mom shook her head and mouthed "No way!" as the ringmaster announced the next death-defying trapeze act.

I loved seeing the little girl in my mom filled with amazement and awe.

Over the next few days, we enjoyed dinners at my favorite Venice Beach neighborhood restaurants, sipped nonalcoholic drinks at the West Beach Café, and chatted with local celebrities at the bar. We drove out to the San Bernardino Mountains and to Glen Ivy Hot Springs and mud baths, giggling like little girls as we covered ourselves in mud and lay on lounge chairs to bake in the sun. She was game for whatever I suggested and was thrilled to have such adventures with me.

I was grateful that Mom and I continued to have such a close, loving relationship.

Usually when Mom visited, we kept things light and fun—but one night over dinner, she cleared her throat and straightened her back, and I knew something serious was coming.

"You know, Wendy, Paul does love you. To him, you are his daughter. You need to fo—"

"I know, Mom," I cut her off. "Focus on his good side." I shook my head. "He does have a good side. But that's what's crazy-making: You never know what the hell is going to set him off, and his crazy side overshadows the good. You can't ignore that, Mom. I'm afraid of him. And I still don't understand why he doesn't have a relationship with his five other kids. Now that they're grown, their mother can't stop him from spending time with them. It's so weird. Why can't we ever talk about these things?"

"I'm working on that, Wendy," she said. "But you have to know that he does love you, and you are his daughter."

Tears filled my eyes, and I reached across the table and squeezed my mom's hand.

Paul had cut down on his drinking in recent years and his angry episodes, according to Mom, now occurred less often. They had been traveling all over the world together—to Thailand, China, Fiji, Australia, New Zealand—and had even gone on motorcycle tours across Europe, Nova Scotia, and one that went from Alaska to Baja, California.

I had no doubt that they loved each other very much. And there was no doubt that it was my mom's love that had saved Paul. But still I worried. Fear permanently resided in my gut and sparked cautionary, protective rumbles. How would I ever be able to trust him? He had shown me who he was since I was nine years old. How could I ever feel safe around him, unafraid that the tiniest thing might set off his violence? Could he ever change?

I was learning that, indeed, people could change for the better, but to do so, they had to work on themselves, take responsibility for their actions. They had to be remorseful for past bad behavior and make amends to those they had hurt.

Paul had never done any of that, at least not regarding the harm he'd done to me.

I stood in front of the mirror in my powder room and studied my eyes. People often commented that I had "David Bowie eyes," since my seeing eye and blind eye were now different colors. I studied my mouth, my crooked teeth.

Before I could become distracted by the tiny, imperceptible wrinkles that I perceived as flaws, I launched in. Gazing into my blue-green eyes, I firmly stated, "I love myself just the way I am"—and burst out laughing.

Why was it so funny to tell myself that I loved and accepted myself? I tried again: "I love myself just the way I am."

It still felt odd and silly, so I tried again: "I am lovable."

I burst into tears.

I had just joined a woman's group based on the work of self-help pioneer and writer Louise Hay, whose recent book *You Can Heal Your Life* was a groundbreaking bestseller in the burgeoning field of the mind-body connection. In the women's group, I was learning and practicing principles intended to help me change the messages I had received from my family all my life.

As I read the book, I wondered about the sources of my family's traumas and afflictions. Mom had only recently confided to me at seventy years old that she had been sexually assaulted as a little girl. Was it possible that her childhood affliction with St. Vitus dance—the neurological disorder that kept her bedridden for a full year when she was eleven, unable to control her jerking limbs—was due to that trauma? And was it possible that my sister's trauma had contributed to her Crohn's disease?

As I learned new ways to perceive injuries and how to heal them, I practiced a forgiveness exercise where I imagined Paul as an innocent five-year-old child. According to Louise Hay, that would help me facilitate my ability to forgive him. Although I didn't know all the details, I knew he had been repeatedly beaten by his father as a child and kicked out of the house as an adolescent and had to go to work for a neighboring farmer and lived in his barn. I understood he didn't know how to deal with the rage and hurt he felt toward his own father. He didn't know how to heal himself. Although his childhood trauma did not excuse his adult behavior, it helped me to think of him as an innocent child so that I could forgive him. Not for him but for myself, to let go of the burden of my anger and pain and grief.

Through this work, I realized that I wanted to be a kind and compassionate daughter. I couldn't change Paul or tell him how to act, but I could choose to act in the way that *I* wanted to. Mom had chosen him not only to be her husband but also to be my father, and I wanted and deserved to have a father.

I only had this one chance, this one person, who could be my father. And maybe, if I could finally embrace Paul as my dad, I would get to spend more time with my mom. Maybe we could be a family after all.

I held my breath as I dialed.

I'd been practicing the forgiveness technique for a month, and now I'd finally summoned the courage to call Paul—who, I was determined to call "Dad" from now on.

"Hellloo," Mom's deep, resonant voice vibrated through the line.

"Hi, Mom, it's me," I said. "I want to talk to you too, but I've called to talk to Paul . . . umm, to Dad. Is he there?"

"Why sure, he's right here. Let me put him on."

"Hey, Wendy Beth, how you doin'? What's going on?" Dad was upbeat and chipper and sounded happy to hear from me.

Haltingly, I began slowly—and then the pent-up words burst out of me. "Dad, I'm calling to let you know that I have been seeing a therapist to understand how my childhood has affected my adulthood. I realize that I have difficult relationships with men. My therapist believes that it stems from my relationship with you and that has caused me to believe that I am not worthy of love and finding a wholesome partner. I have never really felt loved by you. You always act like you're mad at me. I feel that I am unlovable. I feel like it is always my fault if someone is mean to me or doesn't love me."

I paused to catch my breath, shaking with fear. I had never had an authentic, heart-to-heart conversation with Paul. He'd never heard me talk about my feelings, nor had he ever asked about them. How was he going to react to all this?

In the silence, I could hear him breathing and sucking on his teeth. Finally, he quietly said, "Oh, that's not true. I love you, and you deserve to have a good relationship."

I was stunned—couldn't believe my ears. It was the first time he had ever said that he loved me. It was the first time he had said that I deserved something good in my life.

Tears welled up in my eyes. "Do you really mean that?" I asked, choking on my words.

"Well certainly, of course I do."

What I really wanted was for him to repeat over and over that he loved me, to make up for all the years I had missed hearing it growing up. I wanted to hear him apologize for all the years he'd terrorized me with threats of violence, and for the time he'd hit me. I wanted to hear him say he would never do it again. I wanted him to tell me why he drank, why he was so angry, and how he had been hurt as a child. I wanted to hear him say that he would quit drinking and go to Alcoholics Anonymous and work on himself.

But I knew that those three powerful, little words "I love you" were monumental, and I was afraid to ask for anything more. I wanted to believe him. I wanted to believe, too, that with those three words my wounds might be instantly, magically healed.

To my disappointment, I did not feel magically healed. I did not feel immediately whole. I had so many bad memories stored in my bones and my brain, so much fear and anxiety pulsing around my heart and through my blood. I was well trained to hold my breath and tiptoe around like a dancing poodle in a tutu.

But right now, in this moment, I wanted to hold my breath and preserve this moment of rare vulnerability, honesty, and love.

"Okay, thank you. I'm glad I called. I love you too. Talk to you later," was all I could manage to say before I hung up.

HANBLECEYA

"In order to truly know yourself, you need to take the time to listen to your Higher Wisdom, that part of you that knows your weaknesses, mistakes, and fears but also your strengths and potential," Grandpa Marcellus "Bear Heart" Williams, a Muskogee-Creek medicine man and elder, explained to our small group gathering. "We live in noisy modern times with so many distractions that we can barely think straight. One to four days of vision quest allows you time to meditate, alone out in nature, without distractions and creature comforts so that you can focus on the voice of your Higher Wisdom."

I had been attending many different Native American ceremonies, and in that community, I had found people that I felt were my chosen family. That was good, because I needed a village to maintain my sobriety and continue to work to heal myself, and when it came to my own family, nothing had changed all that much through these years. My relationship with Sharon was strained at best, with Mark it was distant and awkward, and with Paul it was tentative and cautious.

"During a vision quest, you fast without food or water," Grandpa Bear Heart continued. "To receive something, we must make room for it. We must empty ourselves first. By fasting, not only do we empty ourselves physically but we also empty our minds to receive new ideas and insights."

Grandpa Bear Heart then announced that he was supporting a vision quest in the fall in a remote area of New Mexico.

The *hanbleceya* in Lakota or "vision quest" was a ceremony that many Native American tribes practiced. I learned that they typically took place on a high hill or mountain. This was meant to give the individual on the quest a better perspective of the world, and that was why it was referred to as "going up on the hill."

At the end of our meeting, I humbly stood before Grandpa Bear Heart.

"Grandpa, would you do me the honor of putting me up on the hill?" I nervously asked as I handed him a bundle of tobacco, following the traditional protocol of making an offering to an elder or teacher when asking for help.

He smiled widely, his kind brown eyes crinkling, and shook my hand. "That's good," he said in his resonant southern drawl. "Yes, granddaughter, I will."

In the few months before vision quest, Grandpa Bear Heart instructed me to make the appropriate number of prayers ties to rim the blanket I would use on my site as well as one large, three-foot-long prayer tie of red wool secured with an eagle feather and an abalone shell. I was told to bring a Pendleton wool blanket to sit on; a sleeping bag and jacket to keep warm in the cool mountain evening climate; my *chanunpa*, or pipe; and tobacco—nothing more. As I prepared my prayers ties, I prayed that my dedication and commitment to this sacred ceremony would heal me and make me stronger and wiser.

"A vision quest means you are questing for or searching for something. What you are searching for is insight into who you are as a human being. While questing, it is helpful to meditate on these three questions: Who am I? What have I done with my life so far? And what is my purpose?"

I was in a rural, mountainous area a few hours from Albuquerque, about to embark on my vision quest. I sat in a sweat lodge with Grandpa Bear Heart and my fellow questers, listening hard as Grandpa talked about the purpose and sacredness of vision quest and how to set our intention for humble requests and answers.

"You can learn a lot about yourself by asking questions and listening for the answers," he told us. "Who am I? What do I believe in? What do I stand for? What have I accomplished so far? Am I in the right place and in the right job? Am I a role model to anyone? Why am I here? What is the purpose of my life? How do I fulfill my potential? Ask yourself these questions while you are on the hill. Then be quiet and listen for the insight and the answers. Communication may come to you in the form of ideas, a realization, a dream, through a bird or animal or plant. If you encounter any animals, observe their qualities and think about how you can incorporate those qualities into your own life."

As I listened to these deep questions, questions I'd asked myself many times before, I wondered if I'd find more answers, or at least clues to those answers, on my vision quest.

Grandpa Bear Heart told us that the sweat lodge fire was the heart of the vision quest, and that it would be maintained the whole time we were on the hill. He assured us that he would work with the fire for our protection, and he would keep an eye on us all night long until he came to retrieve us from our site. "I travel psychically on the smoke of the Sacred Pipe and surround questers with protection," he explained.

When our vision quest was finished, he would find us and bring us back to the sweat lodge, where we would tell him everything that had happened to us. He would then help us interpret the meaning of the experience and determine how we could use this guidance in our lives.

Grandpa Bear Heart and I walked quietly and reverentially past manzanita low shrub, cactus, sage brush, cypress, mahogany, and juniper trees on the way to the site he'd selected for me. I was carrying all my belongings, and I kept clumsily dropping articles of clothing and dragging my blanket on the ground like Linus from *Peanuts*.

I glanced up at Grandpa Bear Heart's scrutinizing expression, and it was clear that he knew I was nervous.

Not nervous—downright scared. Scared of being alone with my thoughts, scared of the dark, scared of whatever animals would come to my space, scared of not doing it right, scared of being a hack, a wannabe, an imposter. Scared of being with my fears that I wasn't lovable. All my fears of everything that I had ever feared seemed to be bubbling up and sitting in my heart and my throat.

Grandpa cleared his throat and, in his sweet Oklahoma drawl, said, "Granddaughter, it's good to be a little bit afraid. You will do many things in life that give you some fear. That fear keeps you aware, on your toes, and ready. It can motivate you. It can give you strength and energy. It can propel you into action when needed. But if you have too much fear it will paralyze you from acting when you need to. It drains your energy. So have a little bit of fear, but not too much."

His gentle patience calmed me. *I can do this*, I told myself.

When we arrived at my site, Grandpa told me that he had faith in me, that I knew what to do, and that I should pray for guidance if I felt unsure and afraid. "You won't see me, but I will visit you and check on you. You are alone but not alone," he reassured me—and then he walked away.

I took a breath, slightly comforted but still scared, and began to set up my space: I placed my blanket on a soft, smooth spot on the ground in partial shade; I strung my multicolored tobacco prayer ties around the perimeter; I arranged my ceremonial objects as instructed and picked up my pipe, my *chanunpa*, to pray.

As I did all this, a blue dragonfly darted around my site as if welcoming me and inspecting my handiwork. Dragonflies symbolize change, transformation, and self-realization, so I was thrilled to see it. "Thank you for visiting me, Dragonfly," I said before it flitted away.

I looked up at the high sun in the New Mexico sky to gauge how much daylight was left. Then I cast my gaze out at the purplish light on the mountain range, covered in a blanket of pinyon-juniper woodlands. I inhaled the fresh, astringent scent of the mint-green sage brush surrounding me and felt fresh and clean. Tender, white cumulous clouds drifted through the breathtaking cornflower-blue sky; they morphed into a calf jumping over the moon and the outline of a cow skull, then melted and instantaneously morphed into something else.

With a sudden realization of the intensity and seriousness of my commitment, my eyes filled with tears. I was crying for a vision, crying for my life, and crying for health and help with all the pain and fear I still experienced. Thinking through my whole life story—the trauma and tragedies, the heartbreak and sorrow of the deaths of my dad and niece, the trauma of Paul's alcoholism, the misunderstandings between all the members of my family, the lack of honesty and direct communication that had always troubled me, the painful secrets I'd learned over the years, and the unanswered questions about why my siblings were so distant toward me—I talked and prayed out loud to the Universe, the Great Spirit.

My intention for my vision quest was to ask the Great Spirit for insight into myself, into my family, into what it meant to have a family and to belong to a family. I also had a long list of requests: I prayed for health and help for my mom, for her inner-wounded-child and the woman who'd lost a husband. A woman now married to a man she deeply loved despite his alcoholism. I mourned for my dad, Burt, who didn't get to see his children grow up. I asked for help for Paul and his wounds, and for Mark and Sharon, and for my niece Jessica. Though I was sober from alcohol use, nicotine still had a heavy grip on me, so I prayed to be cured forever of addiction to alcohol and nicotine. I also asked the Universe to give me a loving, supportive partner and a healthy child—or, if that was not meant to be, to please take that desire away from me.

I prayed out loud for what seemed like hours and then fell silent, listening for the response from the wind, the earth, the sun, the sky, and my own inner wisdom.

Suddenly, a single hummingbird appeared over my head and stood still for a moment, appearing to stare right at me. I knew the hummingbird was one of Grandpa Bear Heart's spirit animals; I laughed out loud and said, "Thank you for checking on me, Grandpa." My body relaxed with relief, and I was filled with love and peace and tenderness.

A moment later, the desert stillness was pierced by the high, shrill whistle of a raptor. A red-tailed hawk floated high above my head, circling around and around my ceremonial space.

Hawks can see eight times as far as humans. Their eyesight is the best in the entire animal world. Despite being blind in my right eye, I realized, I did have the power of the hawk to see things more deeply and more clearly and more completely than a lot of other humans. Perhaps, I thought, this was due to the early childhood trauma of losing my father and then living in a home where I had to be hypervigilant and sensitive to my environment. Or perhaps the fact that I was blind in one eye had helped my other senses develop more acutely. Or maybe I'd just been born to be a sensitive, empathetic, and intuitive human. Whatever its source, I realized that my superpower was the ability to see the big picture and the long-range view. I felt deep in my heart that to continue to strengthen this power I needed to spend time in solitude, in nature; I needed to quiet the world and my own thoughts so that I could listen deeply, to see more clearly, even with just one eye.

As the sun set in the west, I gazed as far into the horizon as I could and practiced the eyesight of the hawk, scanning the dark purple silhouette of the mountain range; then I turned that gaze inward and felt such a deep love, empathy, and compassion for myself and all the trials and tribulations I had gone through in my life. I was proud of myself for what I had accomplished so far and how far I had come despite my challenges. My "vision" was recognizing that I had the love, the innate gifts, and the power within myself that I needed to fulfill my best human potential—whatever that might be.

When the sun fully set behind the glowing orange and purple mountain range, pinpricks of bright stars filled the sky—a black velvet backdrop darkened by the new moon. As the temperature plummeted, I wrapped my sleeping bag around me, recalling that cold motorcycle ride years earlier after my three-day Zen "sessin" meditation retreat in Humboldt. In this moment it was clear to me that my years of Buddhist meditation studies and my Native American spirituality were intertwined and symbiotic. Vision questing and meditation were both a means to purify and to empty one's mind and heart in order to hear and know one's own inner wisdom.

I relaxed and curiously investigated the sensation of cold on my nose and cheeks. I inhaled one and exhaled one, embracing the present moment and the next and the next. A peaceful awareness overcame me as I metaphorically strung my pearl necklace, one breath at a time. I lay back on my wool Pendleton blanket, giving my body a rest after hours of sitting cross-legged, and watched my breath turn to mist in the cool mountain air. With the solid earth beneath my back, I felt grounded and supported, and the presence of the nearby grazing cows, the hummingbird, the dragonfly, and the hawk made me feel safe. Shooting stars streaked across the black sky like a hypnotic visual lullaby, and my eyes grew heavier and heavier until I fell into a deep and healing sleep.

I dreamt I stood in a pool of light, surrounded by a meadow of flowers, while hummingbirds circled my head, creating a jewel-toned crown.

At the end of my vision quest Grandpa Bear Heart came to collect me, and we walked reverentially and silently down the hill and into the sweat lodge.

Only then did he ask me to share about my experience. "Granddaughter, in order to interpret your vision quest, tell me what you heard, saw, and reflected upon while awake and in your dreams."

In only twenty-four hours on the hill, I felt transformed. Like a snake that had sloughed off its old skin, I was reborn, fresh, and clean. The New Mexico altitude and the purifying scent of the big sage brush had expanded my lung capacity. Even my bones felt lighter.

Grandpa Bear Heart nodded and smiled as I told him how the hummingbird, the dragonfly, and the hawk had visited me, and the insight I had gained through my prayers, my dream, and my reflections.

After a thoughtful moment of silence, he placed some dried cedar on the glowing red-hot basalt stone lying in the center of the earthen sweat lodge pit. "May you always have the power of the sight of the hawk," he declared as the cedar crackled and evaporated into smoke. "May you always have the long-range vision and insight to see things deeply and clearly from a higher and broader perspective. From now on, when you speak to the Great Spirit, introduce yourself as the woman you have become—Ayo Hokte, or Hawk Woman—and the Great Spirit will recognize you and welcome you and hear your prayers. *Ho mitakuye oyasin.*"

ASPEN

During my vision quest, I'd had a strong vision that it was time to quit smoking . . . again. As the saying goes: "It's easy to quit smoking. I've done it a million times." This time, though, I really wanted it. During the vision quest I had envisioned my life without smoking, and it was good.

Now five years sober, I was finally ready to break free of addiction to nicotine, however difficult that might prove to be.

Ironically, given how agnostic I was, I found a Quit Smoking program through the Seventh Day Adventist Church. The minister of the church, Rocky, did not try to convert or proselytize. His only mission was to help the participants quit smoking.

Rocky explained at our first meeting that each night of the free weeklong program, he would show us films, explain how nicotine affected the body physiologically and hijacked the brain, and give us tools to avoid smoking one day at a time.

"Rocky, I am making you my higher power," I declared that night, feeling vulnerable and skeptical about the efficacy of the program since I had failed at all my other attempts. "And I only promise not to smoke for twenty-four hours, until I see you again. After that I might smoke again."

"Sure! When you feel like lighting a cigarette, turn it over to me, your higher power. I can handle it." He flexed his bicep and smiled.

Rocky said that each evening he would send us home with a gallon of water to drink over the next twenty-four hours; a lunch bag filled with gum, toothpicks, and hard candy; and a list of things to do instead of smoking, like calling a friend, going for a brisk walk, or taking a shower. Also included in that week would be two Nicotine Anonymous meetings held at the church.

I wasn't sure exactly why, but I knew I was in the right place.

At the end of the evening, Rocky had us gather in a large circle, hold hands, and yell out together, "I choose not to smoke! Keep coming back. It works!"

Our loud, unified declaration made me emotional, and the deep desire of everyone in the group to stop smoking made me feel even more determined.

We collected our gallon water jugs and goody bags and sent each other off with good luck for the next twenty-four hours.

When I returned the next evening, I told Rocky, "Okay, I didn't smoke for twenty-four hours! Help me make it another day!"

That's how many Twelve Step practitioners abstain—one day at a time.

Quitting nicotine brought me to my knees. Only a few days off cigarettes I wanted to smoke so badly that I had to do everything on Rocky's list—brush my teeth, drink water, suck on red-hot hard candy, chew gum, chew on toothpicks, go for a power walk, call a friend, take a shower—and then do it all again just to keep from lighting up. Every day, I broke down and sobbed more than once. I was so exhausted from the agonizing desire for a cigarette I wanted to crawl out of my prickly skin. The tumultuous emotions of my past—the pain, the angst, the years of hurt—that smoking had subdued bubbled up, and sometimes all I could do was to lie in bed until the pain subsided.

I cried every day for three months. At first it was a trickle, then a babbling brook, then a raging river, then a geyser. And after I released that first layer of general sadness, a layer of gut-wrenching grief emerged. Layer upon layer of sadness and pain bubbled up until, finally, anger began to erupt. At one point I saw myself as a fire-breathing dragon. I hated everyone and wanted to incinerate anyone in my path with my fire breath.

I envied friends who could smoke only occasionally. For me it was only all or none. Success or failure. Win or lose. I could not manage my cigarette consumption. Cigarettes ruled me. I felt anxious if I didn't know where my cigarettes were. I made sure I had a full pack of cigarettes before I went home at night. I smoked even when I was sick. Everything about my habit was unmanageable.

I analyzed my addiction. In addition to the extreme physical addiction, I realized, I was psychologically addicted. Besides suppressing my sadness and anger, smoking was a big "fuck you" to everyone who didn't love me. But I realized it was like what the Buddha said about anger: "Holding on to anger is like grasping a hot coal with the intent of throwing it at someone else; you are the one who gets burned."

I was only poisoning and hurting myself, no one else, by smoking—and I didn't deserve to be poisoned. I deserved to live my best life. Something that could not include smoking. One day at a time, I believed, my life was changing for the better; my best life was coming, and I had to be ready for it.

I asked the universe for health, help, strength, and guidance—and the universe heard my plea.

"What the hell am I still doing in LA, Dyanna?" I wailed. "I'm so sick of being alone in this life. I want a companion. I want to be with someone who loves me. I deserve to be with someone wonderful, don't I?"

Dyanna was a dear friend I'd met when I first moved to LA. She'd since moved back to Colorado, where she had grown up, and we shared a love of the state. I'd visited her there a few months back, and we'd stayed up late into the night, dreaming of a bed-and-breakfast we'd run together in the Rocky Mountains.

Dyanna had known Big Toothy Writer and had heard about all my failed LA relationships. This call was the umpteenth time I'd called her crying about the state of my nonexistent love life. Exasperated, she exclaimed, "Has it ever occurred to you that your soulmate is not in LA, and he never will be?"

No, that had never occurred to me. I had long thought I would meet him in LA and only then, together, would we make our escape—to Europe or Santa Fe or Aspen or any place other than LA. But at thirty-seven years old, the dream of finding my soulmate seemed to be slowly fading.

Dyanna was an intuitive, but because she knew me so well, I'd always feared her own agenda might color her advice to me, so I'd never asked for a "reading" or consultation before. Now, however, I was desperate. "Okay, Miss Intuitive, then where is he?"

"I know you think I may be saying this to get you to move to Colorado," she said calmly, "but he's in Aspen."

When we hung up, I challenged the Universe out loud: "Okay, Universe, if I am supposed to move to Aspen, then help me get a job as a DJ on the radio."

I didn't even know if there was a radio station in Aspen. I just had long desired to become a DJ, and I thought that after years of working in the music industry in LA, I might be a bigger fish in Aspen. By this point I'd worked at two of the preeminent independent record companies, and I had years of experience and connections in the industry.

Why not at least give it a try?

The next week, I flew to Colorado.

"Good morning, Wendy Moore here on KSPN-FM Roaring Fork Radio."

The program manager of KSPN had hired me on the spot when I'd come in looking for a job. I'd immediately gone back to LA, sold everything except my books and clothes, and then headed to Aspen, ready to start my new life, have fun with Dyanna, and meet my true love.

As the newbie on KSPN, I had to work the ungodly overnight shift: two to six in the morning. The program manager had informed me that I would most likely hear from Gonzo journalist Hunter S. Thompson, who lived in the area, at some point.

The call came at about 4:00 a.m. early in my tenure.

"Yeah, hey, how ya doin'?" Hunter mumbled. (Insert snorting, coke-sniffing sound.) "Can you play me some Warren Zevon—'Lawyers, Guns and Money'?"

I played Warren Zevon for him that night and for many more nights thereafter.

A few weeks after that first call, Hunter came into Chefy's, the restaurant in Basalt where I waitressed to make ends meet.

I hurried to his table, thrilled to have the opportunity to introduce myself. "Hi, Hunter, besides being your waitress today, I'm Wendy Moore, the late-night DJ on KSPN who plays Warren Zevon for you."

"Oh, yeah, that's you, huh? How're you doing?" He seemed amused as he sat back in his chair and gazed at me through his sunglasses. "You're a good DJ. I like what you play. Nice to meet you." He had a more gentlemanly air than I expected.

In between serving him his lunch, I chatted with Hunter about how I'd gotten to Aspen and about my years in the LA entertainment and music industry scene. When he was finished with his lunch, he lit a cigarette, held by a clear cigarette holder, and placed $150 cash in the leather check holder—$100 more than the total bill amount. "Keep the change," he said.

Stunned, I stuttered, "A . . . are you sure?"

He nodded, and I could see his eyes twinkling behind his signature amber Ray-Ban Aviators. "You know, I need an assistant. Are you interested?"

A million thoughts flashed through my mind in a millisecond: *Is he hitting on me? He seems like a gentleman. Would he be content to keep the relationship professional? Did I just show up at the perfect time when he needed an assistant? What an incredible opportunity. Since I want to write more, maybe I could learn something from him.*

"Yes, absolutely," I said, pushing my anxieties aside. "I would love to work with you, Hunter."

With the directions Hunter had scratched onto a napkin, I found my way to his home: Owl Farm in Woody Creek, not far from where I lived. Getting out of my car, I was greeted by the screeching of his guard peacocks.

Hunter told me to have a seat at the island of his iconic, cluttered kitchen. Cable news blared from a small TV at the end of the counter.

"Have you read this?" he asked as he handed me a copy of his book, *Fear and Loathing*.

"Honestly, no. I'm sorry. I haven't read it," I admitted, embarrassed.

"That's okay." He shrugged. "So, Hollywood is gonna make a movie from my book. Here's the first draft of the film script. I just want you to read my book and then read the script and tell me what you think."

"Okay," I said eagerly. "You want me to start reading now, or wait until I'm at home?"

"You can read it at home," he said. "But do you have a flashlight in your car?"

Unclear what the connection was, I told him I had misplaced my flashlight.

"Well, then, we have to go to Wally World for flashlights!" he declared, already getting up to go.

I quickly learned that my job as Hunter's "assistant" would not be a conventional job. I also learned that Hunter had his own names for things, like "Wally World" for Walmart and "Hilly and Billy" for President and First Lady Bill and Hillary Clinton.

We often had lunch at his beloved Woody Creek Tavern, where he usually hung out, but one day we went to the swanky Snowmass Club for lunch. We sat at "Hunter's Table" by the window in the posh restaurant, and Hunter immediately began to shamelessly use a credit card to cut lines of cocaine and snort it off the table in between sips of his cocktail and drags off his perpetual cigarette, stuck into its holder.

"Hunter, um . . . people are watching you," I whispered haltingly as the other patrons gawked and I nervously picked at my expensive shrimp Louie salad.

"Oh yeah, well, I'll give 'em something to gawk at then," he said loudly as he snorted up another line and chuckled, a big, impish grin on his face.

I had to hand it to him. My perception was that he really didn't give a crap what other people thought of him—at least not total strangers. I wished I had such disregard for what other people thought of me.

After lunch, Hunter, a bit inebriated and high, drove us down the steep road back toward Owl Farm in his 1973 Chevy Caprice—he called it the Red Shark—with only one hand on the steering wheel. Seconds in, he started reaching with the other hand for the cooler on the leather back seat to get his whiskey bottle.

Terrified of his erratic driving down the winding mountain road, I climbed over the seat to get the whiskey bottle for him.

Somehow, we got back to Owl Farm in one piece.

One night after going through and organizing numerous boxes of papers, Hunter asked me if I would like to go to the backyard to shoot his guns. More specifically he said, "Do you want to go blow something up?"

I politely declined.

I was very fond of Hunter, even though he loved alcohol, nicotine, cocaine, and guns—and I did not. I didn't begrudge him his beloved vices. And besides the guns, he didn't offer me any of those substances. I was beguiled by his charming presence.

We were an odd couple, though, even for just a professional relationship. I wasn't impressed by—nor did I know a thing about—cars, sports, or politics, and I needed to sleep like a normal person. We were quite ill matched in many ways.

Except there was something that connected us: He was a kindred spirit. Despite his notorious reputation, he was always kind and generous with me, and I connected with his sensitive side. I saw through his stealthy armor—the opinionated, outspoken, tough, caustic, brilliant Hunter that protected his soft, emotional, and vulnerable side. I saw his pain, just below the surface. I enjoyed his wit, humor, and intelligence. Our relationship was strictly platonic, but I got to know him well enough to understand that he was a remarkable human being, a one-of-a-kind person. And just like when I'd met and spent time with Joni Mitchell, I felt a tender kinship with Hunter and was grateful for his kindness to me.

Like Joni, Hunter made me feel special and unique by allowing me into the out-of-this-world orbit where he lived for the brief but spectacular amount of time I got to spend with him.

There were many interesting people like Hunter who called me on KSPN, usually to request a song. One night, six months into my gig and after a promotion to the 10:00 p.m. to 2:00 a.m. slot, I got a call from a guy with a beautiful Spanish accent.

"Goood evennning," he said with a lilting tone. "Would you pleeease play me some Phil Manzanera, a song called 'Criollo' from the album *Primitive Guitars*?"

Amused with his formality I replied, "Well, good evening to you too! But who is Phil Manzanera?"

"He is a Colombian guitarist and producer who plays with Bryan Ferry of Roxy Music," he explained.

"Oh, I just played 'Love is the Drug' by Roxy Music," I said, intrigued by this guy. "What are you doing up so late?" It was past midnight.

"I'm an architect, and I'm writing a grant for a nonprofit organization providing housing for the Latino community in the Roaring Fork Valley," he said.

I was a volunteer for Grassroots Aspen, a nonprofit that brought inner-city kids to Aspen for summer and winter activities; I wondered if he might be interested in volunteering. It seemed that more women than men volunteered, and I felt it would be nice to have more balance there. And since he spoke Spanish, he could be a huge help.

"Where are you from?" I asked.

"Mwakee," he answered, just like how people from Milwaukee pronounce Milwaukee—leaving out numerous letters.

I burst out laughing. "You are not from Milwaukee! Where are you from?"

"Well, Mwakee is my first American home, so I consider myself a Cheesehead," he said, chuckling.

I laughed out loud, a rare occurrence, understanding the reference to Wisconsin cheese.

"I am from Buuu-ca-ra-man-ga," he said, enunciating every syllable.

Since I had lived in Southern California for thirteen years, I asked, "Do you mean Rancho Cucamonga?"

"No, Bu-ca-ra-man-ga," he repeated, as if the word was like honey on his lips.

"Where in the world is Bucaramanga?" I asked, embarrassed by my ignorance.

"Co-lom-bia," he answered, sounding like he was tasting a delectable fruit meant to be savored.

"Oh, my favorite coffee is from Colombia!" I sincerely announced.

"Well, you know, Juan Valdez is my uncle!" he quipped without hesitation.

Oh my god, this guy was a comedian—hysterical! Since I was chronically depressed most of my life, I was taken aback by how easily he made me laugh. *Who is this guy?* I wondered.

Mind you, I was running a radio station. It was the middle of the night. There was no one else there. I never, ever sat down during my shift, because I was constantly moving—pulling CDs from the library, writing down every song I played, highlighting every other song I played from the current rotation bin, announcing station ID and PSAs, and playing with knobs and equipment all around me. But I didn't want to stop talking to this guy.

I grabbed Elton John and Bernie Taupin's rock epic "Funeral for a Friend/Love Lies Bleeding"—an eleven-minute-long song—so we could keep chatting off-air a bit longer.

As the song played, I asked my mystery caller, "What is your name?"

I had to write it down: Ignacio Correa-Ortiz. I had never heard such a name. It was quite a mouthful for a gringa.

I kept repeating much of what he said. I had never heard these words before.

"Ignacio means 'fire,'" he told me. "Like 'ignition'; they both come from the same root."

The guy also knew Latin. Oh wow.

I put him on hold several times to do the usual station ID/PSA/lost dog/fires/elk crossing the highway/Movieland announcements. After chatting for a long time, I realized I'd better hang up and keep the line open for emergencies, so I asked if I could get his phone number. He gave me both his work and home numbers.

When we hung up, I played the Phil Manzanera song "It's Just Love" and sent it out to Ignacio.

Days passed, and I kept hearing this nagging little voice in my head that said, *"Call him, he might be the one."*

Really, voice? Come on!

But it persisted.

Well, at least he might be a friend I could practice Spanish with, I reasoned, not wanting to get my hopes up. *Okay, voice, here goes.*

I called both numbers he gave me, and they just rang and rang. What was going on? Had this guy given me bogus numbers?

A few more days passed, and that nagging voice brought him up again: *"Call him."*

I did call him! And there was no answer! I argued with the voice.

But it was relentless. *"Call again,"* it insisted.

Fine. I called his office number—and the receptionist answered right away and put me through to him.

He explained that there had been a big storm that had knocked out all the phones in Basalt. Wow, and I'd almost thrown away his number!

"Hello, Wendy Moore," he said, just as charming as he'd been the first night we talked. "Can I invite you to dinner—or to lunch, if that is perhaps more politically correct?"

This was 1994. Who talked like that back then?

"Dinner is fine," I quickly replied.

We decided to meet at Caribou Coffee in Caribou Alley on Hopkins Street in Aspen.

"How will I know you?" I asked.

"I look like a Latin Jesus," he said.

I burst out laughing. "Well that's good, because I look like Madonna!"

As in the *singer* Madonna—I had short, bleached blonde hair and dressed like . . . well, like I was in the music industry: leather, lace, and cowboy boots.

There was a saying in Aspen about dating: "The odds are good, but the goods are odd." So I knew better than to get too excited. But I was looking forward to meeting this Latin Jesus.

I rounded the corner that Friday night, April 8, at the agreed-upon time, and when I saw Ignacio peering out the window, I instantly knew it was him.

When he saw me, he quickly dismissed his friend who had come along just in case.

His description of himself as a Latin Jesus was accurate. Shoulder-length, coal black hair; full black beard; deep brown eyes specked with honey.

But that's where the comparison ended. He also wore wool trousers with hiking boots and a wool cape. A *wool cape*. He was adorably nerdy, in a mountain man kind of way. I was immediately smitten.

We had a quick coffee and moved on to dinner at the only Thai restaurant in town.

"So, tell me all about you," I said after we placed our orders. "Let's start with growing up in Colombia. How many siblings do you have?"

That was a great conversation starter, since he had four sisters and three brothers, all with not only proper names but also nicknames, many with partners and children.

"Oh my, I need a flow chart for all these names," I exclaimed. "What is your nickname?"

"Nacho," he said.

My eyes widened with surprise.

"The proper nickname for Ignacio is Nacho," he said, grinning. "So the guy who invented putting Wisconsin cheddar cheese over corn chips and throwing some jalapeños on top was obviously named Ignacio and called his creation 'nachos,'" he explained.

I marveled that he knew such things.

As dinner was wrapping up, I wondered if he could salsa dance. I had taken a few salsa classes at a club in Santa Monica and loved it. I didn't want to presume, just because he was Latino, but . . .

"Do you know where we might go salsa dancing?" I ventured.

He looked at me with a mischievous grin and a twinkle in his eye. "Actually, I do!"

Ignacio escorted me a few blocks away from the restaurant to a little cabin.

"I used to live here with a roommate," he told me. "She sings in a band, and she's working tonight."

Back then people didn't lock their doors in Aspen, and we walked right in. Nacho turned on the first cable radio station without DJs I had ever heard of and put on the salsa station.

Yeah, he knew how to salsa.

After two hours of dancing in Nacho's friend's house, we walked to the Paradigm Club in town and kept the party going. Dancing to every song, we closed the joint down.

Since Nacho didn't own a car, I offered to drive him down valley to his place in Basalt.

As we set off down Highway 82, he asked, "Hey, do you want to go visit a friend of mine who lives in a teepee?"

"Umm, well, yeah!" I exclaimed, thinking of the time while in college I had spent an independent studies semester researching Native American genocide and lived in a teepee in Oregon, planting trees with the environmental group the Hoedads. I was more than game to meet another intrepid, teepee-living soul.

Following Nacho's directions, I turned off Highway 82 and headed up winding Castle Creek Road.

As we rounded a curve, Nacho pointed to a small turnout. "Pull over here."

We got out of the car and started walking. The full moon reflected off the snow-packed trail, lighting our path.

For a fleeting moment I thought, *Okay, either this is really cool, or he's a psycho killer.*

But just then I saw two teepees and a cabin in a clearing and caught a whiff of soothing campfire fragrance.

Nacho scratched on the canvas of one of the teepees as if knocking on a front door.

"Come on in," said a male voice from inside.

Once inside Alejandro's teepee, I was amazed to see a glorious fire crackling in the wood-burning stove, a hearty pile of aspen and fir logs, a comfy upholstered couch, a bed, and a makeshift kitchen.

Alejandro served us chamomile tea and we talked comfortably, cozy on the couch, until 4:00 a.m.

At one point Alejandro tilted his head and looked at us quizzically. "Wait," he said, "how long have you guys known each other?"

Ignacio and I looked at each other, laughed, and said simultaneously, "We met today! Or technically yesterday!"

From that first date, we were never long apart.

Nacho had gotten his double master's in architecture/urban planning at the University of Wisconsin in Milwaukee and had already accepted a job in Chicago at Skidmore, Owings & Merrill (SOM)—the big firm responsible for the Sears Tower and Hancock skyscrapers and other enormous projects all over the world—before we met. Because he was from Colombia, however, the firm's attorneys were working out the details of his visa, delaying his start date by several months.

Which was a good thing, because it gave us April to September to hike and play and backpack and fall in love.

While we courted, we discussed commitment and marriage. At first, Nacho said he wasn't sure that he wanted to get married. When I said that since he wasn't sure, we should break up, because I did want to get married, so he relented and said he did too. When I asked if he wanted to have a child, he said maybe someday. When I said that I absolutely wanted to have a child, and that at almost thirty-eight years old my "someday" days were running out, he backpedaled and said, "Okay, sooner than someday!"

We backpacked to breathtaking, turquoise blue Geneva Lake. We hiked to Crystal Mill and Marble. Lost Man Loop. The Grottos. And on one weekend, we hiked from Maroon Bells to Crested Butte and back—eleven miles each way, through wildflowers and lightning and aspen groves.

After spending the night in Crested Butte and hiking the eleven miles back toward home, Nacho stopped to take in the stunning aspen grove we were standing in and tenderly smiled at me. "When my visa is approved, I'll move to Chicago to work for Skidmore. Will you go with me?"

I studied the sincerity in his loving, deep brown eyes. I knew what he meant, but I needed him to say it. "Well, I've been around the relationship block a few times," I said slowly. "Many times. I'm not moving to Chicago to play 'house' with anybody."

"No, I don't mean play 'house,'" he said. "I mean, it's you and me together. You know, committed."

Together for what? I thought, waiting for the *M* word.

"I mean, let's be engaged," he said, obviously meaning we would get married at some point and have a child at some point.

"So, we are engaged, and we are going to get married in Chicago, and we will have a child together soon?" I asked, realizing I would have to be the one to spell it out.

"Yes!" He beamed, excited that I'd said the words for him.

He didn't have a ring, but neither of us was very traditional. I didn't care about diamonds or gold bling. What was more important was that I knew what was in his heart. I knew he was committed to our relationship. I knew I would move to Chicago with him. And I knew I would eventually get him to say the *M* word.

"I need you to understand what you're getting yourself into with my family," I said hesitatingly, feeling vulnerable and scared, as we quietly chopped vegetables for dinner that night.

Nacho came around the table, hugged me, brushed the hair out of my face, and gazed into my eyes.

I started to cry.

Over dinner, I told Nacho the whole story of my family. The trauma. The history. The personalities. The violence. The drinking. The crazy. What to expect. What to avoid and watch out for. My absent brother. My angry sister.

"You are the most important person in my life," he reassured me. "Don't worry, your family can't scare me off. *Cuando te casas con alguien, te casas con toda su familia.* That's a Spanish saying, which means, 'When you marry someone, you marry their whole family.' But really, it's just you and me. If they are well behaved, we'll let them into *our* family," Nacho said with a smile and a wink and a hug.

I'd found my soulmate, just as Dyanna had predicted. Ignacio was kind and loving and funny. He was a jokester and made me laugh like no one ever had before. He nourished me with his love and his fabulous cooking. Being from the Andes, he loved the mountains, nature, and hiking as much as I did. I had never met a smarter, better-educated, more worldly person in my life. He was deep and lighthearted at the same time. And he loved me, in a way I had never been loved. Unconditionally. Completely. He accepted my beauty and my warts. He accepted my anxieties and worries about my family.

I had just turned thirty-eight years old. I had spent years in LA feeling invisible and in fear that my dream to have a partner and a child would never come true. But here Nacho was, promising me all of it.

After we became engaged, I played "Nick of Time" by Bonnie Raitt on KSPN every chance I could. It was my song, my story. I'd found him. I'd found love in the nick of time. I had a future I hadn't been able to imagine before, a partner. And he wanted a child.

Mom and Paul visited us in Aspen while on yet another one of their road trips out West. Chef Nacho cooked a delicious dinner and made them feel at home and at ease. Around Nacho, Paul's charming side shone through.

The four of us went to Black Canyon of the Gunnison to camp. In the photos from that trip, I am smiling broadly, but I can still remember how, as I stood next to Paul with his barrel chest and beer belly, I was stiff as a board. Holding my breath. In fight or flight. Waiting for the other shoe to drop. Hoping Paul wouldn't do or say anything to embarrass me—to drive Nacho away.

I let out a sigh of relief when Mom and Paul finally got in their car to drive away.

"Did you notice how edgy Paul got sometimes?" I asked Nacho as we waved them off. "Kind of in a weird, authoritarian, bully kind of way?"

"Yes," he said, "but you don't have to worry. I'll stay beside you, hold your hand, hold your heart, and have your back, through thick and thin. Everything is going to be okay."

I wanted to believe him.

The visa paperwork was finally approved. Nacho was officially hired by Skidmore, Owings & Merrill in Chicago, and slated to begin work in a few weeks.

Facing our imminent move away from our beloved Roaring Fork Valley, we decided to complete one more hike: the enchanting Mount Sopris in Carbondale, nearly thirteen thousand feet above sea level and a six-and-a-half-mile hike straight up.

Halfway up, we passed the breathtaking, teal blue Thomas Lakes—just a stone's throw from Williams Lake, where John Denver had penned the iconic "Rocky Mountain High." I began to sing the song, loudly and gleefully.

We'd gotten a very late start, so it was near sunset when we arrived at the rocky summit. We were the only ones there, so we disrobed and stretched out our arms to the breathtaking panoramic scene before us: a 360-degree view of White River National Forest, a watercolor-painted sky, and a waning sun. On the spot, we made up vows for our "spiritual wedding" as the brilliant September Colorado sun dipped into the western horizon—declaring our love and commitment to each other.

Although Nacho stuttered on the *M* word, it was clear we weren't just moving to Chicago together to play "house."

For twenty years, I'd lived far away from my parents; now, they would be only ninety miles from our new home in Chicago. I still clung to the fantasy that once I was married and had a child there might still be an opportunity for healing and closeness—to finally have the family I had longed for.

We packed up our meager belongings in a U-Haul and headed east to Chicago to start our life together. Our life. Together. A family of two.

Hopefully soon, three.

Finally, I belonged somewhere: with Nacho.

MY FUNNY VALENTINE

Nacho and I settled into our new life together in Chicago and soon had conversations about when and where we would get married. Oftentimes we had our big-topic discussions over Saturday morning coffee, sitting at our thrift store bistro table in our tiny 1920s Lincoln Square second-floor walkup apartment kitchen, complete with the original porcelain sink and cabinets.

"I've always fantasized about wearing a white, Victorian, high-collar, lace wedding dress with satin buttons and my hair piled high into an elegant updo," I told Nacho one morning. "Oh, and the multitiered raspberry and white chocolate cake, the wedding band playing all my favorite Motown and rock 'n' roll hits, the funny snapshots of the happy couple dancing, and all the traditional fuss." I took a sip of my Colombian coffee—and then, as I remembered that booze is usually served at weddings, began to feel panicked and burst into tears.

"What's wrong? What's happening, Wendy?" Nacho came around the table to hold me.

"Booze is served at weddings!" I exclaimed, still crying. "I can't have a wedding."

"What do you mean? Why?" Nacho asked, confused and concerned.

"I can't have a wedding," I repeated, "because I can just see my dad getting drunk and ruining my wedding. And then I'd spend the rest of my life reminded of that horrible event on every anniversary. No, I can't have a wedding like that. I need it to be free of trauma and drama."

Nacho took my hands in his. "You know what? Neither of us is traditional. We don't need the big wedding and reception. Let's save our money for a honeymoon trip to Colombia so that you can meet my family." He looked into my eyes. "I have an idea. Let's just keep it simple and get married at the Cook County Courthouse on Valentine's Day. Let's elope while your parents are snow birding in Baja."

"Oh, that is the perfect idea!"

Immediately, my tears dried up. I loved the idea of getting married on Valentine's Day to my forever Valentine.

I had called Sharon when Nacho and I had decided to get married during our hike from Maroon Bells to Crested Butte. She knew about all my disastrous relationships, especially with Big Toothy Writer, so she knew how monumental this was to me. I hoped she would be excited for me. And I hoped my marriage would add some joy to our family.

"Sharon, I have some wonderful news to share with you! I'm engaged!"

There was total silence as I nervously twisted the phone cord around my finger.

I took a deep breath. "Did you hear me?" I asked. "I said, I am *engaged*! To Ignacio! Isn't that wonderful?"

Sharon emitted a little laugh, then paused before she blurted out, "*Oh*, I am *too*!"

Never mind that that she was barely dating anyone, so of course she wasn't really engaged. I wondered why she couldn't let me have my moment of happiness without trying to compete with me.

Needless to say, when I called her to tell her we were getting married on Valentine's Day, I was protective of my special day.

"Oh, well, I'll come down to Chicago for the wedding," she said immediately.

"No, that's okay Sharon," I said. "We're just getting married at the courthouse."

"But you need a witness," she insisted. "And I could take pictures."

"Okay," I finally said, trying to mask my ambivalence. "I'd love for you to come."

Maybe sharing my special day with my sister would help us feel closer to each other, I rationalized, hoping I hadn't made a bad decision.

Nacho and I arrived at the Cook County Courthouse in downtown Chicago early on a snowy, cold-to-the-bone February 14.

I was dressed in my consignment store black velvet skirt and tunic and wearing a white fake pearl necklace and bracelet. Nacho was polished in a navy-blue pinstripe suit, crisp white shirt, and blue bowtie.

Sharon arrived late. When she found us in the long, crowded line, she loudly announced, "Oh my God! The traffic coming from Milwaukee was awful! And then I couldn't find any place to park!"

She continued to complain, flustered and sweating in her white fur coat, for the next few minutes.

It has always been her nature to be loud and make a scene, I thought. *But I am not going to let her tarnish my wedding day.*

"I'm sorry you had such a tough time getting here," I said to Sharon. "But you're here now, so you can relax."

To my surprise, she stopped complaining.

Finally, we made it inside. When our turn came, a scowling gray-haired judge snapped his fingers at us, sternly said, "Come on, kids," and walked into a small room.

Nacho followed him inside—but before I could join him, Sharon stopped me.

She held up my Instamatic camera. "How do I work this? How do I take the pictures?"

I paused to show her how to push the only button on the camera as the judge began the ceremony without me.

By the time I made it to Nacho's side, the judge had already finished with Nacho's vows. He then turned to me and asked, "Wendy, do you take Ignacio to be your lawfully wedded wife?"

I was so happy and nervous and wanted to memorize every moment of what was happening, but when I heard what the judge said, I looked at Ignacio, who also caught the judge's error. Laughing, Nacho said, "Wife? Wife?"

Either the judge didn't notice what he'd said, or he didn't care. He just looked at me impatiently.

"Yes, I take Ignacio to be my lawfully wedded wife," I said—and Nacho and I burst out laughing.

It was over as quickly as it had begun, and now we were married. My dreams were coming true. Everything felt perfect, like all the stars and planets aligned. Our love was like being wrapped in a warm and comforting shawl; Nacho made me feel safe, adored, and cherished.

The judge moved on to the next couple, and we ran out giggling about the grumpy judge who didn't even know what he was saying. Although Sharon was tired and whiney, I ignored her cranky attitude and invited her to accompany us to the Art Institute to take in some beauty.

She came along for a little while, but ultimately took her leave of us in the Impressionist gallery. We spent the rest of our blissful wedding day exploring our city, watching the ice skaters twirl, and dining in a romantic, candle-lit fondue restaurant.

We were madly in love, content, and filled with hope.

To this day, we claim that we were the first lesbian couple ever legally married in the State of Illinois.

Months later, after plenty of trying, I finally missed a period and bought a pregnancy test. Standing in our tiny bathroom, Nacho and I held our breath as we watched two pink lines appear, indicating a positive test.

"Positive!" Nacho cried out and burst into tears, hugging me. "We're going to have a baby!" He kissed me, tears now streaming down his face.

Elated, I said out loud to Spirit, my Higher Power, and God, "Thank you, thank you, I am so grateful. Thank you for blessing me with this wondrous gift!"

At thirty-nine years old, I imagined that this pregnancy was potentially my last viable egg. I was grateful that my body had been sprinkled with this one star-dusted miracle.

I peered out the window of the cab as we drove along a lush, winding, mountain road. Humid tropical air poured in through the open window, infusing my skin with its sensuous moisture.

I was five months pregnant, and Nacho and I were in Colombia, on our way to his parents' farm for the Christmas holiday. After all he'd told me about his family, I couldn't wait to meet them.

We turned off the main road and twisted and turned on a few dirt roads until we reached the driveway, the property bordered by a row of tall bamboo. Ignacio pointed out the EL TOBOSO sign—they'd taken the name of the farm from *Don Quixote*—at the entrance. His mother had painted the red outline of an old-fashioned windmill against a white background and painted the name below it in black letters.

I felt like a child, asking every ten seconds what this and that was; luckily, Nacho was my eager tour guide. The beautifully designed, three-block-long driveway was lined with hundreds of Cattleya trianae orchids—the national flower of Colombia—growing on totumo (gourd) trees, which produced small round gourds that would eventually be dried and fashioned into bowls.

Nacho's mother had planted those orchids in the Y of the trees, and they were her pride and joy.

We passed the farm's original hundred-year-old adobe home with a clay tile roof, where Nacho had lived by himself while in college, and suddenly the most delicious and comforting scent wafted through the open window.

"What is that amazing smell?" I swooned.

"Inhale deeply, my love!" Nacho smiled. "You are smelling tangerine blossoms! There are over a hundred tangerine trees on the farm, and over one hundred cacao trees for making chocolate. You're going to love the delicious fruit here."

Similarly to when I had finished my first meditation retreat in college, with my senses heightened as I embraced the cold and felt so alive on the back of my friend's motorcycle, I felt every cell of my body bursting with joy as these new sights, sounds, and smells bombarded my senses. Cradling my pregnant belly, I said out loud to my baby, "Darling, I know you can feel the beauty through me!"

At the top of the hill stood a large log cabin with an A-frame entry. Nearby was an inviting pool and thatch-roofed cabana surrounded by towering palm trees and large cedar trees dripping with Spanish moss—a sight right out of a tropical holiday postcard.

As the cab pulled up to the house, my in-laws emerged from the cabin to greet us, bright smiles on their faces.

My mother-in-law, Ines, was classically beautiful and had kind, soft brown eyes. The love emanating from her as she hugged me drew tears to my eyes, and she smiled and met my tears with her own. Rafael, my father-in-law, grabbed me with a deep, hearty chuckle after he hugged Nacho, and he caressed my face with both hands as he spoke to me in rapid Spanish.

"He is saying how happy he is to meet you, that you are welcomed into this family, and he thanks you for bringing his son and grandchild to him." Nacho beamed as he translated for me what his father had said.

Ines smiled as she took my arm to guide me into the cabin, gazing into my eyes and speaking to me in Spanish as if I completely understood every word.

"Mami is saying that she has prepared our 'honeymoon suite,' and wonders if you would like to take a nap and get settled," Nacho explained as he set down our luggage and hugged me. "Welcome to El Toboso!" he said proudly.

The clean, simple room included a private bath and intricately hand-carved oak wood headboard. The bed was covered in a white crocheted bedspread and pillow covers and draped in mosquito netting. Mother Mary looked down protectively from the only picture in the room.

I was too excited to lie down, however. I wanted to explore and fully absorb my surroundings. I looked at Nacho. "Can we walk around a little bit?"

"Of course!" he said, and he led me back out of the house.

We toured the grounds holding hands as he named all the flora, fauna, and fungi for me. Surrounding the house were gardens of poinsettia, hibiscus, anthurium, and *guayacán* trees with brilliant pink and yellow blooms. There were various species of palm trees, including corozo palms, which were adorned with large clusters of sweet, grape-like fruits along their limbs and long, porcupine-quill-like thorns protruding from the trunk. Walking along, we stopped to admire each plant and tree and taste their fruit.

Next was the *madroño*, or strawberry tree, with its dark green foliage and a sour fruit that made a tasty jam. A few more steps farther, and we reached a tangerine tree; Nacho picked a ripe fruit, peeled the rind into a perfect circle, and popped a delicious, juicy wedge into my mouth.

"Wow, this is my favorite fruit in the whole world," Nacho said as he stopped in front of yet another tree and pulled a three-foot-long bean pod from its branch. "This is called *guama*," he said and cracked the pod open to expose a white, fluffy, velvet-looking substance.

He placed a piece of it into my mouth. The texture felt like cotton candy and smelled and tasted like rose petals might taste. The seeds looked like little black mussel shells. (Later that day, my comedian husband would take those seeds and stick them on his eyebrows, ears, and nose to entertain everyone.)

From our vantage point we could see rolling green hills covered in eucalyptus groves, pineapple plantations, and—far in the distance—chicken farms. This lush landscape was perched high on the *mesa* above Bucaramanga, a large, bustling city nicknamed the "City of Parks."

Nacho had joked with me more than once that he'd grown up in a mango tree, and now I believed him.

Just then the sweet song of a great thrush a few feet away caught our attention. I looked up; hawks and buzzards circled high above. I'd arrived in paradise: Soft tropical breezes caressed my skin; my senses were filled with exotic sights, smells, and tastes; and orchids grew on trees all around me. I was in awe of this magical world where Nacho had grown up, and I couldn't help but feel a little envious of the richness of life that he had been raised within.

The next day Nacho's parents threw a lively party for us at the farm, complete with musicians and a catered traditional Colombian barbecue that included criollo potatoes and corn arepas. All seven of Nacho's siblings attended, including the three who were married and their children.

As a flood of siblings, spouses, and children arrived and greeted me, each one hugging me tightly and welcoming me to the family, I felt stunned and overwhelmed by their attention and kindness.

The musicians played traditional Colombian dancing music called Chucu Chucu, and everyone danced. Dozens of extended family and friends filled the long tables, and Nacho and I enjoyed every moment of the merriment as we danced, savored delicious food, and greeted our warm well-wishers.

Although the family mostly spoke in Spanish and Nacho couldn't translate everything for me, I understood enough to observe that the whole family constantly laughed, joked, and acted silly in a slightly competitive kind of way, all of them striving to entertain each other.

Soaking up the lighthearted warmth and ease Nacho's loved ones enjoyed in each other's company, I knew I'd married the right man and into the right family.

"Do you still want to know the sex of your baby?" our midwife asked through the speaker on the phone, double-checking our previously stated desire, just as Ines walked in the door coming back from an errand.

Nacho and I were together at his parent's apartment in Bucaramanga, and our midwife had just called from Chicago to tell us the results of the amniocentesis I'd had weeks before.

We motioned for Ines to join us as we stood anxiously by the phone.

"First, what are the results of the amnio?" I needed to know immediately.

"The baby is perfect," the midwife assured us. "Nothing showed up on the amniocentesis."

"Oh, thank you, thank you, thank you," Nacho and I exclaimed, sighing with relief and clutching our hearts as Nacho quickly translated the wonderful news into Spanish for his mother.

"So, are you ready for the sex?" the midwife prodded.

I could feel her smile though the phone.

"Yes!" we exclaimed in unison.

"It's a boy! Congratulations! You are having a baby boy!"

We thanked the midwife for her call and hung up as the three of us held each other in a circle—hugging, laughing, crying.

We began an impromptu little bouncing dance as we caressed my belly and sang in jubilation together, "It's a boy, it's a boy. His name is Mateo! Mateo, Mateo, Mateo!"

We had already decided that if we were having a boy, we would name him Mateo based on a dream I had had. Mateo meant "gift of God," which for me was the truest name we could give him.

On Christmas Eve the whole family gathered at El Toboso for the holiday weekend. Before opening gifts and after a delicious meal of seafood and meat paella cooked in a giant round pan by my father-in-law, the family gathered in a large circle.

"This is a longstanding family tradition," Ignacio explained as we sat down. "Before we open gifts, we take the time to acknowledge and have gratitude for all the members of our family."

As Nacho translated for me, my mother-in-law poured a small glass of red wine and began, "I want to thank my husband for his love and devotion to me and to our family. It fills my heart with warmth and gratitude to have my children and their spouses and grandchildren all gathered here in El Toboso. And a special blessing to my son Ignacio, who traveled from Chicago with his lovely new bride, Wendy, and our growing new grandson, Mateo."

With this last statement, everyone let out a cheer; they had not known the sex of the baby until that moment.

"Christmas is a time to celebrate the love of family and to welcome new life and possibility into our lives," Ines continued softly. "I love you all with all my heart, and I am so grateful that you are my family."

When she finished speaking, she took a sip of wine and passed the glass to my father-in-law, who spoke of his love for the family. As Ignacio translated for me, I choked up with emotion.

When it was Nacho's turn, he turned to me and, in English, said, "I love you with all my heart. I am so grateful to have found you, and I can't wait to be a father to Mateo. Thank you for joining me on this journey of life. We will have so many wonderful adventures together."

As he repeated what he had said to me in Spanish for his family, I couldn't hold back my tears. I knew of course that he felt that way, but to hear him declare his love in front of his entire family in this way was too much. I could hardly accept the joy of experiencing so much love.

After Nacho spoke, it was my turn, but I was a sobbing, blathering mess. I touched the glass to my lips without taking a sip and, through my tears, thanked my new family for unconditionally surrounding me with their love, kindness, and support while Nacho translated my words to Spanish. Looking around the room at all their beautiful, kind faces, I realized I was not the only one crying—we were all crying through smiles of love.

The ritual continued, with all the family members, from the oldest to the youngest siblings and all the grandchildren, taking their turn. I had never seen anything like that in my life. I had never seen a family declare their love, respect, admiration, pride, and gratitude for all their family members. I couldn't imagine that ever happening in my family.

In Colombia, a country I barely knew, I finally was being embraced by the family I'd long wished for.

BREAKING THE CYCLE

Just after Nacho and I returned to Illinois from Colombia, my mom was scheduled for bypass heart surgery. Sharon came from Milwaukee to be with her; Nacho and I were both working, so we weren't planning to see Mom until the weekend.

After Dad had called to let me know that Mom's surgery had gone well and that she was recovering, I got another call from Sharon, who I had assumed was at the hospital too.

"Wendy, I need to tell you what happened last night."

"What?" I was confused by her tone, since I knew that Mom was okay. "What do you mean what happened?"

"I was getting ready for bed to get up early to go with Mom and Paul to the hospital, but it was hotter than hell in there, and I couldn't sleep," Sharon said. "I went to check the thermostat, and it was eighty degrees!"

I thought my parents' house was always so hot because they were getting old and had poor circulation. But I also wondered if it hearkened back to when Dad had to live in a barn as an adolescent after being kicked out of his house by his vicious father. Perhaps he'd sworn to himself then that someday he would never be cold again.

"I said to Mom and Paul, 'You guys, it's eighty degrees in here! Can we turn this down?' But Paul blurted out, 'Don't you dare touch that goddamn thermostat!' I said to them, 'But you guys, it's too damn hot in here!'—and Paul jumped up and chased me into the bedroom. He pushed me down onto the bed and held me down. My arms and face are all bruised!"

Heart pounding, I said, "Oh my God, Sharon. I can't believe this is happening. Goddamn it. You're lucky it's just bruises! What happened then?" My hands and legs were shaking uncontrollably with fear.

"I left the house and drove the ninety minutes back to Milwaukee. By then the bruises were bad, so I called the police to press charges. But then Mom called me and pleaded with me to drop the charges."

"We have to do something, Sharon," I said. "We can't just let this slide."

My heart sank. My dream of surrounding my baby with a cohesive, loving family was shattered.

Mom had been at home for a few weeks, recovering from her surgery, when I called.

"Mom, I've been waiting until you were feeling better to talk to you about what happened," I said. "We need to go to family therapy to discuss Paul's violence. After all the years of being careful and cautious and avoiding him but also wanting to heal my relationship with him, I can't believe this happened."

I was living a split life: In a nightmare on one hand, with my family of origin; and in a beautiful dream on the other, with Nacho and my growing baby. I worried about protecting my son from his own grandparents. This was exactly what I'd feared and warned Nacho about—that Paul might become violent again.

Nacho had become a buffer between me and my family, and since Paul hadn't had a violent outburst in years, I thought our family had healed, as much as we could. I'd thought that the violence was in the past. But I was wrong.

I hadn't experienced this kind of violent behavior from Paul since he'd struck me when I was sixteen. In the years after that he had frequently stomped around, acted moody and threatening and being verbally mean, making me hold my breath around him—but this was a new low.

"Okay, Wendy," Mom said. "I'll talk to him. I'll tell him we're going to therapy."

I felt a gnawing angst hearing how weak and depressed she sounded. I wanted to hold her accountable, but I also wanted to protect her. Paul made doing both things impossible.

Sharon found a family therapist in Riverside and made an appointment.

Nacho and I drove from Chicago to Riverside and joined her, my parents, and the therapist in her comfortable office. Mark joined by phone from Indiana.

When Sharon described to the therapist what had happened, the therapist stated the obvious—that domestic abuse and violence were to never be tolerated and was unacceptable.

Suddenly, Dad spoke up: "I won't ever touch anyone in the family again," he said firmly. "It won't ever happen again, and that's that."

And that was the end of family therapy. I don't believe he ever said the words "I'm sorry." According to him, no further discussion was needed. End of story.

But for me it was not the end. This incident had triggered my fear, reopened my wounds, and deepened some desperate need to figure him out and to fix it. I was diagnosed with tachycardia and put on medication to be taken until after the baby was born.

There must be a reason. There must be an answer. I didn't, couldn't, understand why our family wasn't like Nacho's family: unconditionally loving, supportive, and civil. I thought again about Paul's painful childhood. Was it solely that or did something else happen to him that made him so angry and violent?

Although Mom seemed powerless to stop his violent outbursts, she also seemed to be the only person who could save him from himself. She had gotten him to cut down on his drinking, so why couldn't she convince him to go to therapy to get to the bottom of his alcoholism, violent behavior, and anger issues?

But also, I wondered, why did I so desperately want, need, and give so much of my energy trying to keep this family together?

Even all the stress surrounding my family of origin couldn't dampen my excitement about the baby. Ignacio and I eagerly learned all we could about birth by attending a twelve-week Bradley Method birth preparation class.

Eight days before my due date, I awoke at 6:30 a.m. with my womb contracting and my lower back aching. I knew labor had begun with that first contraction.

Trained well from the Bradley class, Nacho began writing down the time and length of all my contractions, and I labored at home in the bathtub until around 2:00 p.m., when the contractions got to "411"—as in, four minutes apart, lasting a minute, for a solid hour.

It was time. We left for the hospital.

Only ninety minutes after arriving at the hospital, after laboring more in water and with Nacho constantly at my side, I gave birth to my darling Mateo. I put him to my breast, skin to skin. He was a beautiful baby, with a head of thick black hair like his father, his papa, and wide open and alert deep blue eyes.

Nacho stroked my hair and looked lovingly into my eyes. "You are amazing. You were so powerful and strong as you birthed Mateo. You're going to be a loving, powerful, and strong mother too. I love you so much!" he cried, rejoicing.

Life couldn't get any better than this. With the love hormone oxytocin coursing through my blood and my heart, my dedicated husband at my side, and my perfect baby in my arms, I had never been happier, more exultant, in my whole life.

For me, the deep love and contentment I derived from caring for Mateo filled in the empty, wounded, sad spaces from my childhood and family. When I met Nacho, I'd felt like a rose that was wilting on the vine, and he revived me with his love. There were many years in LA when I'd felt lonely, off track, unremarkable, and invisible—but with Nacho and Mateo, I was seen. In the light of their adoring eyes, I was my authentic self; they saw deep into my soul.

While I recovered from delivery and learned to breastfeed Mateo, Nacho fed me bites of dinner he'd prepared and held Mateo when I needed to shower. He created lullabies on a handmade flute to calm and uplift our little family. My heart soared as I watched him speak lovingly to Mateo in Spanish as he bathed him, dried him tenderly, and gently rubbed baby lotion on his little legs, arms, and tummy. I knew that somehow there was grace and magic in my choice of husband; a good, solid, and dependable man and the most loving and doting father there ever was.

Marrying Nacho, becoming pregnant, and giving birth to Mateo was what I'd prayed for all those years in the sweat lodge and on my vision quest. I trusted in my prayers. There was a small flame flickering in my heart that was meant only for Nacho, my soulmate, as my friend Dyanna had envisioned. And for years before I'd met Nacho, when meditation helped quiet the chattering, fearful voices, I'd often heard a tiny whisper telling me to have hope, that everything was going to be okay. Perhaps that tiny whisper had been Mateo saying, "Hang on, Momma, we'll be with you soon."

BLACK AND WHITE AND GRAY ALL OVER

In my continued quest for a wholesome, close-knit, Norman Rockwell family, I asked Mark, now a Methodist minister, to participate in Mateo's blessing ceremony.

In the twenty years I'd lived in California, I typically hadn't heard from Mark unless I called him, and many years had gone by where we hadn't spoken at all. But since we'd lived in Chicago, he had come for a few visits. I hoped Mateo's birth would increase the frequency of those visits; I felt that even if he didn't care much for me, he would at least want to be an uncle to my beautiful baby boy. He had married for the first time at fifty and had some step kids now, but no children of his own.

Everyone in my immediate family attended Mateo's blessing ceremony. My family had not all been together since Casey's memorial eleven years prior, so I was especially touched that my niece Jessica and her fiancé made the trip from California and that Casey's high school boyfriend, who now lived in Chicago, also attended.

Before the ceremony began, everyone took turns holding Mateo and commenting on his sweet and alert demeanor.

"He's the happiest baby I've ever seen!"

"I think he's an old soul!"

"He listens to every word I say and talks back to me in baby gibberish!"

But no one was prouder than my dad. In his eyes there was no such thing as blood is thicker than water. Mateo was his grandson, and no one could dispute that.

We chose John Lennon's heartwarming and magical song "Beautiful Boy" to close Mateo's blessing ceremony. As the minister sang, I thought that perhaps the birth of my beautiful boy might be the healing that was needed to bring my family closer.

Since we lived in Chicago, only ninety minutes from my parents' house in Biscoe, Illinois, we often visited them on the weekends. Whenever we arrived, Dad cheerfully greeted us, eager for me to put Mateo into his arms.

"How's my little buddy Mateo been? Did you miss your grandpa?" he'd coo to Mateo as he kissed his little hands.

I barely recognized this man: sweet, tender, loving, and doting. I had never seen him fuss over anyone like this before.

As Mateo grew bigger, Dad loved to play with him, often holding him so that Mateo's little feet could "walk" across the grass. He bought a kiddy pool, and as a toddler, Mateo laughed and laughed when his grandpa poured little buckets of water on his arms. Out on my parents' pontoon boat on the Rock River, Dad made sure that Mateo's life vest was snug and put him on his lap so he could hold on to the large steering wheel and pretend to drive the boat. Mateo also loved the cowboy game: When Grandpa put his little legs into his big adult cowboy boots and placed a grown-up's cowboy hat on Mateo's head, they both howled with glee.

When Mateo was three, Mom told me that Dad's daughter, Teri, who was forty-six, had tracked him down. My understanding was that Dad had not seen his five biological kids since they were five and under, except for the times he'd tried to see them and his ex-wife had called the police.

Dad refused to talk to Teri whenever she called, but Mom encouraged her to keep trying and developed a phone relationship with her.

A few weeks before Mateo turned four in 2000, Mom told me that she'd invited Teri to come to a big cookout with all of Dad's family and Nacho, Mateo, and me on Mother's Day, which was also Dad's mom's birthday. She'd decided not to tell Paul.

The whole family was already gathered when Teri and her husband arrived. As they walked down the long sidewalk toward everyone seated at patio tables, Mom looked up and nonchalantly announced, "Paul, look who it is. It's Teri!"

Dad raised his head from the grill and responded equally casually, "Oh, Teri," as if he had just seen her last week and not forty-three years ago.

Mom introduced Teri and her husband to everyone. It was surreal to watch her shake hands formally with her father, grandmother, aunts, uncles, and cousins. I silently wished her luck in her reunion with her father—my dad.

Three months later, Nacho was offered a great job in Florida, and we picked up and moved.

Life was good in our new city. In Chicago I'd attended birth doula, hypnobirthing, and yoga teacher trainings and written articles for *Mothering Magazine*; now, in Tampa, I completed additional training as a childbirth and breastfeeding educator and carved out a successful cottage industry assisting women and their partners in "the childbearing years."

I had a large following as a doula and teacher of prenatal and mommy-and-baby yoga, childbirth education, breastfeeding, and infant parenting. I also developed my own "Comfort Measures for Labor" workshops. I loved helping women create the very best birth experience possible—a positive beginning for both child and mother to grow from.

I also attended nine months of massage school and quickly added trainings in prenatal massage, hot stone, and Ashiatsu—a barefoot massage technique originated by Buddhist monks. Within months of our move, I started teaching yoga at Mateo's school and at numerous preschools as well as prenatal yoga at a facility for pregnant homeless women. I had deeply studied and contemplated the roots of childhood trauma and wanted to develop resources that would empower families to make informed decisions about their children's births, health, and early years to build a strong foundation for bonding and parenthood.

Meanwhile, we were seeing even more of Mom and Dad since our move, since they lived in Pine Island, Florida, for half of the year.

It was apparent that to Dad, the sun rose and shined on Mateo. I know he truly loved my son. Perhaps he was looking for redemption and a parenting redo—a chance to excel as a grandfather where he'd failed as a father.

I was heartened and delighted to see that side of him, but I still didn't trust him with my child. I couldn't. The fear that had been instilled in me growing up still lived in my bones, and that nagging fight-or-flight fear prevented me from ever taking my eyes off Mateo the entire time his grandpa played with him.

"Get that shit out of here, goddammit!" Dad roared.

A familiar, cold fear gripped me.

We were visiting my parents in Illinois prior to driving together to a family reunion in St. Louis. Six-year-old Mateo was happily watching loud cartoons in the living room; the rest of us—including Gerry, the tenant who lived downstairs—were out on the large sunroom. Ignacio had found some bird feathers in the yard and was sitting at a table, fashioning a miniature bow and arrow for Mateo from the feathers.

Now Paul stood, face red, pointing a shaking finger at my husband.

Looking confused, Nacho asked, "What are you talking about, Paul?"

"You could be bringing goddamn West Nile virus into my goddamn house from those goddamn feathers," Paul roared.

"Actually, Paul, you don't contract West Nile Virus from touching bird feathers," Nacho said matter-of-factly. "You contract it through a mosquito bite."

Nacho had barely finished his sentence when Dad grabbed him around the neck from behind, putting him in a deadly karate headlock.

Realizing he was in a dangerous position; Nacho went limp to protect his neck.

I jumped up, screaming, "Dad, what the hell are you doing? Let Nacho go. Stop it!"

"Paul, Paul, stop it now," Mom said firmly. "Calm down."

Luckily, that was enough for Dad to release him and walk out of the room.

Nacho and I were both frozen, stunned by Paul's attack. My heart pounded as I wondered what the hell had just happened.

Fight or flight kicked in after I saw that Nacho was okay, and I ran to the living room to see if Mateo had witnessed his grandfather attacking his father. Our little boy was, thankfully, blissfully unaware, bouncing on the couch and laughing at the TV.

A volcano of emotions erupted and shook me to my core. I wasn't sure which emotions to feel or in what order: disbelief, anger, sorrow, panic, terror? I was furious but felt gagged, claustrophobic, and trapped. My face and throat burned with the words I wanted to say but couldn't.

It had been five years since Paul had promised in therapy that he would never attack anyone in our family again. But now he had physically assaulted my wonderful and loving husband, his son-in-law.

In shock, I didn't want to believe that this was happening again.

"Come on, sweetie," I said, rousing Mateo from the couch. "Let's go for a walk."

Nacho and I took Mateo down to the river, and while he was distracted by sticks and rocks, we discussed what we should do.

Deep sorrow that this could happen released my tears, shame, and guilt. Crying through my words, I said, "Nacho, honey, I am so sorry. I never dreamed you would be subjected to Paul's violence. This is a nightmare. He promised. Oh my God, not again. What should we do? How do we protect Mateo from all of this?"

My sweet husband wiped away my tears and looked at me. "Do you remember the Spanish saying? *Cuando te casas con alguien, te casas con toda su familia*. When you marry someone, you marry their whole family. You told me what to watch out for years ago. Although no one should have to, I should have been more careful and not let my guard down with him. I also know how much you've endured throughout your life and how badly you've wanted to fix your family. And I know you want Mateo to have grandparents who are physically closer than mine. Let's just take some deep breaths. We'll figure it out together."

Shaking my head, I said, "I'm sorry that both of us are married to this family. This is not your fault or anyone's fault, except for Paul's."

Nacho took a breath and exhaled slowly. "Let's go to the family reunion, and we'll decide what to do next once we get back to Tampa."

I was caught in a horrible cycle of trauma and abuse. The fear of losing my mother since my dad's death when I was seven had kept me stuck: If I wanted to be in relationship with my mom, then Paul/Dad came with the package—my mom would always back him up—and I loved my mom and wanted her in my life. It was an impossible, inescapable dilemma. And to complicate matters, Dad could be so charming, generous, and helpful for long periods of time—until, well, until he wasn't. I wished it was black and white, that he was either all bad or all good, but it was just gray all over.

I felt guilty and responsible—scared, sick, and dirty that I was subjecting my husband and son to these crazy patterns. I knew by now that traumatized children who got the message that they weren't good enough could spend a lifetime trying to prove that they *were* worthy. They stayed quiet; they didn't rock the boat or speak up for themselves. It felt dangerous to express healthy anger when someone crossed their boundaries, because they feared rejection. They constantly worked to prove that they were worthy of love.

All that was true—but what was also true was that I was flat-out terrified of Dad and heartbroken by him.

Back in Tampa, I taught and practiced yoga and meditation and attended a six-week class called "Mindfulness-Based Stress Reduction" to soothe my bruised central nervous system. Reading Zen Master Thich Nhat Hanh's books, I imagined being a white lotus blossom thriving in a muddy pond. Smudging myself with sage, I prayed to be released from the unrelenting waves of fear and anxiety.

I attended a three-day Vipassana Buddhist meditation retreat but struggled to meditate. Closing my eyes was too claustrophobic. I tried to engage in deep yogic breathing, inhaling one and exhaling one, but my breath remained shallow and shaky. Attempting a "progressive relaxation" technique that I taught in my childbirth classes—a practice where you methodically focus on individual body parts, moving from your head to your toes, and consciously relax them—I still couldn't stop trembling.

My brain resisted the silent retreat; it desperately wanted and needed to talk and connect with another human being. Someone who would listen to my dysfunctional family story and tell me I was not alone. I wanted someone to say that my dirty little secret was quite common, and that it was perfectly normal to strive for peace and harmony and connection in one's family. That I was not crazy for wanting to find a way to stay in relationship with them.

Raw and on my last nerve, I cried at the slightest provocation and felt layer upon layer of new grief emerge, bubbling up from what felt like a bottomless pit of sorrow.

"Dad attacking Nacho was the last straw," I told Mom in a quavering voice. "If he can attack Nacho, he might also harm Mateo, and I will do *anything* to protect Mateo. Including keeping him away from his grandparents, if that's what it takes."

Nacho and I had sought the advice of a Buddhist psychotherapist the previous week. Within fifteen minutes of meeting us, he'd said that we should cut all ties with my parents. His advice had put us between an emotional rock and hard place. To cut off Dad would be to lose Mom. Although I knew Mom was a grown woman making her own decisions, I also felt sometimes that he was holding her hostage. But maybe she was a willing hostage?

"Oh, he would never hurt Mateo," Mom scoffed angrily.

"Well, Mom, I never thought that he would hurt Nacho either," I retorted. Gathering my courage, I said, "I'm sorry, but a therapist told us to cut ties with you, which breaks my heart—but I'm scared for my family! I think it would be best if we don't see you for a while."

With that, she hung up on me.

I had never been the subject of Mom's anger before. I tried to call her back, but she wouldn't answer the phone.

I was heartbroken. Now, because of Paul, I was losing my mom, my worst fear. Why couldn't she stand up to her husband—not even for her children and grandchildren?

Why couldn't she protect me?

Yes, my mother was culpable. Yes, she was codependent. But she was also my mom whom I loved deeply. The only person in my family who'd ever consistently shown me love.

My mom who had subjected me to Dad's explosive, violent

rages since I was nine years old was also the loving, kind, affectionate, and generous mother I so cherished.

I was so conflicted. I loved my mom. She was good to me. So I resisted looking at her complicity, her responsibility. Wasn't she a victim too?

My whole life I'd kept forgiving and forgiving and focusing on the good.

Was it time to stop?

A few months later, Dad sent a card to Nacho, a cartoon donkey with a goofy look on his face on the front. Inside it said, "I am a sorry ass." He signed it simply, "Paul."

At six years old, Mateo didn't know anything about his grandpa's violent behavior. We had even managed to protect him from knowing about the horrors of 9/11 that occurred when he was five. We agonized over how to allow our son to see his grandparents and have a relationship with them and simultaneously keep him and us safe.

We decided we would allow some visits—but they would have to be short and sweet and few and far between.

In December, nearly six months after the attack on Nacho, Mom and Paul wanted to see Mateo and bring him a Christmas present. Nacho's sister Mechas was visiting from Colombia, and we decided that they could visit us for the day while she was there. We would be in our own safe home and on our turf.

"Grandma! Grandpa!" Mateo screamed, jumping up and down, when my parents arrived at our front door in Tampa.

Mateo jumped into Dad's arms while Mom repeatedly kissed the back of his head. I burst into tears and hugged them both, elated by the reunion.

"How's my best buddy Mateo been? Did you miss your grandma and grandpa?" Dad asked him—his favorite refrain.

"You betcha I did, Grandpa!" Mateo said eagerly. "I missed you so much!"

Mateo was ecstatic to see his grandparents, who'd brought him a cool four-wheeler to ride around the backyard.

Over the next two days, we opened gifts and enjoyed delicious meals together. Dad taught Mateo how to play chess.

As usual, there was no discussion about the past. We all acted as if nothing had happened; instead of discussing the elephant in the room, we just moved on—which was what being in our family seemed to require and was something that my parents had taught me how to do very well.

MOM

We'd had eight peaceful Thanksgiving visits from my parents in a row.

During that time, we'd moved from Tampa to Denver, and my parents came to us in Colorado every November. Year after year, I recreated Mom's fabulous Thanksgiving dinner spread for everyone. After Dad was diagnosed with diabetes, I proved to him what a good daughter I was by adjusting my pumpkin pie recipe so he could enjoy it—I made them from fresh roasted pumpkin and stevia—and sent them off with an extra pie at the end of the visit each year. Dad continued to teach Mateo new chess tricks, and I think even let him win occasionally. It warmed my heart to see how sweetly he interacted with Mateo; it was a side of him I'd only seen since Mateo was born.

Why didn't he teach me *how to play chess?* I wondered. I was still grieving for the father I never had, and still hoped that Paul would somehow become the father I longed for.

As Mateo got older, Dad taught him all the grandfatherly things, like how to change the oil and a tire on a car. He also played a wonderful game with Mateo every time they visited: He'd hide a large jar of coins (that he'd collected all year for this purpose), and then, just as we sat down to dinner, he'd say, "Cold," and Mateo would light up. We'd all laugh as he moved around the living room and kitchen, getting colder or hotter, searching for the jar of coins.

But all the good times couldn't erase the bad ones. I held my breath with every visit, fearing Dad's mercurial mood. I was unable to control my visceral reactions in his presence. Even when we were having a good time, I had heart palpitations, my stomach knotted, and my hands trembled. After being surprised by his anger so many times in my life, I'd gotten to a point where I could never fully relax around him.

After three days of a pleasant visit for everyone else, Mom and Dad would give us big hugs the night before their departure and then leave the next morning before sunrise. Each time, relieved that there had not been an incident with Dad, I would fall into an emotionally exhausted heap in bed and cry, wishing I understood who the hell my parents were and why they couldn't be something else. I just wanted them both to be reliably loving, supportive, and kind.

I couldn't bear to know who they really were.

Mom was ninety-two that spring when she was hospitalized with congestive heart failure. When she was subsequently unable to graduate to rehab, I had to accept the fact that she was rapidly declining. I steadied myself emotionally for what I knew was coming.

Then, one day, Dad called, and in a sorrowful, trembling voice, said the words I'd feared hearing all my life: "Wendy Beth, you need to come home to say goodbye to your mom."

I'd wanted her to live for as long as possible; I wasn't ready to say goodbye. I had once said to her, "Mom, if you would just give up those McDonald's hamburgers, you could live to be one hundred."

She'd laughed and responded, "Wendy, if I can't have my McDonald's, why would I want to live to be one hundred?"

What I had worried about my whole life was now upon me.

Was I strong enough to bear it?

Mateo, now almost fifteen; my niece, Jessica, now thirty-eight; and I flew to Illinois on the same day. At the hospital, the three of us sat at Mom's bedside, holding her hands and feeding her ice chips and talking to her, while Dad sat on a chair nearby. I wanted to crawl into her hospital bed and hold her.

Most of the time Mom slept and seemed unconscious, but then she would wake up and become quite lucid.

Reminiscing about Mom with Mateo and Jessica, I said, "As far back as I can remember, Mom has had the same hairdresser. She saw her faithfully every Friday afternoon for years to have her hair washed and styled." I paused, trying to remember. "What was her name? It was Scandinavian, I think."

"Oleg," Mom said clearly. "Her name is Oleg."

I was shocked; I hadn't even known she was aware of the conversation. Mom was slipping away, but she wasn't gone yet. I squeezed her hand gently, glad to know she could still hear us.

By lunchtime, Mateo, Jessica, and I were hungry. We had all flown in that morning and had taken the shuttle from Chicago's O'Hare airport into Riverside, so we didn't have a car.

"Grandpa," Jessica said, "can I use your car to go get us some lunch?"

"Well, I'm not hungry, Jessica, but you can use my car," Dad said, and he handed her his keys.

In the last few hours I'd marveled at how Jessica bantered back and forth with Dad, holding her own, like one of the guys at the tavern. But when, after he gave her the keys, she jokingly said, "And I'm going to do some donuts in the parking lot," the tenor of the conversation changed.

"Give me back my goddamn keys," he snapped angrily.

"But Grandpa, I was only joking!" Jessica protested.

"I don't care, goddamnit, give me my goddamn keys," he roared. "And if you want something to eat then I'll take you—and let's go *now*, goddamnit."

My body suddenly had a mind of its own. I had no control as my body shook. My palms sprouted sweat. My heart raced and pounded in my ears. My face burned hot. I was nauseous and held my breath, filled with fear that he might hit one of us.

I wasn't going anywhere with him, and I didn't want Mateo to go either. He was almost fifteen years old and had been told some of his grandfather's history, what to watch out for, and this was the first time he'd witnessed his explosive behavior.

My heart pounded and my voice cracked, as I said, "I'll stay with Mom. Mateo, do you want to stay here with me or go with Jessica and Grandpa?"

Mateo gave me a reassuring look. "I'll go with them," he said. "Be right back, okay?"

I nodded, but when they left the room, I silently sobbed and held Mom's hand. "Mom, oh my God, Mom," I whispered. "Even on your death bed he terrorizes us."

"I'm sorry, Wendy," she weakly responded.

I felt guilty voicing my anger, but I felt I had to speak the truth. I understood that Dad was filled with sorrow that Mom was dying—but then, so were we, and we weren't taking our emotions out on each other. It was implausible to me that he didn't understand his behavior was inappropriate and damaging.

Mom had been on hospice at home for a month when she died. She loved her house on the Rock River, and I was grateful that she was able to spend her last days there. Dad was playing shuffleboard in the sunroom when she peacefully passed in the hospital bed set up by the window in her living room.

I had just finished a busy day with massage clients back in Denver when he called, crying.

He didn't have to say anything. I knew. I had never heard him cry before.

I started crying before he even got the words out. "Your mama's gone, Wendy Beth."

We talked about all her wonderful qualities and sobbed together on the phone for a while, until he said, "I have to go, honey. I'll call you later."

A flash of somatic memories moved through my body. Fifty-five years of touch from a mother who was loving, affectionate, and warm. My heart sank as I realized I would never touch my mom—her soft, delicate skin, her curly hair, or her twitchy "little hand"—again.

"Mommy, oh, Mommy I miss you!" I cried out and started sobbing.

My sobbing was interrupted by a heartening thought: *Thank goodness I captured her adorable giggle.* One recent Christmas, we'd recorded a Hallmark book of *'Twas the Night Before Christmas.* Mom had stumbled on the line "visions of sugar plums" and instead said "visions of Superman," then burst into an uncontrollable giggle. I was comforted by the knowledge that I could listen to the recording over and over again, and it would feel like she was right there with me.

Strangely, however, though I missed my mom, I also felt the weight of heavy dread lift from my heart. Finally, I was relieved of the fear of her dying—the fear I'd carried since I was seven. With her passing, both of us were free.

After Mom died, Dad continued to join us in Denver for every Thanksgiving. I had vowed to myself that if he pulled another violent act, I could finally let him go. I didn't need to appease him or put up with him to have Mom in my life anymore.

The crazy thing was, as soon as Mom died, he started acting like the father I'd always wished he would be.

During one Thanksgiving visit, he and I laughed as we reminisced about Mom and their travels around the world, their tours on motorcycle, and all the travels we did together when I was a kid.

"You remember that time, Wendy Beth, when Mom and I went to Majorca?" he asked me.

"Yes, Dad, but tell me again," I said, because it was one of my favorite stories about Mom and her resourcefulness.

"The airlines had lost our luggage, and they weren't delivering it to the hotel until the next day. We had a big, fancy dinner to attend that night, and Mom didn't have anything to wear. So she took a couple of long white hotel beach towels and made herself a dress. She connected the towels with safety pins, leaving enough room for her arms, and she put a big white flower in her hair. Everyone thought she looked beautiful and elegant."

"Well, she was beautiful and elegant," I said, beaming proudly.

"And then there was the time we were up in Alaska touring around on the Honda Gold Wing. I don't know what happened, but I turned on this curve and the motorcycle just went down and started to slide down a hill. I yelled for Mom to jump out of the way as she slid on her behind in her leather chaps. She jumped right up as I wrangled the motorcycle."

"Wasn't she afraid to get back on the motorcycle after you had crashed?" I asked, but I already knew the answer.

"Nope," he said, wagging his head. "She was a trooper. She was a good ole brave broad, your mom. She jumped right back on and said, 'Let's go!'"

I thought that despite always proclaiming that she lived vicariously through me, Mom had lived her own amazing adventures firsthand.

And as for Dad—it appeared that he was redeeming himself, becoming the dad, father-in-law, and grandfather I had always prayed for.

For the next five wonderful years, anyway.

THE GOOD DAUGHTER

I knew who my dad had voted for in November 2016. I didn't even have to ask. He fit the old white guy profile.

I'd witnessed a lot of noise on social media imploring people to "reach across the aisle, try to understand their point of view." After so many years of good behavior from Dad, I thought it just might be safe to try doing just that.

He arrived on a Monday for Thanksgiving after driving two days from Illinois to Denver. Mateo, now twenty years old and a junior in college, was flying home from NYC that evening.

Dad came downstairs to the kitchen while I was sitting at the counter, reading the latest social media post about the shenanigans of our newly elected president and feeling shell-shocked. It was the videos of misogyny toward women and the degrading and mocking comments about disabled people that made my dad's vote personally painful. Mom with her deformed right hand, her "little hand," might be considered one of the disabled people that Dad's candidate made fun of.

"Dad, what do you think of him making fun of disabled people?" I hesitatingly asked.

"I don't know what you're talking about," he answered gruffly.

"Oh, surely you've seen the video of him making fun of the disabled reporter," I pressed. "And how about his comment about grabbing women's pussies? I'll show you." I moved to open the video, which was trending online.

"Well, he's better than that goddamn n—"

My heart stopped. All the wind went out of me, and my cheeks burned with the fire of disgusted rage. My brain crashed into my body with a frightful exploding impact. I hadn't heard him use that deplorable racial epithet in decades, probably due to Mom telling him to knock it off.

"Please don't say that hateful and repugnant word," I said stiffly. "Not in my home."

"I will because it's true," he shot back. "And if you don't like it, I'll just leave."

With that he marched upstairs and gathered his things while I sat stunned and paralyzed, unsure of what to do, my heart beating so hard I could barely breathe with the pressure against my lungs, the pounding so loud in my ears I thought I might be drowning in my own blood.

Fearful that he might get physically violent but also hoping to save our family holiday, I followed him out to his car. "Please, Dad, can we just calm down?" I pleaded. "It's Thanksgiving. Mateo's coming home tonight. He's so excited to see you," I said, trying to de-escalate the craziness.

"You're all goddamn n— lovers!" he yelled, and then he got in his car and drove away.

I stood in my driveway, shaking and crying and hoping that my Black neighbors—the same neighbors who Dad would usually sit and shoot the breeze with when he visited—hadn't heard his racist rant.

How could I have forgotten that I would always be walking on thin ice with him? How could I have forgotten that although over the last five years he'd acted like a great father, he was still the same person, had not grown, and would never change? I felt ashamed of myself for being naive and blindsided once again. And I was embarrassed that I'd let social media convince me to do something I should have known better not to do.

I hadn't had a panic attack for many years, but I felt the telltale signs coming on: a fear that I wouldn't be able to breathe, that my mouth and throat would shrivel and dry up, that my chest might collapse, and that I might be dying.

I stood alone in my driveway, wondering how this could be happening *again*. Not Dad's behavior, since intellectually I knew that was predictable, but my surprise that it had happened again.

No, it cannot end like this. He was old and sick; I couldn't bear the thought that he might die mad at me.

I tried calling him on his cellphone repeatedly, hoping that he would calm down and come back, but he did not pick up his phone.

I needed to understand: What had kept me trapped in this toxic dynamic my whole life? What kept me hopeful that it would ever be any different?

I felt depressed and ashamed of myself, heartbroken for letting down my guard once again. I needed to understand why I so desperately wanted Paul's love and acceptance. I decided to see a therapist with expertise in trauma.

"Why do I still hope that he will change? That my family dynamics will change? Why do I even want his love? Why do I grovel for scraps of love? What exactly is keeping me hooked in?" I cried, desperate to understand both intellectually and emotionally.

"First of all,"—Marilyn, my new therapist, who had been in practice for over forty years and had extensive training in trauma, spoke softly as she handed me a tissue— "you are not broken. You have not failed. You are not weak. You are not stupid. This is a case of a very primal human need. Humans are meant to be cared for and loved and protected by our tribe. This is how humans survive. You are not wrong to want and need their love." She paused to let that sink in and then continued, "Who did you feel loved by in your tribe?"

That was an easy question to answer. "Really just my mom, I guess. My stepdad could be loving, but then something unpredictable would set him off, and he would explode with rage. My brother was distant and absent, and my sister was angry, jealous, and combative."

She looked at me from behind her square glasses with deep compassion. "And then you were a child when your father died. This is a tremendous trauma for a child. Your first instinct was to care for and protect your mother. A child who loses a parent is understandably terrified that something bad will happen to the surviving parent."

"Yes, it was my greatest fear that she would die too, right up until she did."

"And then your mother chose a man to be her partner and to essentially be your father too. You had no choice in the matter. Unfortunately, your mother chose a man who seems to have mental health issues and alcoholism, yet she turned a blind eye to that and his violence, didn't protect you, and taught you to focus on his good qualities." Marilyn tapped her pencil on her notebook.

"And I knew the message was, 'If I wanted a relationship with my mom then I must accept him too,'" I said, nodding. "And since he was the only father figure I would ever have in my life, I wanted him to be my father. And he wasn't always mean and violent—mostly only when he drank. He could also be charming and fun and adventurous."

Marilyn sat up straight, her blue eyes sharply focused on mine. "Exactly. What happened to you and why you continue to have hope that your relationship with your stepdad will be good again is called intermittent reinforcement. This is one of the most powerful ways that humans are manipulated and shaped. And you've had a whole lifetime of intermittent reinforcement. You had fun adventures with your parents on vacations and on other occasions. Your stepdad could be fun and loving. And then, *blam!* Something sets him off, and you are threatened with violence. But those intermittent good times—vacations, kindnesses—keep you hoping for more of that. Especially in threatening situations, we look for evidence, any small sign of hope, that things will change and improve. And in the last five years, things did improve and seem to change."

"Oh my God. That's the intellectual, psychological part I needed to hear and understand. It's not just that I am stupid or naive or weak or broken." I started to cry harder, now with relief and compassion for myself.

It felt odd, but I was relieved to be reminded that love and protection of family was a basic human need for survival. And it was validating to learn why and how I felt so trapped in wanting and needing the love of my stepdad and my siblings. I wasn't a freak. I was a human.

Marilyn led me through some deep breathing and grounding while I wiped my tears and digested my aha moment and then said, "Wendy, your diagnosis includes anxiety, low-grade depression, and complex PTSD. But there are many tools to help you."

I had heard those diagnoses before, but never dreamed they might pertain to me.

"I don't know what happened to that defiant and courageous girl who drove cross country to California to save her own life. Who was so determined to heal herself, despite her family dysfunction. Now I am so easily startled. Everything frightens me," I cried to Marilyn.

"I think we should try a modality called EMDR, or eye movement desensitization and reprocessing, which is a specialized eye movement technique that helps the brain process traumatic memories," she said. "It has been recognized by the World Health Organization as one of the best treatments for trauma. In addition, I would like to do ImTT, or image transformation therapy, with you, which will also help you to gently process those traumatic memories without having to reexperience the pain and terror."

I was willing to try anything.

Over several sessions, I sat in the leather chair in Marilyn's office, relaying every traumatic experience that had happened to me in my life. As I spoke, I held metal wands in my hands that vibrated left to right, back and forth.

Initially, waves of anxiety clenched my chest and rose in my throat—but slowly, the raw emotion and tears subsided. Everything was the same, the memories were still there, but I felt calmer and more at peace with them. I felt less emotionally triggered by the memories. EMDR helped to take the edge off the intensity of emotions I felt—the sadness and grief.

At home, I practiced another form of EMDR Marilyn had suggested—bilateral music stimulation, a deeply relaxing form of brain healing for stress, trauma, and anxiety—to help myself sleep.

With Marilyn's skillful guidance and expertise, a crack of light beamed into my darkness. I realized that my dad would not change, and I accepted that this was my lot in life. This was my dad, my father, the man who had raised me and was supposed to love me and protect me. This was my beautiful son's grandfather.

It still made me angry, because my son deserved much better and so did Nacho and I, but this was the hand I had been dealt—this was the way things were.

If I was ever going to find peace, I would have to accept what was—exactly what I had learned in my Buddhism studies.

Four months went by. ImTT, EMDR, bilateral music stimulation therapy, yoga, walking, meditation, massage, Buddhist teachings, and CBD drops helped me to move numbly through the day and to perform my daily activities, but I still felt the weight of sadness and dark depression. My last interaction with Dad had ripped open the deep wound of feeling unlovable and unsafe once again.

I wondered if this was when I should really let him go completely. Was this the end of the road for us? After a lifetime of forgiving so that I could have a relationship with Mom, I now felt invested in the lifetime I had spent trying to have a relationship with Dad. He was eighty-five years old, and he had numerous life-threatening health issues; I knew he didn't have a lot of time left on this planet.

"I want him to die not mad at me," I told Marilyn. "And I want my inheritance too."

"There's nothing wrong with that," she assured me. "You deserve it."

I also wanted to see this through to the end because I couldn't shake that desperate, primal need to be loved by the only dad I would ever know. *He doesn't need to be perfect*, I thought. *He just needs to be sane and loving.*

I thought that he could be that father. He had showed me consistently for the previous five years that he could and that he did love me. Every year he sent thoughtful cards for Mateo's birthday, my birthday, Nacho's birthday, and our anniversary, and he signed them "Love, Dad." I cried when I received those cards, and I saved every one of them as proof of his love.

"The cards he sends, the gifts, the acts of kindness, those are perfect examples of intermittent reinforcement," Marilyn pointed out. "That is exactly what keeps you hooked in."

"So intermittent reinforcement has caused me to continue to seek my stepdad's approval and love, and I settled for the occasional compliment, card, gift or 'attagirl!'" I nodded as the facts lined up like a mathematical problem solved, and it all began to make sense.

I had compassion for the little girl inside of me that needed Dad to die not mad at her, to assure her that she was lovable. If I knew that despite everything, he did love me, that would also help me to forgive him. And to know that I was lovable would help to heal my childhood wounds.

I wrote him a letter saying so, telling him that I worried about him and his health, and reminding him that Mom would not want us to be estranged.

Dad called me when he received the letter. "Hey, Wendy Beth, how are you?"

As usual, just like nothing ever happened.

"How is Mateo? How is Nacho? How is the weather?"

We never spoke again of the Thanksgiving incident, and we went back to our easygoing phone relationship.

After Mom died, Dad had asked me to be executor of his will and affairs and told me he was leaving me the house.

"You're going to wish me dead," he'd said then, and laughed.

I'd protested at the time—but he was right. I did wish him dead. Especially after this latest blowup and the reconciliation. I wished to be free of his intermittent explosiveness. I wished to be free of his intermittent reinforcement. I wished to be free of freezing, holding my breath and waiting for the other shoe to drop. I wished to be free of the fear that he would blow up again and reject me. I wished to be free of the anxiety that coursed through my body every time he called or had left a message. I wished to be free of the fear that he might physically attack my family or me. I wished him dead before he ever had an opportunity to be mean or violent toward Mateo.

And I wanted him to die *soon*—while we were still on good terms, and he was acting like the good father I'd once thought he could be.

"I'm struggling with feeling stupid for reconciling with my stepdad," I confided in Marilyn. "I don't want to be the person who keeps going back to their abuser, and I'm terrified of the other shoe falling again, but I also want to be there for him to make sure he has good end-of-life care."

"Let me remind you how normal it is to have a primal, infantile need to be loved and cared for by our parents, even if they are abusive," she said. "Dementia can also affect a person's personality and moods. Many people deal with these issues, especially with abusive aging parents. Culturally and morally, we feel that we should always care for our parents no matter what, that blood is thicker than water and so forth."

"As his medical power of attorney, I keep a record of his medications and speak to his doctors about his ongoing medical issues and needs," I said. "And when the time comes, I will see to it that his 'five wishes,' are met—including his cremation, which he has already paid for. Despite our history, he is my dad who deserves love, and I want to be the good daughter who will make sure he can die with dignity at home on hospice, like my mom."

"You are a very compassionate and good daughter," Marilyn reassured me. "He is lucky to have you as a daughter. Someone else might have given up on him long ago. Please know that and take it to heart." She smiled at me kindly.

I had tried my whole life to diminish my trauma by pointing out others in the world who had it worse off than me. Years ago, I began to accept and honor my pain as I read *Man's Search for Meaning* in which Holocaust survivor Viktor Frankl states that human pain is relative, and each person's suffering is equally significant no matter the cause. More recently Lori Gottlieb addresses the same issue in *Maybe You Should Talk to Someone* by stating that pain is not a contest and that everyone's pain is valid regardless of how it compares to other's pain. And now, with the guidance of a therapist who held a mirror to my pain, I held myself in compassion for all that I had endured: the death of my father at seven; losing my mom to my stepdad at nine; losing my stepdad through alcoholism, mental illness, and abuse; and losing my siblings to family dysfunction. Marilyn also reminded me that the psychological effects of losing a parent during formative years are significant, especially for children who lose a parent before the age of twelve; kids who experience the death of a parent before that age, she told me, were more likely to have depression than those who were older.

Apparently, I was no exception to that rule.

With all this in mind, I forgave myself for wanting my dad to die before he got angry again, which I was able to do because I had finally accepted the truth: There would be a next time.

I studied the results on the screen, brow furrowed with confusion. My biological father, Burt, was German/Dutch, and yet my results showed no German or Dutch roots. Also, I was Scandinavian? To my knowledge, no one on either side of my family was Scandinavian.

A prickly, ugly, and terrifying thought surfaced: *Is my father not my father?*

Nacho and I had taken DNA tests at Christmas, thinking it would be fun for Mateo to learn details of his heritage through his parents. Now, six weeks later, I'd just received my results, and I was perplexed.

Looking at my computer screen, Sharon's voice from forty years prior burst into my mind like a forest fire consuming trees with its fury. *"Well, you're Mr. Lee's daughter anyway!"*

Who was Mr. Lee? Was there any validity to her hurtful statement from forty years earlier?

Of course, Burt is my dad, I told myself. But there must be an explanation for this DNA result.

I hadn't seen Sharon in seven years—not since Mom's memorial—and we spoke only occasionally. But I wanted to know what she knew. I picked up the phone.

When Sharon answered, I didn't bother with warm-up small talk; I launched right in.

"I just received some interesting DNA results," I said. "It appears that either Dad Burt was not German, or Burt was not my father. Looking at the results reminded me of the times you said in anger that I was a Mr. Lee's daughter or the milkman's daughter. Can you tell me who Mr. Lee is?"

Suddenly, Sharon (who often could not remember what she'd had for breakfast) was spilling details about people I never knew existed in a breathless monologue. She reported that Mr. Lee was the father of her St. Louis playmate, Jenny Lee, who'd lived across Sullivan Street from our family. The Lee family had lived down the hall from our maternal grandfather in a two-story brownstone, above a tavern and barbershop that all the neighbors frequented.

When Mom and Dad Burt were building a house thirty miles away in Collinsville, Sharon told me, Mr. Lee brought Jenny to the under-construction house to spend many sleepover weekends on pallets on the newly laid wood floor. Mom and Mr. Lee arranged for Sharon and Jenny to play together, and Mark played with Jenny's younger brother, Terry. Since Mom didn't drive, Mr. Lee would drive Mom and Sharon and Mark back and forth from St. Louis to Collinsville.

"I wondered as an eleven-year-old why Mom was friends with Mr. Lee but not with Mrs. Lee," Sharon mused. "Sitting in the back seat of Mr. Lee's car, I noticed how they looked at each other—how they smiled at each other and flirted. And I wondered why Mr. Lee came to the house while dad was at work. I thought something funny was going on with them."

I sat frozen and stunned as Sharon filled in the details of a family story I had never heard before.

"As you grew into a toddler with your white-blonde towhead hair, I thought you looked like Mr. Lee and Jenny," Sharon went on. "But anyway, it's not fair to Mom to accuse her of anything now, since she's dead and can't speak up for herself. I don't have any proof. It was just a kid's hunch."

By the time Sharon finally took a breath, my mouth was hanging open with shocked disbelief. I didn't trust her, and she'd bad-mouthed Mom all my life, so I didn't know what to believe. I struggled to stay inside my body and feel my feelings.

As I did, anger arose from deep inside my chest.

"I can't believe you are just telling me this!" I said through choking tears and clenched teeth. "These details. These things you've known since you were eleven. I am sixty-two years old and just now learning about this. Did it ever occur to you to tell me this while Mom was alive? Now I can never ask her."

"It was just a hunch," Sharon repeated. "It wasn't my place." I could practically hear her shrugging through the phone.

I hung up the phone and ran to find Nacho to tell him what I had learned from Sharon. He immediately googled Jenny Lee in

St. Louis and found an address and phone number. He wrote them down on a piece of paper, and I posted it on my bulletin board. But I had no idea what to do next.

Over the ensuing months I occasionally stared at Jenny's name on the scrap of paper and asked out loud, "Jenny Lee, are we sisters?"

But I wasn't ready to find out.

In the spring of 2018, a year after a fall that broke his femur, I called my dad after work to check on him.

"Hi, Dad, how are you doing today?"

"Oh, Wendy Beth, I feel awful!"

"What? Why? What's happening?"

"Oh, my stomach is so hard and bloated. I've been constipated for a few weeks, and I've gained about thirty pounds in the last few months," he moaned.

I winced; I could feel his pain through the phone. "Oh my gosh, you never told me this before!" I exclaimed. "You need to see the doctor right away!"

"Well, they said that the first available doctor's appointment was in two months," he said, sounding defeated.

"No, Dad, that is unacceptable! I'm calling the doctor's office right now."

As soon as we hung up, I called his doctor's office, explained what was going on with him, and demanded that he see a doctor right away.

Dad called me back a few hours later and left a message.

"Well, daughter of mine! Daughter of mine! I don't know how you did it, I don't know what you said to them, but I have an appointment tomorrow morning!"

"Daughter of mine." I repeated this phrase over and over to myself, warm all over. His loving words assured me that in his eyes, I really was the "good daughter" I strived to be. But now I recognized that those words were also more intermittent reinforcement.

I also wasn't surprised by the diagnosis he received explaining why his abdomen was so hard and bloated when he went to the doctor the next day: advanced cirrhosis of the liver.

By the fall, Dad was declining rapidly. When he didn't answer his phone, I got updates from his sister Shirley, who lived nearby, and his daughter Teri, who since that first Mother's Day reunion eighteen years earlier had developed a relationship with him and Mom and who now often drove from Wisconsin to check on him.

On his eighty-seventh birthday, Shirley drove to his house to take him out to lunch. She called to tell me that when she arrived, he was sitting on his bed—unresponsive, unable to move. He had soiled himself. Shirley thought he'd had a stroke.

"He kept saying, 'No, no, no,'" Shirley said, crying. "His eyes were open, but he had a blank, ghostly look on his face. It was so scary."

"Shirley, did you call the paramedics?" I ventured.

"Yes, I did, but when they arrived and checked him out, they reported that his vitals were okay. He seemed suddenly fine and answered their questions. They wanted to take him to the hospital, but he refused."

I could hear Gerry, the downstairs tenant, crying in the background. I asked to speak to her.

"Gerry, are you okay? What's going on with you? Why are you crying?"

"I just can't do this anymore," she said, choking on her tears.

Gerry, who was a few years younger than my dad, had been a tenant and friend to my parents for twenty-five years, and since Mom died, she'd often helped Dad with cooking, cleaning, and laundry.

"I came upstairs today to check on him and he was naked, standing next to his bed but not talking. He wouldn't answer me. I can't look after him anymore."

Shirley took the phone back from Gerry. "You *have* to come home *right now*!" she yelled, spewing her anger and resentment at me through the phone. "You need to get home and see for yourself how he is. Gerry can't do this anymore. And I'll tell you what—when he dies, Gerry needs to get something. And I mean money!"

My heart started banging in my ears at the idea of having to go help my uncooperative and combative dad. I didn't know how to explain to Shirley that I had no authority over what Gerry got; Dad had written his own will long ago. And as long as he was lucid, I had no power to help him if he didn't want help. For now, he was still in control.

"Oh," Shirley added, "and by the way, he has a loaded gun next to his bed. He's been so out of it he could shoot and kill someone."

Upon hearing "loaded gun," my fight-flight-freeze kicked in. I was terrified of him even without a loaded gun next to his bed. My chest squeezed as I thought, *I don't ever want to go there again. I can't, I can't.* Just the idea of going there felt debilitating and claustrophobic. I struggled to locate the place in my being that housed agency and autonomy. Anxiety spread throughout my body like spilled ink on paper. I became short of breath and feared that I might stop breathing altogether.

That night I tossed and turned and dripped with sweat, unable to sleep, before finally falling into a fretful, weird, lucid dream state filled with people yelling and physically fighting.

The next few days, I was a nervous wreck. I didn't sleep.

In between my massage clients, I made calls on Dad's behalf and researched symptoms of cirrhosis of the liver. Finally, I found it: He was most likely suffering from hepatic encephalopathy; his body was flooded with toxins that his sick and dying liver could not filter out. Symptoms of hepatic encephalopathy included anxiety, irritability, cognitive impairment, confused thinking and judgement, slurred speech, aggression, somnambulism, and lethargy. All the symptoms he was exhibiting. His already volatile personality and behavior turned up full volume.

I sat in the horror of the reality that my dad was a very sick man with end-stage cirrhosis of the liver resulting in confusion and delusion, while a loaded pistol sat next to his bed. I felt like I was the only adult in the room.

When Nacho came home from work, he found me lying in the middle of the living room floor, mumbling to myself, panting, and trying to regulate my breathing.

"Wendy, what's going on, honey?" he asked as he sat down on the floor next to me and lifted me to sit up. Gently, he took my face into his hands. "Look at me, please. Look me in the eye. Okay now I want you to breathe with me," he gently but firmly instructed me. "Inhale deeply. Good. Now exhale."

As he hugged me tight, the floodgates opened, and I shook and cried and began to shiver.

I won't go to Illinois until Dad is in a coma or dead, I told myself, and that made me feel better.

But I knew that, ultimately, I had no choice but to go and help him.

I was the good daughter, after all.

LAWYERS, GUNS, AND MONEY

I put off flying to Illinois for as long as possible, but in October, a few weeks after Dad's birthday, it became clear that it was time. His condition was dire; it was time for hospice.

When I arrived at the house, he was in the sunroom playing shuffleboard with his son Lance, the youngest of his five bio kids, who'd been a baby when he left. Eleven years after Teri had reunited with their father, after Mom died, Lance had started coming around. A retired nurse's aide, he'd been very helpful with Dad's care in the last few years. He'd also assured me that he had moved all of Dad's guns to the basement before my arrival.

Holding on to the shuffleboard, Dad looked emaciated and weak but was lucid and calm.

He lit up when he saw me. "Oh, hi, Wendy Beth."

I barely recognized him, now so thin and frail. On the verge of tears I announced, "Hi, Dad, I'm happy to see you up and playing shuffleboard. Are you winning?" I winked as I walked over to hug him.

Teri and Lance didn't know much about Dad's affairs, nor did they understand what power of attorney or executor meant. Dad had only wanted to discuss that information with me.

I set to work immediately after getting there. Armed with a three-ring binder filled with all his medical and financial documents, I took him to the doctor, met with hospice and set up his care and comfort, and made sure that all the guns were safely stowed in the basement to protect everyone—especially the hospice nurses who would come to the house to care for him, oftentimes letting themselves in with a lock box. (Lance had indeed moved the rifles to the basement but not the loaded pistol that was still next to his bed when I arrived).

I was so relieved to learn that a hospice nurse would visit twice per week, a volunteer once per week, and a massage therapist once per week. Shirley said she would visit on Sundays. Lance said he would come once a week and stay for a few days at a time. That covered the full week. I also hired Gerry's daughter to clean once a week, relieving Gerry of that responsibility so that she could just come up to visit.

Once all those logistics were taken care of, I went to the grocery store and bought all the necessary ingredients to make my hearty chicken soup that Dad always enjoyed. I wanted to invite Gerry up for dinner as a thank-you for all she had done for my dad.

Teri went with me downstairs to invite her. When we walked into Gerry's apartment, she jumped back, crossed her arms tightly against her chest, and began to cry.

Confused, I said, "Gerry, I made a big pot of soup and want to invite you for dinner."

"I don't know how I feel about that," she haughtily replied.

"What do you mean?" Was she having trouble adjusting to the fact that Dad was dying?

"You don't care about your dad. You hate your dad. I know all about it!" she yelled shrilly, still crying. "You're a horrible daughter!"

I blanched. "What are you talking about, Gerry? I am here getting my dad on hospice and making sure he's taken care of!"

"I don't mean now!" she snapped. "I mean from before. Your mom told me all about it. You hate him."

I was getting angry now. "You don't know what you're talking about!" I shot back. "You only know parts of the story."

"Oh, I know all about it," she spat. "I was there when your dad attacked Nacho, and you yelled at your mom that you would never speak to them again. You know your mom thought about suicide over that, because you wouldn't speak to them? How could you!"

"You bet I told them I wouldn't speak to them!" I cried, incredulous. "He had just attacked my husband. A therapist told me and Nacho that we shouldn't have anything to do with them ever again. But that didn't last. I forgave him yet again, and within six months they came to our house for Christmas." I shook my head, wondering why I felt a need to explain anything to this woman.

Gerry gave me a nasty look. "Oh, yeah right."

I shot a glance in Teri's direction. I'd always been careful not to mention my harrowing childhood with Dad, or any of the more recent events, to her. As far as I knew, she hadn't experienced that side of Dad since she'd reunited with him eighteen years prior, and I didn't want to cause any trouble; she deserved to have whatever kind of relationship she could carve out with him, untainted by my own experiences.

Now, hearing all this, her eyes were wide, and her mouth was hanging open.

"Just get out of here. Get out," Gerry snarled.

I'd heard many stories of how badly humans often behave around a dying person, especially when money, lawyers, and wills are involved; now I was experiencing it firsthand. I took a deep breath and tried to deescalate the conversation.

"I have had only complete gratitude for you, for all you've done for my parents as a tenant and as a friend," I said calmly. "I know you cleaned their house for a reduced rent. And since Mom died, I know you have also been doing my dad's laundry and bringing him some meals. Families can have fights or arguments and then forgive each other. It has nothing to do with today. Today, my dad and I are good. And all I want is for him to die in peace—and Gerry, I really hope that's what you want too."

With that, I marched out the door.

Teri hurriedly followed me out. We stopped on the sidewalk outside, and I burst into tears.

"Why did Gerry talk to you like that? And what? Dad attacked Nacho. When?" Teri was pale with shock.

Exasperated, I broke down. I was tired of protecting him. "You don't know anything about my life, about my childhood and adulthood," I said in a rush. "I wasn't going to tell you anything until he was dead, but I guess Gerry spilled the beans. And what happened with Nacho was only one incident."

She looked at me with such a sad look. "But he loves you, though."

I shook my head in disbelief. "How would you know that?"

"Because every time I visit him, all he does is brag about you the whole time," she said. "He talks all the time about what Wendy is doing, how she built a business, where she is going, on and on. And I always wish if only he would love me half as much as he loves you."

I was stunned. I was heartbroken. The tears fell harder, and Teri started crying too. We fell into each other's arms, sobbing.

"We're the same," I told her through my tears. "We're both wounded women who wished our father loved us. Your father abandoned you, and my father treated me like he hated me."

Sharing with Teri the truth about my dad as a father and how much I had suffered, I felt a great weight lift from my shoulders. I'd always sensed that she envied me my childhood with him since he'd abandoned her and her siblings, five kids all under six years old, so I was relieved for her to know that she hadn't missed out on a fantasy childhood after all.

I had put together a solid plan for my dad's care: He would have a lot of help going forward and could still be independent and comfortable in his own home.

It was time for me to go home.

As I walked out the door and onto the sidewalk, I turned to look at him standing in the doorway, knowing it could be the last time I would see him.

"I love you, Dad," I said, tears welling in my eyes.

He was gaunt and frail, a skeleton of the strong man I knew from my childhood, and there was a pained and achingly resigned expression in his hollow eyes, as if it was suddenly crystal clear to him now how much he might have done differently.

The slump of his shoulders that said there was nothing he could do about it now.

"I love you too," he choked out before I walked to the rental car.

It was only the second time in my life my dad had said those words to me.

NOT FULL SIBLINGS

I was burning with curiosity over whether there was any truth to Sharon's "Mr. Lee" story. Researching online, I found another way to reveal the truth: I could do a sibling DNA test with Sharon. If we were full siblings, that would dispel the Mr. Lee theory and exonerate my mom.

Because I hadn't seen Sharon in seven years—not since Mom's memorial—when she and Jessica expressed a desire to come to Denver for Thanksgiving from California, hesitation growled in the pit of my stomach. But then I agreed, deciding that I could then collect her DNA myself. I called to ask if I could take her DNA sample when she arrived, and to my surprise, she readily agreed.

Unfortunately, my gut fears were realized, and that Thanksgiving was marred by more of her disparaging name-calling: "You're mentally ill. You're passive aggressive. You're rude. You're just like mom," she berated me on the last day of her visit. "Oh, you're a yoga teacher and massage therapist? Well, you have no compassion!"

I admit, after years of her verbal and emotional abuse, I couldn't muster the compassion and empathy I had tried so hard to hold for her, given her many traumas and life challenges. I couldn't respond to her derogatory and hateful lashing out with the skillfulness, patience, or grace that I learned through yoga and meditation. But at least I got her DNA.

When I received the email that the test results were in a week later, my heart caught in my throat.

My hands shook as I logged on to the website. I held my breath and read the results over and over before it finally sank in.

Nacho walked over to me to wrap his arm around my shoulders and confirm that what I was reading was real. At the top of the DNA report were three devastating words: NOT FULL SIBLINGS.

I realized I had been holding my breath; I sucked in air like someone revived from drowning, desperate to give my brain the oxygen it needed to try to comprehend what this meant. *Sharon is not my full sibling. Meaning, then, that Burt was not my father.*

I couldn't grasp the implications. Had Mom really had an affair, as Sharon suspected? Was John Lee my father, or was it another man?

Who am I if I am not my father's daughter?

After receiving the sibling DNA results, I spent days walking around in a daze, mouth slack like a zombie. I stayed in my body, but it was numb and tingling. I thought I must be watching a black-and-white foreign film about someone else's life, in a language I didn't understand.

I tried to forget what I now knew. I imagined turning back the clock to the time before I saw the results. For a fleeting, content moment when I first awoke, as I sifted through the images of my dreams, I really would forget. But then, with a stun gun like ZAP, the truth would invade my consciousness and my body, and my eyes would fill with tears. I could not unsee what I had seen. I could not unknow what I knew. Over and over, the taunting words on the DNA results repeated in my mind: NOT FULL SIBLINGS.

Sharon looked exactly like Burt, the man I'd always thought was my father—her brown eyes and auburn hair, her body type and short legs, even her ears and receding chin. There was no question that she was Burt's daughter. *I* was the one who looked nothing like him; I was the one who was not Burt's daughter.

Was I Mr. Lee's daughter? Or was my bio father another man?

I decided that the only way to find this out was to take another DNA test, this time with Ancestry.com, the company with the largest database of people, who also connect you to DNA matches, which the first genetic test I took did not. I wished I'd used them to begin with.

As I spit into the tube, I wondered how I could contain myself for the next six weeks as I waited to receive the results—and the answer to who I was.

Meanwhile, my dad was steadily declining. In late January, Nacho, Mateo, and I went to Illinois for a few days to say goodbye to him—a visit that proved to be a powerful time of beginning to heal and let go for the three of us.

A few weeks later, back home on February 13, I had an intuition that Dad's death was very near, so I called the house and asked Lance, who was staying with him, to put the phone up to his ear.

Dad had been for the most part unconscious and nonverbal for several days, barely taking sips of water.

I told Dad that Mom was there with him. I described the two of them sitting on the couch holding hands and watching TV, something that they'd done nearly every day for forty-six years together. Then I told him that Nacho, Mateo, and I loved him.

"I love you, Dad," I repeated in case he hadn't heard me.

Weakly but clearly, he said, "I love you too."

I cried as I hung up the phone. This "I love you" before he died was what I had prayed for these many months. Years. I had spent nearly fifty years in self-discovery, in self-healing—through nature and hiking, Buddhist meditation and retreats, Native American ceremony, AA and Nicotine Anonymous, psychotherapy and EMDR, yoga, writing, grief and inner-child-healing workshops. I had managed, despite my wounding, to build a loving, solid marriage, and raise a beautiful, well-adjusted son.

I had made such huge strides in my inner healing that I would have been complete without that final "I love you," but it was a bonus healing gift for me. My inner child wish—just to be loved by both of my parents—had finally come true.

Even so, I was filled with regretful questions. Why couldn't we have had this parent-child love between us, this stability, consistently throughout my life?

Why did his love have to wait for his deathbed?

"Wendy, honey, what's happened now? Is it Paul?"

My loving, supportive husband had come home from work early to take me out for our twenty-fourth Valentine's Day wedding anniversary (one day early, since February 14 was always too busy)—only to find me again on the living room floor in fetal pose, sobbing. He stooped to sit me up.

"I just can't," I cried, the emotions roiling my guts. "It's all too much. I'm overwhelmed with sadness and regret. The only father I've ever known is dying."

"I know, honey." Nacho wiped away my tears. "This is tough. But together, we'll get through this."

"You know, therapy has really helped me to understand why I have had such an urgent need to heal the past with him and to be free of the pain of trauma and rejection," I told him. "But the finality of his impending death is just gripping my heart."

"You know, I'm going to miss him too," Nacho admitted. "The good side of him, that is."

"And that's what makes me feel so crazy!" I wailed. "The conflicted feelings about him, the complicated grief. I feel angry for the pain he inflicted on me and our family my whole life. And then I have feelings of love and tenderness toward him despite the trauma."

"He is absolutely the most complicated person I've ever met.

You loved him as best you could. You've been a good daughter, even to the end." My sweet husband smiled and hugged me.

I was so grateful to have Nacho's compassionate ear as I uncoiled the knot of my grief. "I keep thinking about his 'good side,' like Mom always wanted me to focus on. The wonderful memories of travel and vacations with them when I was a child and adolescent. And he was such a loving caregiver to Mom as she declined. That's the dad I'm going to miss."

Nacho added, "And then he was always a loving and doting grandpa to Mateo. That's the grandpa I'm going to miss too."

We stayed home instead of going out, and Nacho made us a delicious anniversary dinner.

Later that night, just as I was about to shut down my computer, the email from Ancestry.com that I'd been waiting for arrived. The subject line read: YOUR RESULTS.

Holding my breath, I nervously clicked on the link. My eyes and fingers shot to "DNA Matches," and I clicked on the tab. Scrolling through my matches, I saw cousin's names that I recognized from my mom's family—but then I saw people's names I did not know. *Who are these people?*

And then, there it was. There it was! My mouth fell as I saw numerous people with DNA matches to me with the last name "Lee."

I said out loud, "Well *that* explains a *lot*."

Reality was a bucket of ice water over my head. I was a pinball machine, and the truth was a pinball bouncing around in my brain. My body didn't know if it should laugh or cry. It felt absurd, like some bizarre Fellini movie, that at sixty-two years old I was finally finding out who I really was.

February 13, 2019. That date would live forever in me as a day of waking up to truth. My dying dad, with whom I had a deeply complicated relationship, had given me the gift of love and healing by saying those three little words, "I love you." And Ancestry.com had given me the gift of truth, of identity—a limb of my family tree I'd never known existed.

Questions bombarded my stunned brain. *Did Mom know that I was Mr. Lee's daughter? Did she suspect? Did Mr. Lee know? Did Dad Burt know?* Sharon had said that I looked like Jenny and John Lee. With my white-blonde hair, had I been the elephant in the room? *Did Mom share her secret with anyone? Did my dad Paul know?*

Looking up from my computer screen, I looked at my husband loading the dishwasher. "Ignacio," I said urgently.

He stopped what he was doing, stood up straight, and looked at me fully, inquisitively, ready to listen.

"It's true: I am John Lee's daughter," I said—and burst into tears.

A week later, Dad died, and Nacho and I flew to Illinois to begin the grueling, months-long task of taking care of his cremated remains, my parents' house and its contents, and their estate.

Our first task was to go to the bank and go through the safety deposit box. What I really wanted was to find a letter from my mom, telling me about John Lee. Certainly, I thought, she'd planned to at least tell me after she had died.

It was the largest safety deposit box the bank offered. Nacho and I divvied up the stacks of papers and sifted through over fifty years of bank statements, deeds, mortgages, insurance policies, purchases of machinery for their business, titles to numerous cars, RVs, motorcycles, and real estate transactions.

We moved through the stacks meticulously, but there was no letter. There was nothing about John Lee.

Back at the house, I cleaned out my mom's desk. Perhaps she'd left it there, the letter I so wanted to find.

Among the scraps and scraps of paper; bank deposit slips; odd, random ephemera; and notes, I found a piece of my parents' company stationery, folded in thirds. I opened it to find a page of her handwriting. I began to read the words and held my breath as I thought for a moment these were her words, perhaps a poem she'd written.

But reading along, I realized these were not her words, they were the lyrics to a song. A Willie Nelson song. She'd loved Willie Nelson and Rod Stewart. I could tell by her scribble that she'd been listening to the song and quickly jotted down the lyrics that spoke to her. I realized this song summed up her regrets. Perhaps it was Mom's mea culpa, her acknowledgment of the choices she had made in her life. The title of the song is, "Nothing I Can Do About It Now."

Going through Mom's photo albums, I smiled at the hundreds of photos of her and Paul in countries all over the world, often touring on motorcycle. There was one of Mom riding a camel. There they both were, sheepishly smiling and energetically dancing at someone's wedding reception.

While sifting and sorting and pulling grainy images of elaborate dinners in Europe, Asia, and Australia out of yellowed plastic sleeves, I found a one-inch-square scrap of brittle newspaper behind another photo. Mom had written *June 14, 1974*, on the backside. That was right before I'd left home at seventeen for college in California.

It was a notice of filing for divorce. Mom had charged Paul with mental cruelty and sought injunction, alimony, attorney's fees, house, furniture, car, and equitable interest in savings. One time a few years after I'd left home, she'd told me that she had thought of leaving Paul, but I never knew that she had filed for divorce until this moment. I knew how bad living with Paul had been for me, but I didn't know how bad it had been for her.

I sat and bawled my eyes out for Mom. Who did she have to tell her regrets to? Whose shoulder did she have to cry on? Who could she share her secrets and her shame with? Who did she trust to be nonjudgmental? No one. I don't think she had anyone. Perhaps she shared some of her secrets with my stepdad, her true love, despite her one time filing for divorce, but I didn't know that for sure, and I never would. My heart broke for her.

"Mom," I cried out loud. "I love you. It's okay. You're just human. I do hope you loved John Lee. I wish you had felt safe enough to tell me the truth. But it doesn't matter anymore. I'm happy to be here. I'm happy the two of you gave me my life. I forgive your choices. I forgive that you chose Paul to be my dad in our family. I know you loved each other deeply—two wounded souls who comforted each other. I forgive him too. Be at peace. You did your best."

I started to gather the things I wanted to keep. The things I felt so tender toward were strange: their passports, their driver's licenses, the deed to their house, the deed to their business. The things that meant so much to them. The things that summed up two long lives.

Shirley came over to choose something of Dad's as a keepsake. I watched as she, her husband, and Nacho played shuffleboard in the sunroom. My dad had found this seventy-year-old, twenty-two-foot-long Rock Ola Standard shuffleboard in an auction years ago. It was from a bar in Wisconsin that his parents had frequented, and it was certain that they had played on it.

"I just wish this shuffleboard could remain in the family," Shirley lamented, sighing.

It was totally lost on her, apparently, that my decision to keep the shuffleboard and drive it cross country in a U-Haul to my home in Denver *was* "keeping it in the family." Although her brother had raised me since I was nine years old, I was still an outsider to her.

When we had a moment alone, I took the opportunity to ask her the one question on my mind: "Shirley, I have waited fifty-four years to ask someone who might know: What happened to my dad? Why was he so angry? Why was he an alcoholic?"

My mom had only told me that his father was a son of a bitch who beat the shit out of Paul and his mom and had later spent time in an institution. But Shirley had witnessed it; perhaps she'd even been beaten herself, I didn't know. She was younger than my dad, and she might be the one to know details of what had happened.

When I asked her that question, even though her mother and father and my dad were all dead and seventy years had passed since her childhood, her voice quivered as she responded. "We had a terrible childhood. I still have nightmares. My brother Ernie still has nightmares, and I'm sure your dad had nightmares too. It was horrible, so please don't ask." Although she was approaching eighty years old, the unhealed trauma was as raw as if it had happened yesterday.

No details were shared. Nothing illuminating about her and my dad's father's behavior was forthcoming. All I would ever know was that my dad's childhood had been horrible, and that he'd been kicked out of the house as a child and had to live in a freezing barn.

Twenty minutes later, Shirley nonchalantly mentioned that her grown son had purchased a "weighted blanket" for her, for her anxiety, and that sometimes she couldn't wait to go to bed at night to be comforted by that blanket. Then she added, "You know, Wendy, maybe you should get a weighted blanket too."

Looking at Shirley's forlorn face, I recognized how deep the intergenerational trauma ran in her and my dad's family, and how even time, distance, and death couldn't heal those deep childhood wounds.

I was grateful that as a child I had recognized the wounding in my dad and had vowed all those years ago that it would end with me.

Now it was time to focus on my own healing, and eventually I, too, would get a weighted blanket.

Part III

BELONGING

THE TRUTH WILL SET YOU FREE

After my dad's death and learning about my true paternity, I was emotionally raw and fragile. I needed to understand what happened to my family—and to me. It felt like I was a box of puzzle pieces, thrown upside down onto a table; the pieces were there, but I didn't know how to put myself together.

I understood that I was in the grip of not just grief but *complicated* grief. I clung to the words of the beloved Zen Buddhist teacher Thich Nhat Hanh in his book *No Mud, No Lotus*: "The art of happiness is also the art of suffering well." He taught that to suffer less, we must first acknowledge, allow, and embrace our suffering. Only then can we transform suffering into understanding, compassion, and joy for ourselves and others. The beautiful lotus flower, he said, grows out of mud. The practice for not getting stuck in the mud is to sit with our suffering with gentle, loving kindness, and to sit with those emotions that arise with steady, focused mindfulness and breath without trying to push them away.

In the throes of my grief, this simple-sounding practice was harder than it sounded. Sometimes I could only sit for a few minutes before a tsunami of emotions threatened to drown me, and I would jump to my feet. I imagined holding the grieving part of me in the arms of my stronger, wiser self that gently assured the grieving part of me that it was okay, that I had a right to those emotions, and that they could pass through me without hurting me.

Then, like a prayer answered, I found a grief recovery workshop based on a book by John W. James and Russell Friedman, founders of the Grief Recovery Institute.

During that six-week workshop, I found ways to understand that although I couldn't change the past, I could change my current reaction to what happened. That if I took responsibility for even 1 percent of what was incomplete, I could claim some agency and control over what had happened. But if I thought that others had complete and total control—say, by waiting for an apology that would never come—then I might always feel like a victim and be unable to heal that wound.

During and after that workshop, I found so many helpers in my healing journey. I surrounded myself with uplifting and positive messages from many Buddhist teachers, including through the use of the daily meditation app Happier™ (formerly 10 Percent Happier). I took classes online with Insight Meditation Society teachers Jack Kornfield, Joseph Goldstein, and Sharon Salzberg, whose wise and kind words were balms to my nerves and my spirit. "It's okay to feel this," Joseph gently encouraged, giving me permission to acknowledge and accept my strong emotions without judgment. I burst into tears when I heard Sharon say, "Sometimes life just hurts," acknowledging that there are times that all I can do is to accept life's challenges with mindfulness, kindness, and self-compassion. And Jack reinforced these simple but profound words of wisdom with, "Healing is possible. It begins with allowing ourselves to feel what we feel and to be what we are."

I read Donna Jackson Nakazawa's book *Childhood Disrupted* and was astounded to learn about adverse childhood experiences (ACEs)—how stresses, losses, and challenges that children face early on in life become chronic, and that these environmental/psychological experiences impact our biology and can often be traced as the major determiners of our health into adulthood.

The research on ACEs was incredibly affirming and validating. I saw myself in every page—my fear of my mom dying and my hypervigilance, yes, but also my desire to learn and grow and live a fulfilling and productive life are common characteristics of someone affected by ACEs. Many people who have had adverse childhood experiences are more empathetic to others and seek to have more authentic and intimate relationships with others, I learned, as well as to enjoy the simple pleasures of life. In some ways, I realized, trauma—or at least the way I had processed that trauma—might have made me a better person.

As Peter Levine, author of *Waking the Tiger* and *Healing Trauma*, writes: "Trauma is a fact of life. It does not, however, have to be a life sentence."

As I lifted the heavy cardboard cylinder filled with Dad's ashes, I registered how heavy a human body reduced to ashes was.

Four months had passed since I'd learned the truth about my paternity, and during that time I'd been consumed with settling Dad's affairs—holding an estate sale, getting the house ready to be sold. Nacho and I had made numerous trips to Illinois to fix up and clean out the house and meet with the realtor, accountant, insurance broker, and estate attorney. But this was to be our last trip, and I had one last task to complete, per my dad's wishes: to spread his ashes under the tree he'd planted for Mom in their yard, just as we'd done with her ashes.

I hefted up the cylinder, tipped it forward, and poured the ashes into the ground at the base of the tree. As I watched them settle into the soil, I began an impromptu ceremony: "Mom and Dad, you are together now forever. You are a part of nature: the earth, the wind, the sun, the sky. You are freed of all your earthly concerns. You are free to ride your motorcycle together on grand adventures, riding from star to star, all over the universe."

I paused and poured some more ashes, then paused again to wipe cool tears off my cheeks that I hadn't even realized were there.

Then, I started to laugh.

I hadn't planned what I was going to say, but what felt right was to speak to them as if they were sitting on the grass with me: "Hey, guys, I have this fantasy that when we die, we are given a kind of exit interview—you know, like in the movies, when people see their whole lives flash by them. But in my fantasy, the people who should have loved us but instead wounded us learn at their deaths how they could have done better. And then we get to see how we wounded others with our own wounds and how the cycle continues unless someone says, 'Enough of that.' Mom and Dad, I said 'enough of that' a long time ago."

I took a deep breath and gazed at a single blade of dark green grass. "Dad, I hope that in your death you were able to see how you might have done better. How you might have been a better father, not only to me but to all your kids. I hope you had an aha moment and regretted the things you did to hurt so many of us. I know that you loved me despite the trauma you inflicted on me, but it was hard sometimes to love you because of that."

The leaves on the tree, gently flickering in the bright sunlight, caught my attention as I once again pondered the conundrum I had struggled with my whole life: How could I love a person that I was afraid of and couldn't trust?

"Did you really want me to be afraid of you? I'm happy that Mateo was never afraid of you. I think you redeemed yourself at least a little by the way you loved, respected, and treated him. You were a good grandpa to him, and I am so grateful for that." I reflected on the hundreds of canceled checks I'd found in the boxes in the attic—fifty years of contributions to a South Dakota Native American school and numerous other charities. Despite not liking to be separated from his money, Dad could be very generous.

Touching the intricate design of the bark on the tree that I imagined my mom was now a part of, I looked at the house on the Rock River, with all the memories it contained, and thought about what to say next. Mom had never spoken to me about her relationship with Dad Burt, except when I'd asked her specific questions.

Recently, Mark and Sharon had told me that they thought Burt had loved Mom, but Mom hadn't loved him. Now I just wanted to ask her everything about John Lee.

"Mom, I hope and believe that you loved John Lee and that is how he became my bio father. I wish you would have told me the truth. I know you had your reasons for not telling me. Perhaps you both agreed it would be better for everyone to not know the truth, but for me it was not better. Why didn't you leave me a letter explaining your relationship, your reasons for not telling me . . . anything, really? On your deathbed, you told me you were sorry. I thought then that it was for my traumatic childhood, but maybe you were saying sorry for not telling me the truth about John Lee too." I laughed through my tears. "But guess what, Mom? Your tenacious daughter went and found out the truth. There were whispers in my soul my whole life, a nagging voice about pieces not quite fitting, about me not quite fitting in, and then a louder and louder voice that pushed me to finally seek the truth and find the answers that became a doorway to healing. But now I need your help. I need to find Jenny Lee. I want to meet my sister and to see a photo of my dad."

I sat thinking about what to say next. The beautiful Portuguese word *saudade*, which I felt described me perfectly, came to mind. It means a vague, melancholic longing for something that does not and may never exist. That was how I felt about my family of origin. Intuitively, I'd always known there were missing puzzle pieces in my family, in myself; I'd felt it in my heart and blood and bones. I'd seen it in the mirror.

I gazed up at the crystalline, cerulean-blue sky filled with peaceful, fluffy, cotton ball clouds that were perched like bystanders, witnessing my speech. I wanted so much for Mom and Dad to be alive again, just for a moment, so that we could speak heart-to-heart, honestly, with each other.

"Mom and Dad, I'm sorry that we couldn't talk openly to each other when you were alive. It breaks my heart. All I wanted from both of you was honesty and authenticity and to feel safe with you.

Perhaps then we might have been able to heal your wounds so that you wouldn't have inflicted your wounds on others. But you are free now. Be at peace. Rest."

I patted down the ashes around the base of the tree and brushed the ash dust onto my heart.

"I need to go now. I'll talk to you later. We must get this beloved shuffleboard to Colorado." I laughed—and then started to cry again. But I managed to finish with, "I forgive you both. I love you both. I promise when I've healed more, I'll remember and focus on the good times and the love we shared, especially our travels on vacations. Thank you both for all the good things you did. Mom, your orchestrating Paul being reunited with his bio kids after forty years was one of the most generous and big-hearted things you ever did. Bless you forever for that."

Just then a perky, red-chested robin landed in the tree, and I felt it was a signal that the ceremony was complete. I felt sorrow in leaving them there, but I still had some of Dad's, Mom's, and my niece Casey's ashes to spread in Colorado, where they would always be close to me.

I climbed into the passenger seat of the cab of the U-Haul and Nacho hugged me. We both took one long last look at the home on the Rock River that had meant everything to my parents—the house where they had both died, peacefully and in the same spot in the living room—and slowly drove away.

I was filled with *saudade* leaving the place where I grew up, knowing I would never return.

"Hi, Wendy! I received your letter on Ancestry.com. I'll talk with my family this weekend. And I hope to hear from Jenny soon. She'll be happy to learn this news. Looking at the photo you sent, I'll say your son looks very similar to some young Lee men. At least to me. Talk soon!"

Once we were back in Colorado and installed the shuffleboard safely in the basement, I had emailed my bio father's family tree contact on Ancestry.com, who turned out to be my great-niece, Marissa. I explained how I was connected to the family, and she was immediately accepting, warm, and welcoming and said that she would contact my sister, Jenny.

Marissa was young, Mateo's age, so she only knew some basic details of the family, but she allowed me access to her Ancestry.com family tree and confirmed what I had uncovered through my own research: that my bio father and his wife had already passed. She also shared that all my half siblings, except for Jenny, had already died.

I felt like an intruder—like a stalker watching a family who were strangers to me—but on the other hand, I felt an urgent need to know them.

"Aunt Jenny will outlive all of us," Marissa reassured me, but since Jenny was the only surviving sibling and fifteen years older than me, I worried about her health. I had spent my whole life not knowing she existed. What if she died before I got the chance to meet her? I had to make it happen as soon as possible.

Thinking about her and wondering what she might think of me was agonizing. My fear was that she might wish I would just go away.

I took deep inhales and exhales to soothe my ragged breathing as the thought occurred to me that I might never know anyone from my bio father's family. I willed myself to push away that painful and disheartening thought.

I looked on Ancestry.com at the names of these strangers that I was blood-related to and wondered who they were and how we might be alike. What characteristics did we share? Would they like me? All I wanted was to meet my sister and to see a photo of my bio father and see myself in their faces.

As months passed and I didn't hear from Jenny, I often scoured the family tree connections on Ancestry.com. Sometimes, I would suddenly stop and berate myself. *Wendy, what did you expect? Did you really think that Jenny and the rest of the Lee family would immediately respond with, "Oh my God, we have a long-lost sister and relative! When can we meet you?" Maybe this was a mistake.*

Although I had done many things to heal my past traumas, the revelation of my paternity was another unexpected trauma and layer of shock that I had not expected. As time passed, my desperate need to meet my bio father's family only grew stronger. I was convinced that if I met them and looked into their eyes, it would give me the closure I needed. Despite having the most wonderful husband and son, I still felt the sadness bubble up whenever I saw close, loving families or I thought of my parents, my siblings, and the Lee family I did not know.

But what if they didn't want to know me?

Even as I wondered about the family members I'd never met, I continued to wonder about the family I did know. Sharon had often said negative things about Mom, so I knew where she stood with her. But I did not know where Mark stood. I had always thought that it was Paul who drove him from our family. Was that the case?

As I pondered this, our visit to Dixon State Mental Hospital when I was seven crossed my mind. I wrote an email to Mark, asking if he remembered why we'd gone.

His email response was almost entirely in caps and bold.

"Why not drop your seven-year-old daughter off to be cared for by the Walking Dead? You want to know why we went there? Because mother was the queen of the inappropriate. And it was deliberate. Sorry. You did not know my mother."

He went on to say that he thought she was mentally ill. He thought she expected it to be a disturbing experience for us. He said that she'd humiliated him his entire life, and that was why he'd left and stayed away. He laid out his experience with a mother I had never witnessed. I had no idea who he was talking about.

I remembered back to the last time I had spoken to him on the phone years before. I had once again been the one to reach out to maintain a connection. His wife had answered the phone, and we chatted pleasantly for a moment before she handed the phone to Mark. Instead of saying, "Hello, nice to hear from you," I could feel his irritation through the phone as he angrily barked, "Yeah?" as if I was bothering him. At the time, it felt like the nail in the coffin of my attempts to claim his as my brother, but now with his vulnerable admission, I only felt sadness and compassion and forgiveness for him. A tiny window seemed to open between our hearts, and I felt closer to him in that moment than I ever had.

I told him I was very sorry to hear his story, and sorry that our family was so dysfunctional. It was painful to hear how he had been treated and how he'd felt in the family.

After taking in what he'd said, I gazed out the window and cried for my family. For all of us. It was heartbreaking to think that my mom had treated him that way—that our family had been so damaged even before Paul came along.

For so long, I had obsessively sought answers for what happened to my family. Now that I was finding out, I felt I was living proof of what Joe Klaas wrote in his book *The Twelve Steps to Happiness*: "The truth will set you free, but first it's going to piss you off."

LITTLE SISSY

As the months went by and I didn't hear from Jenny, I became more distraught that I might never know my half-sister. When I checked in with Marissa each month, she told me that she had left messages for Jenny but had not heard back from her. I wondered if she was trying to stall or to let me down easy—perhaps she knew that Jenny didn't want to hear from me. And I felt that I shouldn't ask her directly for Jenny's phone number; the one Nacho had found had been disconnected, and I wanted to be respectful of privacy and to not be pushy or overstep boundaries.

The internal emotional pressure of needing to meet Jenny intensified every day. I sat on my couch, tearfully watching episodes of *Long-Lost Family* and *Finding Your Roots*, wondering who I was and who my ancestors were.

Finally, I couldn't take another month going by. I asked a writing teacher of mine who had been a private investigator if she could find Jenny.

Within twenty-four hours, she'd located Jenny's correct contact information.

The next day I emailed and snail mailed a letter to Jenny explaining who I was, the DNA results, what Sharon had told me, and a photo of myself with Nacho and Mateo.

"Please know up front that I don't want anything except to meet you and to have a photo of your dad, John Lee, my bio father,"

I wrote. "I am sorry if this information is hurtful or painful to you. I have gone through many feelings and emotions over the past eleven months since learning my true paternity. I am sure that you will too. But I have decided that my mom and your dad were human, and that you and I are not responsible for their choices and actions. We both have a half-sister in the world that we never knew existed. I am almost sixty-four, and you must be in your late seventies. I'd like to meet you while we are young (☺). Once you have had an opportunity to absorb this news, I hope that you will want to meet me. I really want to know you."

I received Jenny's phone call the next day.

"Hello," she said. "This is Jenny Lee. I got your email."

I burst out crying with relief. She confirmed everything I knew and apologized for not returning Marissa's phone calls. Her husband had been very ill and hospitalized numerous times over the months.

"Of course," she said, "I remember your mom, dad, Sharon, and Mark." Her distinct memories flooded into the present. "I remember how pretty and sweet your mom was and that she made excellent coleslaw. She always wore the cutest short shorts, and she had those long legs. But I also remember that she always seemed lost in thought. As a child, I played with Sharon on Sullivan Street in St. Louis and at the new house your parents were building in Collinsville. I even remember your mom being pregnant with you. One time, Daddy asked me if I wanted to go visit the new baby. You were about nine months old, dressed in an adorable little pink corduroy jumpsuit and standing barefoot in your crib, holding on to the railing and bouncing and laughing."

The details of what she remembered were at once enlightening, overwhelming, and a balm for my soul. It was all true. I was the product of Mom and John Lee. And he'd known that I was his baby.

Jenny was happy to tell me all about my bio father—and what a joy it was to hear about him finally!

"He was a kind and gentle man," Jenny said. "He was a soft-spoken southern man from North Carolina. He had dignity and class. Later in life he was an entrepreneur who owned properties, fixed them up, and rented them out. And despite a limited education, he watched the evening news and read the newspaper and studied finance and the stock market."

I could just see him through her words, sitting in his chair and reading the paper.

"He loved the St. Louis Cardinals baseball team," she went on.

"Oh my gosh, so did my mom," I exclaimed, visualizing them bonding over their team. "Was he religious?" I ventured curiously.

"He didn't go to church, but he was spiritual. He was a man of few words, but the words he spoke were true and honest and meaningful. He had fabulous southern aphorisms for every situation. With his sweet North Carolina drawl, he delivered pearls of wisdom that usually began with 'honey' or 'sugar.' Whenever I complained and compared myself to someone else, he'd say, 'Now, sugar, the sun doesn't shine on the same pigs behind every day.'"

I laughed out loud. "Oh, I love him already."

"You know," Jenny said, "the photo you sent reminds me of myself, and you have daddy's chin."

To hear that I had my bio father's chin took my breath away and confirmed for me that I was part of him.

"I wish you could have known him, little sissy," she said. "He would have enriched your life."

With that, my eyes burst with tears and emotion filled my lungs—not only to hear that my bio father would have enriched my life but also because she was calling me her "little sissy." I had never been called "sissy" before; it felt like she had bestowed upon me an honored title.

We compared our traits and found so many we share. We both love to learn and read, think deeply, and meditate. We both love inspirational quotes and human-interest stories. We are empaths who need time alone to revitalize ourselves. Like our father, neither of us goes to church, but we both still consider ourselves connected to a higher power, a higher wisdom. We sort things out in a candlelit bath and talk to dead people. We inherited our paternal grandmother's short legs, have blue-green eyes, and had been towheaded little kids. We have crazy cowlicks on our hairlines and at the crown of our heads. We've been known to accidentally wear articles of clothing inside out and backward. One of us has even left the house with two different shoes on.

What is remarkable, what is the miracle, is that Jenny immediately fell in love with me. The whole thing could have gone completely sideways, and I was prepared for that. But she had no animosity toward my mom or her dad—our dad. She acknowledged and accepted that my mom and our dad were human. She called him Daddy, and started correcting herself to refer to him as "our daddy," which was exceptionally loving and kind and generous of Jenny, even though he would never be my daddy. My daddy died when I was seven, and even with this heartbreaking revelation, he would always be my daddy who died when I was seven.

John Lee would always be the phantom father whose unknown love I longed for, who I occasionally glimpsed the presence of just out of the corner of my eye like a ghost, who never gave me his name but gave me life itself.

Jenny confirmed that her parents and other siblings had died years before (Jenny being the only member of her family who did not smoke and drink) and said that she felt sad and alone to be the last one left in her family. But she had long had a feeling, an intuition, that something wonderful was going to happen for her. That there was another chapter to be revealed. She hadn't known what that chapter was before, but now she knew.

It was me. I was the something wonderful she had been expecting.

Jenny and I spoke on the phone at least two times per week. I was crushed when the COVID-19 pandemic broke in March 2020, a mere month before I had planned to visit her in St. Louis, but in the meantime, we settled for phone calls.

We both felt an urgency to know each other and spoke for hours at a time, trying to fill in the years, the lifetime of connection we'd been denied, as if we could stop the clock and reclaim the past we'd missed together.

"I get so excited talking to you. I'm completely twitterpated," Jenny exclaimed during one call.

"What is that?" I asked, laughing.

"And then I forget to breath and bubble gush all over the place," she added.

"Sissy, I don't know what those words mean!" I howled with laughter.

"Oh, sissy, haven't you seen Bambi and Thumper?"

I had not, but promised I would watch the old Disney movie soon, knowing how much she loved all things Disney.

"In my prayers at night I thank God for letting me have my sissy in this lifetime," she told me. "I wish I could have come into your life sooner. I would have loved you how you deserved to be loved, and taken care of you and protected you."

Like the day when I heard Nacho's family acknowledge their love for each other that very first Christmas I spent with them, Jenny's words were a balm to all my healing wounds. But when she continued, it was almost unbearable to hear her kind words and praise of me.

"You are God's diamond," she said tenderly. "You are beautiful. You are precious and unbreakable. I am so delighted to have you in my life. You are part of who I am. We are part of each other."

Both of us had lived our whole lives feeling there was a mysterious hole in our hearts, shaped like a "something is missing" feeling—and that hole had been immediately filled in with the outline of each other's love.

After about six weeks of twice-weekly phone calls with Jenny and feeling so elated by her acceptance and love, I found a letter from Sharon in my mailbox.

With a wince, I wiped down the letter with a valuable and coveted antibacterial wipe. Information about the virus was so new that we were still wiping down our groceries and mail. This act felt so weird, so odd, and I wondered if the ink would run, but it didn't.

I hadn't spoken to or communicated with my sister for almost a year and a half—not since that sad and horrible Thanksgiving in 2018 where she'd berated me to the point of my having a panic attack. Now, shaking with anticipation, I felt hopeful that the letter was an attempt at reconciliation and an apology for her name-calling, hostility, and disparaging comments about my character and mental health.

Nacho sat with me while I read the letter out loud to him.

The first paragraph of my sister's letter seemed hopeful. She said that she had been reflecting on "our childhood" and her relationship with me and our mom (I thought it a bit strange that she wrote "our childhood," since she was twelve years older than me and her childhood had a completely different set of circumstances, including being raised by a different father and, as I was learning, a different mother). She referred to "her relationship" with me and Mom as if Mom and I were the same person.

As the letter went on, my sister's language became increasingly caustic, accusatory, and hostile—more of the same shaming, blaming, finger-pointing, venomous words that I had endured for the past forty years. First, the same old "you're mentally ill," "you're passive-aggressive," and "you're just like Mom, you think you're so perfect" and "you always wanted Mom to love you more" tropes; then, flat-out bizarre accusations. She accused me of trying to come between her and Casey in the years before Casey's death (although I'd lived in California in those pre-Internet and long-distance phone charges days and had been busy living my own life); she accused me of forgiving my dad before his death only for my inheritance; she accused me of not wanting to continue a relationship with her and Jessica "because we have nothing of financial value to offer you"; and she even went so far as to absurdly blame me for some crazy and deplorable things my dad had done . . . The list went on.

What I knew for certain about Sharon was that she could say hateful things in a fit of anger, reminding me of the proverb "the tongue is sharper than the sword" but then try to soften it later. But this was a letter; she'd taken her time, she'd chosen her words carefully, she'd spent hours, maybe days, writing it. She was showing me with her own words the truth of her character and her feelings.

Nacho put his arms around me. "Maybe you should put the letter down and take a break."

"No," I said, my voice trembling. "I just want to finish this so it's over. She's telling me how she really feels about me. And I need to finally believe her."

Sharon finished with, "I hope you will not expect an apology for a family upheaval brought on by yourself."

Once again, she was blaming me for everything—her little sister, the "pretty baby" she couldn't stand.

I shook through the entire reading but near the end of the letter the shaking became uncontrollable. Sharon's final words were the tipping point to a full-on panic attack. I had never had one like this before. I had to put the letter down and hold on to the counter to breathe.

Nacho squeezed me tighter and murmured, "Look at me, breathe"—but it was too late. Although it was seventy-four degrees in the house, I felt like someone had stuck me on a snowbank, naked, in below-zero weather. I was shivering so hard that my teeth started chattering.

Nacho grabbed two blankets to wrap around me. I was so cold that I couldn't speak without my jaw bouncing and my teeth crashing into each other with each word.

Finally, wrapped in the comforting blankets and soothed by my husband's sweet embrace, I began to warm up. As I did, I broke down in tears.

After a few minutes, the crying gave way to long, heaving, grief-filled sobs.

"Why does she hate me?" I asked Nacho pleadingly. "Why does she say such hateful and mean-spirited things to me? What the hell did I ever do to her except be born?"

He just held me, letting me get it all out.

That letter was devastating. But after the rage and grief subsided, in a way I was grateful Sharon had sent it. The truth was that it wasn't just my dad to whom I felt I needed to prove my lovability to, but I had also tried my whole life to prove it to my sister. One time I had wanted to give her an opportunity to apologize for her disparaging name calling, suggesting that perhaps her anger was misdirected at me. No, she said, her anger was placed exactly where she meant it to be. And instead of apologizing she took every opportunity to look for proof that I was a horrible person. As painful as it was to read that letter, it got me to where I needed to be—finally able to accept who Sharon was and what our relationship was. The two of us were not loving sisters. We never had been, and we never would be.

After all these years, I could finally let go of that dream.

"I couldn't be happier to have you as my sissy," Jenny said to me during our next call. "I am so blessed. I thank God every day to have you in my life."

My feelings of not being loved by my other siblings melted away a little more with each phone call with Jenny. The agony of wondering what it would be like to belong to a close-knit, loving family began to soften. Jenny described the family she grew up in as well as their personalities and quirks. And although she loved all her siblings, she said, she felt a special bond with me: We had an immediate spiritual closeness and authenticity with one another.

"I could never in a million years say or do anything to hurt you," she told me. "I just want you to be happy and safe. I know your husband and son adore you. You're my three peas in a pod. The love you have for each other just radiates."

The wounded and broken places in my being that had wondered my whole life what it might have been like to have a sibling who cared for, protected, doted on, and loved me unconditionally began to glue themselves together in the face of her precious love. Like the Japanese art of *kintsugi*, where broken objects are repaired by filling the broken places with gold lacquer, she stitched me back together with her golden words and love.

"You deserve to be loved, cherished, appreciated, validated, and respected. You are beautiful inside and out." Although she had begun confiding in me about her own human flaws, fears, and challenges, Jenny's words soothed me as if she was a bodhisattva, the Buddhist name for a person who has evolved enough that they could reach nirvana or freedom from suffering, but who chooses to stay in human form out of compassion to help suffering human beings.

I wrote down each beautiful sentiment Jenny shared with me and read those words repeatedly, absorbing them into my being so that I could believe and accept what I was hearing. She was my sibling dream come true. I felt the ball and chain of feeling unloved loosen from around my heart and watched the metal pieces fall away. I felt myself lighten and become a person who knew the love of a sibling. I felt myself changing, gradually shedding the weighty armor that had surrounded me my entire life—armor that had attempted to protect me from the pain of feeling unloved by my family.

That armor had served a very important protective function. Now, however, I hoped I didn't need it anymore. Since I had been shaped to expect rejection and abandonment from my family, a tiny protective voice still whispered the fearful thought that Jenny might do the same. But as I absorbed her loving words into my heart, I decided that even if for any reason I never spoke to her again, she had already provided the healing I needed.

In August 2020, in the middle of a worldwide pandemic and pre-vaccine, Nacho, Mateo, and I drove twelve hours to St. Louis to meet Jenny and spend a few days with her. Once we took COVID tests and our temperatures, we drove to the St. Louis Botanic Garden, where we could spend time together outdoors and mask-free.

Jenny and I held hands as we walked and barely took our eyes off each other. I marveled at how I could feel so connected to a stranger I had only gotten to know over the phone the last six months.

She, of course, had already fallen in love with Nacho and Mateo before ever meeting them.

My intuitive sissy, Jenny, like our deep-thinking and perceptive daddy, also had several beautiful and philosophical aphorisms and metaphors. As she took Mateo's arm and gazed into his brown eyes that day, she said, "You know, we are all just a thread in the tapestry of life. But I do believe that my nephew Mateo is one of the golden threads."

We bubble gushed and twitterpated our way through the rest of our time together.

As we drove the twelve hours back home to Denver from St. Louis, I gazed across the endless flat miles of golden grain, vacillating between happiness that I'd learned the truth and found Jenny and a surreal, disembodied, existential experience. I silently repeated the facts of this new reality: This was my true story. I had painstakingly and tenaciously searched for the buried secrets that refused to stay buried. I'd patiently unearthed them and held them to the light, and then I'd held them to my heart.

I imagined growing up in a home where the father used sweet southern aphorisms to instruct his children on how to be better humans—phrases like "When they go low, we go high" and "You know, sugar, a fish wouldn't get caught if it kept its mouth closed." In my magical thinking, Jenny's father sounded like the one I'd always wished I'd had. How I'd always yearned for the doting, soft-spoken, gentle, supportive father she described.

"I wish you would have known him," Jenny had said to me more than once. "He would have enriched your life." And she would have been that doting, loving sissy who would have played games with me, read to me, taught me things, curled my hair, and painted my nails. I mourned what I felt I'd lost—or, more accurately, never had. Again, that *saudade* feeling of missing something that never was.

But I also realized that I would not be who I am had it been any other way, and I am grateful for who I've become.

That gratitude balances the *saudade* sadness—gratitude for who I am, what I have made with my life, gratitude to know the truth of my paternity, to know who my ancestors are, and that I now have a sissy named Jenny, who loves me deeply.

Like my bio father and my sissy, I, too, like aphorisms: Better late than never. Glass half full.

EPILOGUE

As I poured my stepdad's ashes into the ground around the tree to join Mom's, I spoke to them about my fantasy of having an "exit interview" when we die—a chance to see what we might have done better. But now I wonder if this "exit interview" isn't really a task for the living. To pass the human test, to get the promotion, must we strive to forgive both the living and the dead for their earthly human transgressions? Do we have to consider that they really did the best they could with the resources they had, even though their best was sometimes not good enough?

Maybe they were ignorant and didn't know better. Maybe they only knew how to lash out like a wounded animal. Maybe they were mentally ill or had a drug or alcohol addiction. And so, for those reasons, perhaps it is necessary to try to find a little compassion for them and forgive them.

Because, you see, forgiveness is for the living. It's necessary so that we can go on and live our lives. Forgiveness is for the forgiver, not the transgressor.

But forgiveness is not a single act. You may forgive and think that you are complete, but then another surprising layer of hurt and pain bubbles to the surface, and you must forgive again, and again, and again as you tend to your own wounds. Forgiveness is a practice like meditation, yoga, prayer, or playing a musical instrument: Each time we practice, we strengthen and elevate our own body, mind, and spirit.

As Buddhist teacher and psychotherapist Jack Kornfield explains, "Forgiveness is fundamentally for our own sake, for our own mental health. It is a way to let go of the pain we carry." According to Buddhist psychology, forgiveness is a way to end suffering and to bring dignity and harmony to our life. We must also forgive ourselves for any role we may have knowingly or unknowingly played by staying too long in an abusive relationship, or waiting for an apology that will never come for example, and acknowledging that we may have hurt and betrayed others just as we have been harmed by them.

I forgive myself, and I hope others have forgiven me as well.

Forgiving to free yourself is illustrated by the story of two ex-prisoners of war:

"Have you forgiven your captors yet?" the first man asks.

"No, never," the second man says.

"Well then," the first man replies, "they still have you in prison."

I still believe that everyone has the right to forgive on their own terms and time, or not to forgive at all. Some things may in fact be unforgivable. But if you are able to forgive, you will give yourself the gift of peace and freedom.

Forgiveness does not condone the actions of others, nor do we have to forget what occurred in order to forgive. Forgiveness does not necessarily mean reconciliation either. As a wise person once said, "I may forgive someone, but that doesn't mean I want to have lunch with them."

The weight of my family trauma has lifted. Many secrets were uncovered and traumas exposed. Although this was initially shocking and life-changing, I rest easier now in the truth. My lungs are more expansive. I'm more aware when I hold my breath, and I can breathe more deeply. I can exhale longer, let go, and send peace and compassion to all the members of my family with the loving-kindness meditation I practice. All of them wounded. All of them filled with shame and secrets and painful memories. The suffocating darkness, heavy sadness, and grief that followed me and filled my psyche my whole life has now given way to a lightness I never knew before. I see more clearly. I loved them all the best I could, the best they'd let me.

I can forgive them, but that doesn't mean I want to have lunch with them.

Most of my life I wondered if people could see that I was damaged goods—felt that I must be, since most of the members of my own family had rejected me. Now I hold close to my heart the twelve step mantra "one day at a time," and to the Buddhist mindfulness practice of one breath, one moment at a time as I strive to bear witness, embrace, and accept both "the beauty and the terror" of my life as the poet Rilke gently beckons us to do. Now I meditate on my own goodness and value, filling myself with loving-kindness affirmations: "May I be safe. May I be healthy. May I be happy. May I live life with ease." Now I surround myself with people who reflect to me that I am loved and lovable, and I am filled with gratitude.

And I meditate on forgiveness. Not for them but for me. For my own well-being and mental health, for my own heart.

Here is what I now know: I've spent a lifetime striving to put together the pieces of my family puzzle. To cut through the Gordian knot—the unsolvable, troubling enigma—believing that if only I knew the when, why, and what, I could save my family and make it whole again.

Now, I can accept that there are some answers, some solutions, I will never have.

There is much I am sorry for: I am sorry that my mom's actions and decisions hurt people. I am sorry that my bio father John's actions and decisions hurt people. I am sorry that my dad Paul hurt a lot of people, including all his children—bio and step. I am sorry that my dad Burt died at forty-five, and I pray that he didn't know the truth of my paternity.

But I am not sorry that I am here.

I will not carry the burdens and decisions of Mom, Burt, Paul, or John. I won't apologize for being alive. I am grateful to be here.

In the words of sociologist Brené Brown, "When we deny our stories, they define us. When we own our stories, we get to write a brave new ending."

With the truth revealed, illuminated, and embraced, the trauma ends with me.

RECOMMENDED READING AND RESOURCES

BUDDHIST WISDOM

Boorstein, Sylvia. *It's Easier Than You Think: The Buddhist Way to Happiness*. Harper One, 2011.

Chödrön, Pema. *When Things Fall Apart: Heart Advice for Difficult Times,* Shambhala, 2016.

Hahn, Thich Nhat. *No Mud, No Lotus: The Art of Transforming Suffering*. Parallax Press, 2014.

Kornfield, Jack. *A Lamp in the Darkness: Illuminating the Path Through Difficult Times*. Sounds True, 2014.

Wright, Robert. *Why Buddhism Is True: The Science and Philosophy of Meditation and Enlightenment*. Simon and Schuster, 2017.

CREATIVE ARTS THERAPY

Cameron, Julia. *The Artist's Way: A Spiritual Path to Higher Creativity*, thirtieth anniversary edition. Tarcher Perigee, 2002.

Gilbert, Elizabeth. *Big Magic: Creative Living Beyond Fear*. Riverbend Books, 2015.

Guzman, Leah ATR-BC. *Essential Art Therapy Exercises: Effective Techniques to Manage Anxiety, Depression, and PTSD*, Callisto, 2020.

Pennebaker, James W., PhD, and John F. Evans, EdD. *Expressive Writing: Words That Heal*. Idyll Arbor, 2014.

Weymar, Diana (Creator of Tiny Pricks Project). *Crafting a Better World: Inspiration and DIY Projects for Craftivists*. Harvest, 2024.

DEATH, LOSS, PAIN, AND GRIEF

Gawande, Atul. *Being Mortal: Medicine and What Matters in the End*. Metropolitan Books, 2014.

Halifax, Joan. *Being with Dying: Cultivating Compassion and Fearlessness in the Presence of Death*. Shambhala, 2009.

James, John W., and Russell Friedman. *The Grief Recovery Handbook: The Action Program for Moving Beyond Death, Divorce, and Other Losses*, twentieth anniversary edition. William Morrow, 2009.

Kübler-Ross, Elisabeth, MD. *On Death and Dying: What the Dying Have to Teach Doctors, Nurses, Clergy, and Their Own Families*, fiftieth anniversary edition. Scribner, 2011.

Weller, Frances. *The Wild Edge of Sorrow: Rituals of Renewal and the Sacred Work of Grief*. North Atlantic Books, 2015.

MEDITATION AND MINDFULNESS

Fronsdal, Gil. *The Issue at Hand,* fourth edition. Bookland, 2008.

Goldstein, Joseph. *Mindfulness: A Practical Guide to Awakening*. Sounds True, 2016.

Salzberg, Sharon. *Real Change: Mindfulness to Heal Ourselves and the World*. Flatiron Books, 2020.

Suzuki, Shunryu. *Zen Mind, Beginner's Mind,* fiftieth anniversary edition. Shambhala, 2020.

Trungpa, Chögyam. *Meditation in Action*. Shambhala, 1991.

INDIGENOUS SPIRITUALITY

Anderson, Mitch, and Nenquimo Nemonte. *We Will Be Jaguars: A Memoir of My People*. Harry N. Abrams, 2024.

Bear Heart. *The Wind Is My Mother: The Life and Teachings of a Native American Shaman*. Clarkson Potter, 1996

Black Elk, Wallace, and William S. Lyon. *Black Elk: The Sacred Ways of a Lakota*. Harper Collins, 1990.

Kimmerer, Robin Wall. *Braiding Sweetgrass: Indigenous Wisdom, Scientific Knowledge, and the Teachings of Plants*. Milkweed Editions, 2013.

McLuhan, T.C. *Touch the Earth: A Self Portrait of Indian Existence*. Promontory Press, 1971.

NATURE

Li, Quing, Dr. *Forest Bathing: How Trees Can Help You Find Health and Happiness*. Penguin Life, 2018.

Emoto, Masaru. *The Hidden Messages in Water*. Simon & Schuster UK, 2005.

Mann, A.T. *The Sacred Language of Trees*. Sterling Ethos, 2012.

Renkl, Margaret. *Late Migrations: A Natural History of Love and Loss*. Milkweed Editions, 2019.

Solnit, Rebecca. *Wanderlust: A History of Walking*. Viking Adult, 2000

PSYCHOLOGY/PHILOSOPHY

Gottlieb, Lori/ *Maybe You Should Talk to Someone: A Therapist, Her Therapist, and Our Lives Revealed*. Harper, 2019.

Goodman, Whitney. *Toxic Positivity: Keeping It Real in a World Obsessed with Being Happy*. Tarcher Perigee, 2022.

Lembke, Dr. Anna. *Dopamine Nation: Finding Balance in the Age of Indulgence*. Dutton, 2023.

Tawwab, Nedra Glover. *Drama Free: A Guide to Managing Unhealthy Family Relationships*. Tarcher Perigee, 2023.

Watts, Alan. *The Book: On the Taboo Against Knowing Who You Are*. Pantheon, 1966.

SELF-HELP

Carson, Rick. *Taming Your Gremlin: A Surprisingly Simple Method for Getting Out of Your Own Way*. Quill, 2003.

Brewer, Judson, MD, PhD. *Unwinding Anxiety: New Science Shows How to Break the Cycles of Worry and Fear to Heal Your Mind.* Avery, 2021.

Kabat-Zinn, Jon. *Full Catastrophe Living: Using the Wisdom of Your Body and Mind to Face Stress, Pain, and Illness.* Bantam, 2013.

SOCIOLOGY

Brown, Brené. *The Gifts of Imperfection: Let Go of Who You Think You're Supposed to Be and Embrace Who You Are.* Random House, 2020.

Dolan, Eamon. *The Power of Parting: Finding Peace and Freedom Through Family Estrangement.* GP Putnam's Sons, 2025.

Frankl, Viktor E. *Man's Search for Meaning: The Classic Tribute to Hope from the Holocaust.* Rider, 2011.

Haidt, Jonathan. *The Anxious Generation: How the Great Rewiring of Childhood is Causing an Epidemic of Mental Illness.* Penguin Press, 2024.

SOUND HEALING AND MUSIC

Fleming, Rene, ed. *Music and Mind: Harnessing the Arts for Health and Wellness.* Viking, 2024.

Gaynor, Mitchell, MD. *The Healing Power of Sound: Recovery from Life-Threatening Illness Using Sound, Voice, and Music.* Shambhala, 2002.

Gibson, David, *The Complete Guide to Sound Healing*, Sound of Light, 2018.

SOUND HEALING RECORDING

Collazo, Jorge Henderson. *Bilateral Stimulation- Relax and Concentrate.* (EMDR)

Halpern, Steven. *Crystal Bowl Healing 2.0.*

Iobst, Benjamin. *Seven Metals: Singing Bowls of Tibet.*

TRAUMA HEALING

Harris, Nadine Burke, MD. *The Deepest Well: Healing the Long-Term Effects of Childhood Trauma and Adversity*. Mariner Books, 2018.

Levine, Peter A., PhD. *Healing Trauma: A Pioneering Program for Restoring the Wisdom of Your Body*. Sounds True, 2005.

Perry, Bruce D., MD, PhD, and Oprah Winfrey. *What Happened to You?: Conversations on Trauma, Resilience, and Healing*, Flatiron Books: An Oprah Book, 2021.

Siegel, Daniel J., MD, and Marion F. Solomon, PhD, eds. *Healing Trauma: Attachment, Mind, Body, and Brain*, 1st ed. W. W. Norton & Co., 2003.

TRAUMA RESEARCH

"About | ACEs Aware," University of California, accessed April 29, 2025, https://www.acesaware.org/about/

Maté, Gabor, MD. *The Myth of Normal: Trauma, Illness, and Healing in a Toxic Culture*. Avery, 2022.

Nakazawa, Donna Jackson. *Childhood Disrupted: How Your Biography Becomes Your Biology, and How You Can Heal*. Atria Books, 2015.

Van der Kolk, Bessel. *The Body Keeps the Score: Brain, Mind and Body in the Healing of Trauma*. Viking, 2014.

TWELVE STEP

Beattie, Melody. *Codependent No More: How to Stop Controlling Others and Start Caring for Yourself*, revised and updated. Spiegel & Grau, 2022.

Griffin, Kevin. *One Breath at a Time: Buddhism and the Twelve Steps*. Rodale Wellness, 2018.

Klaas, Joe. *The Twelve Steps to Happiness: A Practical Handbook for Understanding and Working the Twelve Step Programs for Alcoholism, Codependency, Eating Disorders, and Other Addictions*. Ballantine Books, 1970.

Knapp, Caroline. *Drinking: A Love Story*. The Dial Press, 1999.
Whitaker, Holly. *Quit Like a Woman: The Radical Choice to Not Drink in a Culture Obsessed with Alcohol*. The Dial Press, 2019.

WRITING INSPIRATION

Almond, Steve. *Truth is the Arrow, Mercy is the Bow: A DIY Manual for the Construction of Stories*. Zando, 2024.
Altman, Elissa. *Permission: The New Memoirist and the Courage to Create*. Godine, 2025.
Karr, Mary. *The Art of Memoir*. Harper, 2015.
Lamott, Anne. *Bird by Bird: Some Instructions on Writing and Life*. Anchor, 2007.
Shapiro, Dani. *Still Writing: The Perils and Pleasures of a Creative Life*. Grove Press, 2013.

YOGA PHILOSOPHY AND PRACTICE

Cope, Stephen. *The Wisdom of Yoga: A Seeker's Guide to Extraordinary Living*. Bantam, 2007.
Iyengar, B.K.S. *Light on Yoga: The Bible of Modern Yoga*. Schocken, 1979.
Lee, Cyndi. *Yoga Body, Buddha Mind: A Complete Manual for Physcial and Spiritual Well-Being from the Founder of the Om Yoga Center*. Riverhead Books, 2004.
Mehta, Silva, Mira Mehta, and Shyam Mehta. *Yoga: The Iyengar Way: The Definitive Illustrated Guide*. Alfred A. Knopf, 1990.

KSPN PLAYLIST

KSPN-FM	Aspen, Colorado	Playlist Shift: 10:00 p.m.
Jock: Wendy Moore	Date: 3/23/1994	–2:00 a.m.

ARTIST	SONG
(10:00 p.m.)	
Counting Crows	Mr. Jones
John Mellencamp	Jack and Diane
The Boomers	Art of Living
The Allan Parsons Symphonic Project	Standing on Higher Ground
Elvis Costello	You Tripped at Every Step
Tom Petty and the Heartbreakers	American Girl
Tasmin Archer	Lords of the New Church

ARTIST	SONG
Peter Gabriel	Blood of Eden
Phil Collins	Please Come Out Tonight
Bonnie Raitt	Have a Heart
Colin James	Cadillac Baby
(11:00 p.m.)	
The J. Geils Band	Freeze Frame
Heart	Magic Man
Bruce Cockburn	Listen for the Laugh
Robert Palmer	Every Kinda People
Squeeze	Loving You Tonight
Michael Penn	No Myth
SYN	Love on my Side
Roxy Music	Love Is the Drug
Bob Dylan	Tangled up in Blue
Tori Amos	God
Harry Nilsson	Jump into the Fire

ARTIST	SONG
(12:00 a.m.) Elton John	Funeral for a Friend/ Love Lies Bleeding
Bruce Springsteen	Streets of Philadelphia
Joni Mitchell	Both Sides Now
John Wetton and Phil Manzanera	It's Just Love
Travis Tritt	Take It Easy
The Firm	Midnight Moonlight
Stevie Ray Vaughan	Riviera Paradise
Roxy Music	Take a Chance with Me
Santana	Oye Como Va
Lenny Kravitz	Let Love Rule
(1:00 a.m.) The Beatles	I've Got a Feeling
David Bowie	John, I'm Only Dancing
The Kinks	The Road
Jackson Browne	My Problem Is You

ARTIST	SONG
The Pretenders	Brass in Pocket
Concrete Blonde	Mexican Moon (Spanish Version)
Led Zeppelin	Ramble On
Koko Taylor	Bad Case of Loving You
Chicago Transit Authority (a.k.a. Chicago)	I'm a Man
Died Pretty	Harness Up
Stevie Nicks	Stop Draggin' My Heart Around
Aimee Mann	I Should Have Known
The Rolling Stones	Sympathy for the Devil

ACKNOWLEDGMENTS

Mr. Rogers encouraged us to look for the "Helpers." I have so much gratitude for the following Helpers on my lifelong journey.

A bow of thanks to Brooke Warner, Krissa Lagos, Megan Milton, Julie Metz, Tabitha Lahr, Leah Lococo, Sterling Hooker and the entire She Writes Press team for bringing *My Pretty Baby* to life, and to Simon and Schuster for getting it into the hands of the readers who will most benefit from my story. Boundless thanks to Brooke Warner and Linda Joy Myers for their brilliant guidance in the "Six Months to Write Your Memoir" intensive, and to Linda Joy for her patient editing and encouragement of my fledgling chapters.

To my She Writes Press sisters, I am so grateful for all of you and your generous support and loving encouragement, especially Leslie Johansen Nack and Barbara Stark-Nemon for our Fall 2025 Cohort.

Many thanks to all the teachers at Lighthouse Writer's Workshop in Denver for over a decade of skillful classes, but especially to Mark Springer and the "Get 'er Done" classes for providing a supportive space for writers to get it all on the page, and to Erika Krouse for not only your masterful classes, but a debt of gratitude for finding Jenny.

Lifelong thanks to all the unsung hero teachers who recognized my thirst for learning and who encouraged and educated me from grade school through college and beyond.

To all my Buddhist teachers who held my heart, hands, and soul through retreats, books, workshops, and Zoom and online classes. Thank you for helping me to find compassion and love for my true Buddha nature. To the yoga teachers whose class or workshop or teacher training I have attended, beginning with the beloved Iyengar teacher Bonita Bradley in San Francisco in 1979.

To all my Native American teachers, but especially to Grandpa Wallace Black Elk, Wesley Black Elk, and Marcellus "Bear Heart" Williams. Your generous sharing of your wisdom through ceremony changed my life. I am forever in your debt. Thank you to my brother Wes for reading and blessing these pages. *Mitakuye oyasin. Wópila.*

To all the friends of Bill W. in the twelve step rooms of AA and Nicotine Anonymous who supported me at my worst and told me to "keep coming back, it works!" It does indeed. Gratitude for the Denver Buddhist 12-Step Sangha.

To all my therapists over the years who gently guided me as I peeled apart the layers, sought the truth, and found healing. Julie Ehlers for the Grief Recovery Workshop, and Nate Postlethwait for the Healing Your Inner Child Workshop.

To all the researchers shedding light on the impact of adverse childhood experiences on individuals and society alike. Special thanks to Donna Jackson Nakazawa for compiling the most recent studies in her book *Childhood Disrupted* and where I found myself on every page.

To Bridey Thelen-Heidel, Kerry Kletter, Kathleen Rose Morgan, Leslie Johansen-Nack, Sharon Salzberg, and Priscilla Warner for your generous and thoughtful blurbs, and to Steve Almond, Erika Krouse, and T. Kira Madden for your ongoing support and kindnesses.

To all my friends who became family, my brothers and sisters who have loved me and held on to me despite my many moves around the country: Norm and Steve, Michele and Philip, Joanne, Patrice, Jan and Jim (my dear Jan, an early reader and steadfast cheerleader), the Hambones, Vicki, Jewel and family, the Angels, and Cara. And to my sister-friend Rose for naming me "Face" and holding my hand countless times over the years as the OG Helper. Dyanna, my dear friend, I miss you every day. Thank you for Aspen and you know who.

To the entire Denver crew for your friendship, support, and community. Thank you to everyone who has ever hiked with me, helping me to heal one boot step at a time. Thank you to those of you who were Mr. Rogers Helpers in real time. Ann, also thank you for reading my manuscript and for your insightful questions. Anita for proofing my ARC. Jennifer M. Koskinen (Merritt Photo) for your gorgeous headshots, even in a heatwave. Thank you to Colorado Public Radio for keeping me company while I write. Many thanks to my attorney David Ratner of Creative Law Network, LLC, and my publicist Ann-Marie Nieves of Get Red PR.

Gratitude to all the fab teachers at Core Power Yoga Central Park. Molly for acupuncture, and Cherie for trading massage. To my awesome massage clients for your loyal support and friendship over twenty years.

To Marissa Lee, thank you for being my great-niece and for your kindness and including me in the Lee family. To my sissy Jenny and her hubby Barry, thank you for wholeheartedly accepting me and opening your hearts to me. My niece Missy, thank you for gifting Ancestry.com to Jenny therefore connecting me to her and hence to my own identity. To my Correa family, thank you also for you know who. I'm so grateful to be included in the Correa family. Kelly Ann, your sweet smile will live in my heart forever.

To my Duclos/Rouensa/Phillipe/Saucier/Smith/Moore/Lee/Franklin family. Thank goodness for hearty, tenacious, and courageous ancestors. I recognize that the land I live on is the traditional territory of the Ute, Cheyenne, and Arapaho peoples.

But mostly, with my hands on my heart and tears in my eyes, a deep bow of gratitude goes to my two favorite guys: my husband Ignacio and my son Mateo; the most loving, supportive, thoughtful, and kind humans I know. My life truly was blessed when you both joined me in this crazy adventure called being human. You are my moon and my stars and my universe; how grateful and lucky I am to have your love, to be your wife and momma. Can't wait for our next adventure.

ABOUT THE AUTHOR

WENDY B. CORREA is a writer, yogi, hiker, as well as a licensed massage therapist. She has worked in the film, television, multimedia, and music industries in Los Angeles and later as a radio DJ in Aspen, Colorado. She holds bachelor's degrees in psychology and theater arts and has contributed articles to *Mothering* magazine.

A wife and mother, she resides in Denver, Colorado, and loves traveling to magical destinations with her family. *My Pretty Baby* is her debut book.

For more information, visit www.wendybcorrea.com.

Author photo © Jennifer M. Koskinen